DIL

An introduction to

Fourth Generation Languages

An introduction to

Fourth Generation Languages

Diane Meehan, B.Sc.
Principal Lecturer, School of Information Science and Technology,
The Liverpool Polytechnic

Stanley Thornes (Publishers) Ltd

First published in 1990 by:
Stanley Thornes (Publishers) Ltd
Old Station Drive
Leckhampton
CHELTENHAM GL53 0DN
England

British Library Cataloguing in Publication Data

Meehan, Diane
    Fourth generation languages.—(Computer science series).
    1. Computer systems. Programming languages
    I. Title   II. Series
    005.13
    ISBN 0-7487-0400-0

Typeset in 10/11½pt Plantin by Tech-Set, Gateshead, Tyne & Wear.
Printed and bound at The Bath Press, Avon.

Editor's note

The Stanley Thornes Computer Studies Series is a series of text books with a modular structure aimed at students of computer studies and designed for use on courses at most levels of academic and professional qualification. The focus of the series was originally the syllabus guidelines for BTEC courses and existing books in the series include:

Computer Appreciation and Basic Programming
Computing in a Small Business
Fundamentals of Computing
Computer Systems: Software and Architecture
Microcomputer Interfacing for Control
Structured Program Design
Scientific Programming
Data Processing Methods
Basic Systems Analysis
Basic Systems Design
Management of Systems Development
Case Studies in Business Computing
Basic Principles of Human–Computer Interface Design

As the series has developed and computing has grown as a subject, the need has been recognised for a number of texts which are more specialist and advanced than the earlier ones, though still focused on intermediate level courses in computing. *Basic Principles of Human–Computer Interface Design* focuses on the technological aspects of interaction between humans and computers with sound advice for the system designer on the types of interface available and their appropriateness for particular applications. *Relational Databases* builds on the earlier books which cover database concepts and technology, and provides a deeper practical introduction to the most popular type of database software. *An Introduction to Fourth Generation Languages* does a similar job in relation to the powerful software tools which have come on to the marketplace to aid end-users to develop their own systems and professional staff to build prototypes very quickly.

Barry Lee
Series Editor

Contents

PART THREE   The future

APPENDIX

Tables

Figures

Part One

The current and historical perspectives within the computing industry

1 Setting the scene

Objectives

After you have studied this chapter you should be able to:

★ identify the advent of fourth generation languages within the computing industry and appreciate the need for change.
★ describe the previous generations of computer languages and their characteristics.
★ understand the place of the fifth generation in computing.
★ attempt to define the terms procedural and non-procedural language.
★ appreciate the place of non-procedural languages in the fourth generation.

1.1 Introduction

Fourth generation languages or 4GLs, have generated (and continue to generate) a considerable amount of discussion in the world of computing. At one time it seemed as if every article in the computing journals and magazines was addressing the subject of 4GL use. Yet 4GLs are not new. They began to emerge as far back as the end of the 1970s. By the early 1980s, large numbers of products had flooded the software market and it started to look as if every new and not so new software product was being sold as a 4GL.

Despite this, an air of uncertainty still surrounds 4GLs. They have been overplayed by the media and their manufacturers, with few of the real issues satisfactorily explored. Such questions as 'what are 4GLs?' are difficult to answer, although we shall attempt to do just that later in this book. There are obvious difficulties because of the diverse nature of these products and as yet a general lack of standardisation.

The reasons for the emergence of 4GLs are however, much clearer and are discussed fully in Chapters 2 and 3. Briefly these reasons can be summarized as follows:

★ A change was needed. Much of the software we are using currently in computing has been around for twenty or more years. Often this software has its roots in another era. Some of it has not kept pace with other, important developments.
★ Various problems within the computing industry required a solution. 4GLs offer just one solution to these problems.

This does not imply that the first three generations were without significance. Each new generation of computing languages has brought with it a solution to a particular problem or set of problems, as well as new and (at the time) innovatory ideas. Each generation has strived to make the communication between the machine (computer) and the user (programmer) of that machine easier and more meaningful. In addition, the amount of knowledge about the workings of the machine that the programmer needs has decreased.

An appreciation of this historical perspective is important in understanding the place of 4GLs in computing. For this reason we shall begin our consideration of 4GLs by looking at the previous generations.

1.2 The generations of computing languages

A summary of the generations of computer languages appears in Table 1.1.

1.2.1 The first generation

In the late 1940s, the only means available for programming the first stored-program computers, was to write in machine code. This involves writing direct instructions in the binary digits of the machine's operating codes. Machine code or machine language is by definition machine dependent. Writing programs in machine code demands a thorough knowledge of the workings of the machine, i.e. the machine architecture and organisation.

This low-level access to the processor has the advantage of being very fast. However, machine code is very complex and is difficult for people to read and to use. Hence programming in machine code is tedious, time-consuming, prone to error and labour intensive. One of the main drawbacks is that a change in one machine code instruction results in an amendment to many, or all, of the other instructions within a program.

Despite this, in the first generation issues such as low programmer-productivity were never raised. It was generally assumed that only a small number of expensive computers would exist, that they would be used to solve complex problems and only technical specialists would need or be able to put them to any use. The technology had also not developed sufficiently for any alternatives to exist.

Machine code is still used by computer builders. Table 1.2 illustrates the development of computer languages and gives examples of code from the various generations.

Table 1.1   A summary of the generations of computing languages

Generation	Approximate Date of Conception	Type of Language	Characteristics
1st	Late 1940s	Machine language or code	Written in binary code. Machine dependent. Difficult to use/read, time-consuming to program/debug. Fast and efficient. No translation necessary.
2nd	Early 1950s	Assembly language	English-like mnemonics. Still machine-dependent. Easier to use. Still fast and efficient. Translated by means of an assembler.
3rd	Late 1950s/start of 1960s through to 1970s	High-level languages, application packages and database languages	English-type words/statements. Much less dependency on the environment. More friendly 'interface'. Translated by compiler or interpreter. Generally procedural in nature. Also packaged, re-usable solutions.
4th	Late 1970s/start of 1980s	4GLs; a whole range of languages and other tools, including query languages and decision support tools	English-like key-words. Generally portable across a range of machines. Much more 'user-friendly', some suited to use by non-professional. Translated by compiler, interpreter or both, or uses generation techniques. Many languages relate to specific types of problem. Non-procedural element central to this generation.
5th	1950s–	Languages and tools associated with artificial intelligence	Unlike the conventional programming languages in structure and usage. Includes functional and logic programming languages among others.

Table 1.2 The development of computer languages

Generation	Examples of the code used
1st	011011 000000 000000 000000 000010 000001

could mean place the contents of storage location 129 in the accumulator. The next step was to replace the instruction code by a mnemonic. Here the boundaries of the first and second generations become blurred, i.e. the original code becomes

   CLA 000000 000000 000000 000010 000001

where CLA has replaced 011011 and means clear and load the accumulator. The two instructions are hence equivalent.

| 2nd | Further developments allowed the numbers representing storage locations or registers to be written in decimal form, i.e. |

   CLA 0 0 0 129

Finally came the development of symbolic notation for both instructions and data. Our original instruction now takes the form

   CLA NUM

where NUM is the location in memory of the value of a variable.

| 3rd | This generation saw the development of notation more akin to the language of the application, e.g. |

   LET A = NUM

| 4th | Examples of Fourth Generation Languages will be considered separately in later chapters. Generally it takes fewer lines of code to achieve similar results to those of the third generation. Commands such as 'Compute Sum' are used. |

| 5th | Declarative languages such as PROLOG are just one example of those found in the fifth generation. In PROLOG, facts and rules may be stated, e.g. |

   a fact – owns(john,dog)
   a rule – owns(john,dog):-bought(john,dog,X)

PROLOG has relatively simple mechanisms for handling arithmetic for example.

1.2.2 The second generation

The second generation of programming languages became available in the early 1950s with the development of symbolic assembly languages. These assembly languages use mnemonic codes for each machine instruction. This has the effect of making programs more meaningful to write and to understand and takes assembly languages one step closer to the language of the people writing the programs.

Assembly languages are however, still very closely tied to the machines on which they run. This leaves little or no scope for portability across a range of hardware. Assembly languages require a translation process in order to turn them into machine code. This is done by means of an assembler, as shown in Figure 1.1.

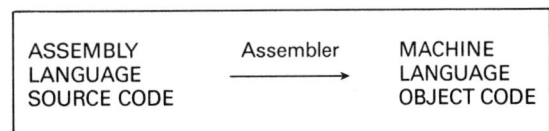

```
ASSEMBLY        Assembler      MACHINE
LANGUAGE        ———————>       LANGUAGE
SOURCE CODE                    OBJECT CODE
```

Figure 1.1 *The translation process for the second generation*

Also at this time significant developments in such areas as operating systems software occurred. Before the second generation this level of sophistication was not required.

Although the second generation brought with it a number of distinct improvements, programmers wanted to be able to do more. For example:

★ To use each other's code. Many programs, e.g. mathematical functions such as square roots, were being constantly re-written because of the unique nature of each assembly language.
★ To use routines which needed tailoring only to specific situations, e.g. sort routines.
★ To use a more natural notation.

Assembly language is now used by programmers building system software. This type of software must be efficient and interact directly with the computer hardware. Both machine code and assembly languages are known as low-level languages. In fact the distinction between assembly language and machine code is often ill-defined. Some people would dispute that these low-level languages were programming languages at all. See Sammet (1969) for a good introduction to the development of programming languages.

1.2.3 The third generation

A. High-level languages

During the late 1950s/early 1960s and into the 1970s a range of languages emerged which are typified by the so-called high-level procedural languages such as COBOL, FORTRAN and Pascal. High-level languages provide a more user-friendly interface between the programmer and the native machine instructions. They are high-level in that they use 'symbols' closer in nature to human language than the language of the machine. No one could argue that in COBOL, for example, words like PERFORM, ACCEPT, ADD, etc. do not look like their counterparts in the English language. However

the construction of the syntax of the language and the way in which it is used does not resemble human language.

Some high-level languages such as COBOL can be used for virtually all applications within a commercial organisation, whereas others such as FORTRAN are designed for more specific use, e.g. scientific applications.

With third generation languages or 3GLs, the software instructions are further distanced from the hardware on which they run, allowing a greater degree of portability across machines than with the previous generations. 3GLs require a translation process which may be achieved by means of a compiler (compilation) or an interpreter (interpretation) as shown in Figure 1.2. A basic appreciation of translation methods is important in our later discussions about fourth generation languages or 4GLs.

Compilers take in the whole of the high-level source code (program) and turn it into the machine language object code which is then directly executable ('runnable') on the machine. Interpreters residing in the memory along with the high-level source code take each individual high-level statement and execute it directly. Interpretation gives the programmer the impression of being brought closer to the machine and is used with the more interactive of the 3GLs, e.g. BASIC. However interpretation is much slower than compilation, as various stages must be constantly repeated.

Although there is a one-to-one correspondence between assembly language and machine code, the translation of each statement in a high-level language results in the production of many machine language statements, i.e. there is a one-to-many correspondence.

Also relevant here is the concept of the language-directed machine where direct execution of the high-level language is achieved without translation. This is because the high-level language is physically implemented in the machine hardware as the machine language. A similar idea is that of the database machine, except that the machine/high-level language is database oriented. The place of such machines in the day-to-day world of computing has yet to

	HIGH-LEVEL SOURCE CODE	Compiler →		MACHINE LANGUAGE OBJECT CODE	
or	HIGH-LEVEL SOURCE CODE	Compiler →	ASSEMBLY LANGUAGE CODE	Assembler →	MACHINE LANGUAGE OBJECT CODE
or	ONE HIGH-LEVEL SOURCE-CODE STATEMENT (e.g. BASIC)	Interpreter →		EXECUTE STATEMENT	

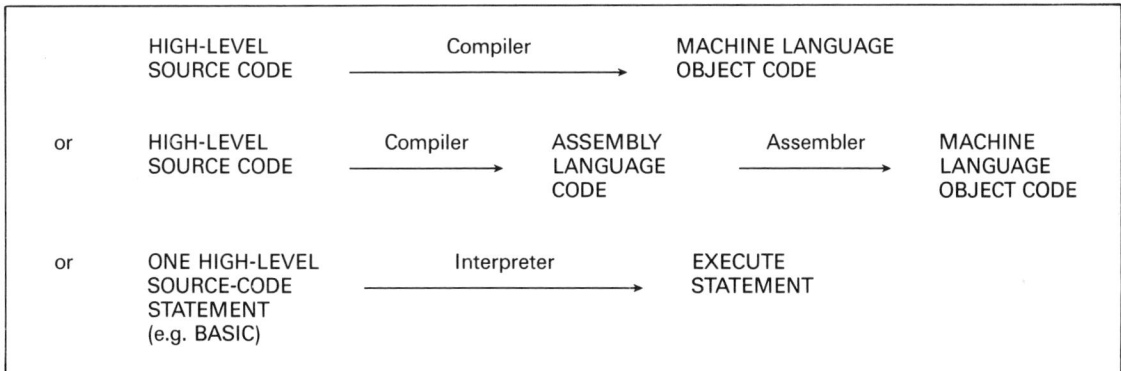

Figure 1.2   *The translation process for the third generation*

be fully established, although there are some commercial implementations.

Most modern digital computers are built around the classic von Neumann architecture and the structure of the conventional languages correspond to this model. The mathematician John von Neumann had the idea of a stored program machine with characteristics such as a single (global) memory, fixed-size memory cells, assignment and sequential execution. A program counter controls the program flow and indicates the next instruction to be processed. This model is currently reflected in most of the computers in everyday commercial use, although alternative architecture types are now being considered, e.g. parallel architectures.

3GLs have encouraged the increase in information processing that has been a characteristic of the last twenty years in computing. They have also, theoretically at least, opened up the availability of computing to a much wider range of people. However, this is probably more attributable to software such as application packages than to languages such as COBOL and Pascal. Most 3GLs are aimed at the professional user and are not readily 'picked-up' by an end-user. A more rigorous discussion of what is meant by end-user computing and its implications is pursued in Chapter 7 of this book.

Most 3GLs are procedural. Procedural languages require the programmer to do two things:

1) To define what is to be done.
2) To control the program flow, i.e. how it is to be done.

Basically the programmer defines a set of executable instructions which are then executed in the sequence defined.

Such languages have a number of identifiable characteristics. Refer to Sammet (1969) for a full discussion. Figure 1.3 summarises these characteristics.

Procedural languages also aim to:

★ be easy to use and to learn.
★ provide a natural, brief notation.
★ provide savings in

  ★ programmer costs.
  ★ implementation time.
  ★ and maintenance effort.

Despite these aims and characteristics, it is fair to say that the use of 3GLs has a number of drawbacks. In general, 3GLs

★ can only be used by trained professionals. The average user will not learn and use COBOL for instance.
★ do provide savings in terms of cost, time and effort, if measured against the earlier generations. However, there is often a

High-level procedural languages	do not require the programmer to have any knowledge of the low-level languages (machine and assembly languages) of the computer.
	are to some degree machine independent, i.e. if you write a program in a procedural language for one machine, it should be directly portable to at least one other machine type.
	use language or notation closer to that of the application area than, say, assembly languages.
	may utilise the process of compilation which results in the production of several machine code instructions for each instruction in the source code.

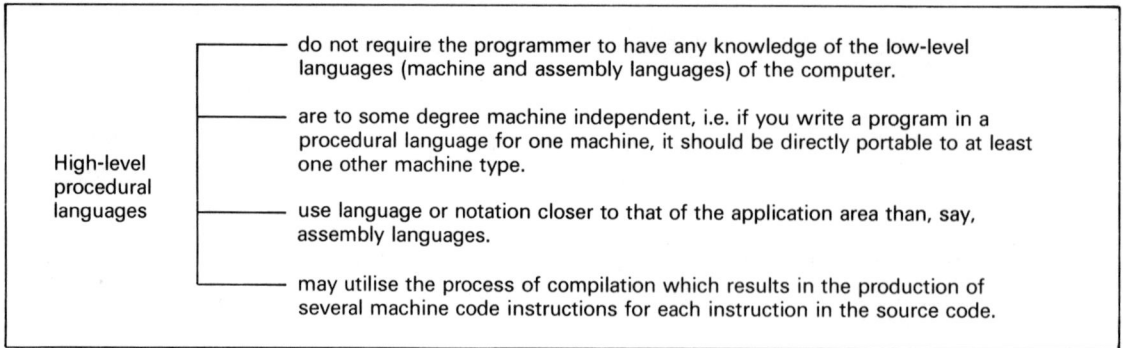

Figure 1.3 *The main characteristics of high-level procedural languages*

large amount of code involved in writing an applications program in a 3GL. This means that 3GL programs are still time-consuming to debug and often difficult or impossible to modify or maintain.

★ have their roots in the batch processing environment of the 1960s.

★ offer quite different facilities across versions despite some standardisation.

These problems will not cause 3GLs to be abandoned. This is particularly true if you consider the fact that the computer industry has invested a great deal of time, effort and money in using languages such as COBOL. However, it is very important to appreciate that they will not always be the best tools for certain tasks. Now alternatives exist which may be more appropriate in various situations. Such alternatives include 4GLs.

B. Other 3GLs

Most of the procedural languages like FORTRAN and BASIC are conventional, sequential languages based around the von Neumann programming model described earlier. However there is a second class of procedural languages which deserves mention. These are the concurrent languages, e.g. Ada and Occam, which have parallel control structures.

These concurrent languages are based on processes with communication and synchronisation facilities. A process in this case is an independent program with its own data structure and sequential code to operate on the data. Concurrent processes work independently and interact by means of the communication and synchronisation mechanisms. Communication methods include shared (global) memory and messages, whilst synchronisation mechanisms may include signals, buffers and queues. Ada is classified as a shared memory language and Occam as a message-passing language.

These languages are outside of the mainstream high-level languages around which our discussion has been based. Perrot (1987) covers many of the concepts raised here, Jones (1987) looks at Occam and Sommerville and Morrison (1987) at Ada.

C. Databases

Whilst a thorough discussion of database technology is not appropriate in this text, basic concepts will be explored at various stages. Databases are also a part of the historical development with which we are concerned. Hence at least a brief consideration of relevant ideas must be pursued.

Prior to the 1960s, the data processing industry used files for the storage and processing of data. As needs changed there was a requirement for more speedy access to and retrieval of stored data. Hence the move was towards the storage of data in a database environment.

What is a database?

The word database was first used around 1963 and an early definition told us:

★ A database is a set of files.
★ A file is an ordered collection of entries.
★ An entry consists of a key or keys and data.

Later definitions are not that much more helpful, e.g. a database is a collection of interrelated data. Martin (1976) expands on this by adding:

★ The data must meet the needs of different types of users.
★ The data is independent of the application programs.
★ New data is added and existing data is modified and retrieved through a common and controlled approach.
★ The database is seen differently by different users (user views).

What is a database management system (DBMS)?

Most of us view a database as something like the diagram in Figure 1.4. The logical structure of the database, i.e. how it is perceived by the applications, is separated from the physical structure, i.e. how it is implemented (which is device-specific). The DBMS allows the logical–physical mapping. It provides such facilities as concurrent access to multiple database users, recovery procedures and retrieval of data.

Many people use the term DBMS to describe the complete database package, i.e. an integrated set of software which provides all the necessary functions of a database: enquiry, storage, modification, security and integrity of data.

The data used by a DBMS may be structured in several ways. The three most common methods are, briefly:

★ Hierarchical – the first implementation of databases in the 1960s was via hierarchical data structures, the idea of a hierarchy being reasonably familiar to most people. The hierarchical model is based on a tree structure.
★ Network (CODASYL) – the approach adopted as the CODASYL (Conference on Data Systems Languages) standard. This involves a more complex structure than the hierarchical approach.
★ Relational – this approach utilises flat files or tables and differs radically from the other models mentioned. The relational model is attributable to E. F. Codd and is being more widely used in database implementation, for reasons we shall discuss in later chapters.

A fourth method, Inverted Files, could also be added to this list. See Date (1986) or Martin (1976, 1977) for a full discussion of these database techniques. We shall return to the use of databases, particularly where relevant to 4GLs, in Chapter 4.

D. Application packages

The origins of the application package also stem from the third generation. An application package is not the same thing as a high-level language. The application package provides a set of routines which allow the user to supply the information or parameters needed for their particular application. (Compare this with the discussion of 4GL techniques in Chapter 3.) This is often done by means of 'form-filling' or a

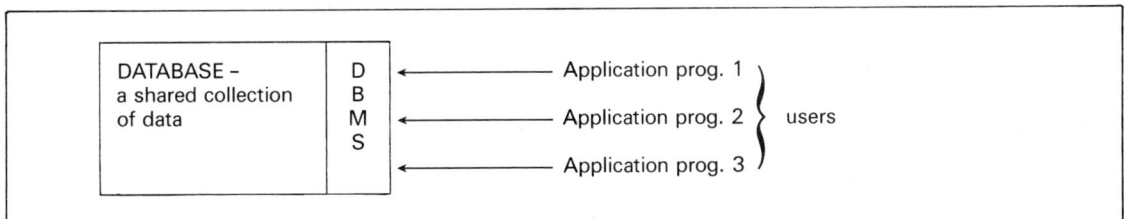

Figure 1.4 *A user view of a database*

similar method. The user may or may not be involved in the specification of the execution sequence of the routines. The application is hence pre-packaged software designed to fulfil a specific business requirement.

Application packages are now commonly used, particularly on micro or personal computers, although obviously on mainframes as well. Such packages include word-processing packages (e.g. WORDSTAR), spreadsheet packages (e.g. MULTIPLAN), graphics packages (e.g. HARVARD PRESENTATION GRAPHICS) and integrated packages which may offer both spreadsheet, database and other facilities (e.g. Lotus 1-2-3). There are a great many low-cost, good-quality packages available which offer certain advantages to the user. These advantages include:

★ faster implementation
★ provision of documentation
★ portability
★ cost – they are often relatively cheap.

Despite these advantages there are also several disadvantages associated with application packages which in general:

★ are restricted to solve particular problems,
★ may not perform all the tasks required by the user,
★ are not easily modified,
★ may not perform tasks to the user's standards,
★ may require specialist skills not easily learned by the user.

1.2.4 The fourth generation

A. 4GLs

We have already defined the majority of 3GLs as being procedural, von Neumann-based languages. One definition of 4GLs (Grindley, 1986) is that they are non-procedural languages, i.e. they instruct the computer by specifying the desired result rather than the actions required to achieve that result. A non-procedural language removes the second of the programmer's

responsibilities, i.e. how the results are to be achieved.

Non-procedural languages are specification languages rather than programming languages. To understand this fully, contrast using a form-filling mechanism within an application package to programming in COBOL or Pascal. In the former you are simply providing parameters from which the results will be obtained. The latter requires the definition of computer procedures.

The term non-procedural is not new and has never been well-defined. This is probably because it is relative to how far away from computer procedures and execution sequences the non-procedural language allows you to go. In the fourth generation the languages labelled non-procedural are not concerned with the definition of procedures at all but with data items and the links and relationships between them. Figure 1.5 reinforces the differences between procedural and non-procedural languages. We shall return to the idea of non-procedural languages in Chapter 3.

It is rather unfortunate that not all the products currently being called 4GLs fit this definition. One of the main problems is of course that no one satisfactory definition, covering all products, actually exists. Nor is there even any one method of definition. If we accept the non-procedural definition then we must also accept that not all 4GLs are in fact rightly named. In any case the non-procedural idea is central to the concept of 4GLs. There is also a problem of standardisation, which also currently does not exist.

There are other problems as well. The term 4GL is not the only one used. Fourth Generation Tool (4GT), Fourth Generation Environment (4GE), Fourth Generation System (4GS), Application Generator (APG or AG) and even command-level language are other (almost) synonymous alternatives. The term 4GL is also associated with a wide range of facilities, leaving the potential purchaser of these products asking many questions:

★ What hardware does the 4GL run on?
Many 4GLs are portable across a range of

Procedural languages	Non-procedural languages
(Programming languages)	(Specification languages)
↓	↓
Programmers must say what the desired results are and how they will be achieved	Specify only what the desired results will be
↓	↓
through the definition of a set of executable instructions which are executed in a predefined sequence	through the passing of parameters by means of a form-filling or similar technique
↓	↓
i.e. concerned with computer procedures	i.e. concerned with the definition of data and the links between them

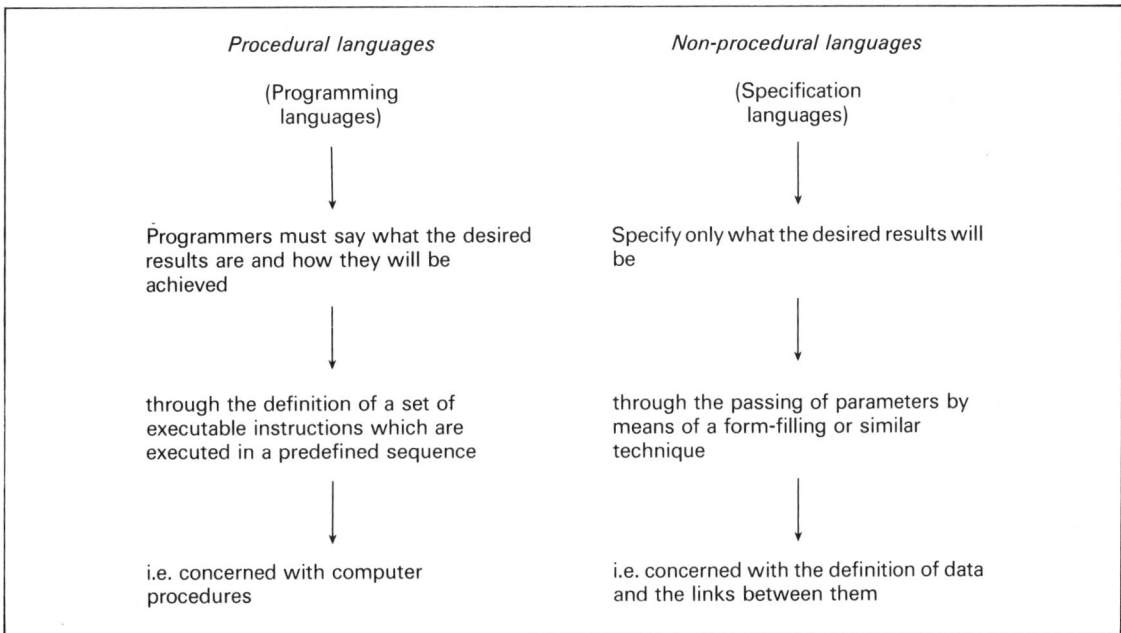

Figure 1.5 *Procedural v. non-procedural languages*

hardware and environments. For example, MIMER runs on Apollo, Concurrent Computer Corp., Control Data, Data General, Digital, Hewlett Packard, Honeywell Bull, IBM, ICL and Norsk Data amongst several other machine types. Other 4GLs are specifically aimed at one manufacturer, e.g. GENER/OL is for IBM mainframes and PCs.

★ Is there a version for personal computers and if so what are the memory requirements? Some vendors of 4GLs also offer a micro-based version of their product, e.g. RAMIS Information System and RAMIS/PC.

★ Can it be used for transaction processing, batch applications or both? EASYTRIEVE PLUS is used for batch processing. Many other 4GLs are aimed at transaction processing systems, e.g. GENER/OL.

★ Is 3GL code produced which must be translated or are machine instructions developed directly? DELTA produces

COBOL or PL/1 code ready for compilation.

★ Does the 4GL offer an integrated set of functions, such as a DBMS, a data dictionary, a report writer, a query language or a subset of these facilities? For example, PROGRESS offers a relational database management system (RDBMS), a data dictionary, an application language, a procedure editor and a screen and report formatter.

No wonder there has been some confusion where 4GLs are concerned. Most manufacturers claim that 4GLs provide a solution to most if not all problems, whilst other people's experiences have led them towards a more cautious view of 4GL use. See Prizant (1986), Steele (1987) and Stahl (1986), for example. It is very important to take an objective look at the issues surrounding 4GLs, which is one of the purposes of this book. We shall return to many of the topics raised in this section in the later chapters that look directly at 4GLs and their use.

B. Other developments

Other developments which may be considered 'fourth generation' include the use of tools to automate the application development process. Various of these tools such as IPSEs (Integrated Project Support Environments) and CASE (Computer Aided Software Engineering) tools will be discussed in more detail later.

1.2.5 The fifth generation

This section is included for completeness and cannot hope to explain all the concepts in detail.

Although 4GLs are relatively new, current developments have moved computer languages into the fifth generation. Fifth generation languages or 5GLs have not necessarily evolved chronologically in relation to 4GLs, but have come to be associated with systems within the field of artificial intelligence (AI), e.g. Intelligent Knowledge Based Systems (IKBS) or Expert Systems. The building of such systems demands a radically different approach from conventional software engineering methods. Hence those languages associated with the fifth generation are unlike the algorithmic, sequential languages of the third generation, although they have more in common with such languages as Occam.

Some of the categories of languages which might be considered fifth generation are:

★ Functional programming languages – which operate by seeing a program as a collection of (mathematical-type) functions. There are two main types of functional language:

(1) Data flow languages, e.g. VAL, ID, which have no concept of variables. Data is passed from one statement to another. Execution of statements is data-driven, i.e. statements are executed when all input values are available.

(2) Applicative languages, e.g. LISP, so called because of their application of functions to structures. The value of an expression is determined solely by its constituent parts. Therefore if it

occurs more than once in the same context it has the same value each time.

★ Logic programming languages, e.g. PROLOG, which is based on Predicate Logic. However in order to use PROLOG as a practical programming tool, a mathematically intensive introduction is not necessary. The idea of using logic as a programming language emerged in the 1970s. PROLOG is a descriptive or declarative language (as opposed to procedural). This type of language allows a set of facts and rules to be described. An example of PROLOG code is shown in Table 1.2 but cannot hope to show all the differences between this type of language and those of other generations. Some of the things it is extremely easy to do in the procedural languages, such as arithmetic handling, are not important in languages such as PROLOG, which provide relatively simple ways of handling arithmetic. This can seem clumsy in comparison to a 3GL. Rogers (1986) provides an introduction to PROLOG, and Bratko (1986) and Clocksin and Mellish (1984) go into more advanced techniques.

★ Object-oriented programming languages, e.g. Smalltalk, Simula, revolve around the concepts of:

★ Objects – an active part of the system comprising some memory and an operation set. Communication between objects is via messages.
★ Classes – a grouping of a set of objects.
★ Instances – an individual object described by a class.

These languages have been useful for sophisticated interfaces and graphics, etc. with objects now playing an increasing role in parallel processing requirements.

The fifth generation basically offers three approaches to producing systems:

1) Languages such as those discussed above.

One or two languages have gained more ground than the others for AI work. LISP, a functional language seems to be particularly popular in the USA and has the advantage of linking to a wide range of support tools. PROLOG is more widely used in this and other European countries. Both have their devotees.

2) Environments which offer a range of facilities, including a language, text editor, etc. These tend to be designed for mainframes or workstations, and are often less portable than languages. Examples include ART and KEE.

3) Shells or Expert System Shells, such as CRYSTAL from Intelligent Environments Ltd, LEONARDO from Creative Logic and Expertech's XI PLUS. These provide a low cost solution to building knowledge-based (AI) systems. Many shells run on personal computers.

1.3 Conclusions

There have been significant developments in programming languages in the last four decades or so, with 4GLs being one such development. Many people are still unfamiliar with the very large number of products which fall into this category. The list at present is almost endless, yet seems to grow by the day, with many 4GLs disappearing as fast as they emerge. Table 1.3 lists some 4GLs which will no doubt already include some languages no longer marketed. Some of these products are considered in more detail in Chapters 3, 4 and 5, as well as in Appendix A.

The origin or current distributor of the 4GL is also included. This too changes, as other companies acquire the rights to various products. There are many, many more 4GLs which could have occupied space in this table equally well.

This is yet another criticism of 4GLs. How does the potential user choose from such a large number of products and will they be guaranteed continuing support if they do make a choice?

People have short memories, however. Asked to list languages from the third generation, most people would include Pascal, COBOL, FORTRAN, BASIC, PL/1, and perhaps one or two others, but how many people remember or have even heard some of those languages listed in Figure 1.6? These are just a few of the some hundred or more languages which appeared during the third generation. Sammet (1969) lists and discusses many of these languages. There is no reason why the same thing should not happen in the fourth generation, until the settling down process is complete.

Adam	Comit	Jovial
Altran	Deacon	Madcap
Amtran	Flap	Map
Baseball	Formac	Stress
Clip	Graf	Treet

Figure 1.6 *Some of the lesser known languages from the third generation*

Perhaps the most important concept is that of the non-procedural language, which although not a new term is still as yet ill-defined. However 4GLs are bringing us nearer to this concept in its purest sense. Non-procedural techniques will form a central theme in our later discussions.

1.4 Follow-up questions and activities

1.4.1 Questions

1) a) Explain what you understand by the terms first, second, third and fourth generation languages.
   b) What are the main differences between these generations?

2) What is the significance of the fifth generation of computing?

3) Third generation languages (3GLs) are often called high-level languages. What is meant by the term high-level?

4) What advantages do 3GLs offer over assembly languages and machine code?

5) What are the disadvantages of 3GLs?

6) Why are application packages by themselves not a sufficient solution to the problems of the third generation?

7) Briefly explain the terms procedural and non-procedural language.

8) What significance do non-procedural languages have in the fourth generation?

1.4.2 Activities

1) Explore the current 4GL market by cutting out or noting the advertisements in computing magazines and journals which are being used to market 4GLs. Take particular note of the variety of products being offered.

Table 1.3   Fourth generation products*

Product name	Developer or UK distributor
CORVISION	Cortex Corporation
DELTA	Delta Software International
EASYTRIEVE PLUS	Pansophic Systems
FOCUS	Information Builders
GENER/OL	Pansophic Systems
GURU	MDBS International Ltd
INFORMIX	Informix
INGRES	Relational Technology International
KnowledgeBUILD	Cullinet Software Inc.
MANTIS	Cincom Systems
MIMER	Mimer Software UK
NOMAD	RCMS Computing Services
ORACLE	Oracle Corporation
POWERHOUSE	Cognos Ltd
PROGRESS	Progress Software
RAMIS	On-Line Software International
UNIFACE	Inside Automation B.V.

*Product names are acknowledged as trademarks of their relevant owners. Some of these products will be considered in more depth in later chapters.

2 Problems within the computer industry

Objectives

After you have studied this chapter you should be able to:

- ★ identify the problems within the DP industry and appreciate the need for change.
- ★ explain what is meant by the term 'traditional systems life-cycle' and describe its associated stages.
- ★ list the advantages and disadvantages of this traditional approach to application development.
- ★ describe ways of tackling the problems identified in the DP industry.
- ★ begin to appreciate the place of 4GLs in this changing environment.

2.1 The current situation

2.1.1 Trends and developments

4GLs are a response to some of the difficulties within the computing industry in general and application development in particular. As we have seen, 3GLs have not only failed to fulfil all of their promises, they have also contributed to a host of problems. It is these problems which we need to address in this chapter.

In addition there has also been a natural evolution in computing that has led to developments and trends which are also relevant to our discussion. These include:

- ★ An increase in the demand for and the emphasis on information. Information is now treated as a resource along with the other valuable resources, such as money, people and raw materials. Organisations need up-to-date, reliable, timely and relevant information to remain competitive and to stay in business. The role of the computer has become vital in the provision of this information.
- ★ The changing face of data processing (DP). This is partially connected to the point made above. It has long been thought that the emphasis in DP should be on data rather than programming. In many organisations DP has become part of the much wider strategy of Information Resource Management. This is often reflected in something as simple as a change of name. The data processing department now goes under titles such as Information Systems Management or Information Services. The increase in end-user computing has also contributed to this changing role. Users need help, advice and guidance from the professionals rather than being isolated from them. The role of the DP department is now that of a provider and supporter of users' needs. This changing role is considered in more detail in Chapter 7.
- ★ The wider availability of computers and computing power. The trend towards smaller, cheaper machines has meant that computing power can now be distributed throughout organisations. Advances in communications have also contributed to this trend. Some companies have even moved towards 'saturation', with every employee having a personal computer (PC) or terminal resident on their desks. This situation is more likely in financial or research organisations, say, than in manufacturing companies. Fawcett (1985) gives the results of a survey related to this terminal usage.
- ★ A significant decrease in hardware costs which needs to be matched by a comparable reduction in software costs. If you only had to pay £1000 to buy a Rolls-Royce, you would not want to pay £10,000 a year for a chauffeur to drive it! Software development costs have not decreased

significantly over the last twenty-five years or so. Figure 2.1 contrasts the differing trends in hardware and software costs.

★ An increase in the level of complexity of the applications requested. Development requirements have gone beyond routine batch processing systems such as payroll and accounts payable. The complexities of on-line and real-time applications, of process control, of integration and of communication networks, etc. now have to be dealt with. This complexity of systems may be viewed as three-dimensional; the increasing complexity of time-dependent behaviour, of data and of functions.

★ A greater demand for applications. Potential users are more aware of what computers can do for them. At a personal level it may mean a move towards greater convenience and speed, while at the corporate level the result could be a reduction in production and administrative costs, and an improvement in competitive status. This includes demands by management for management information systems and decision support systems, which, because of their *ad hoc* nature, tend to be forever changing.

★ An increase in the speed and power of computers, which needs to be put to good use. This is a continuing trend which has yet to achieve its full potential. Recent developments have gone beyond very large-scale integration (VLSI), to transputers and parallel processing.

★ The demand for computer professionals and the scarcity of trained personnel. For example systems programmers are particularly 'thin on the ground'. DP professionals ideally now need a diversity of skills, e.g. the analyst/programmer whose role is discussed in Chapter 7. At the same time the cost of employing such individuals has increased. Figure 2.2 illustrates this trend compared against the decreasing cost of machines.

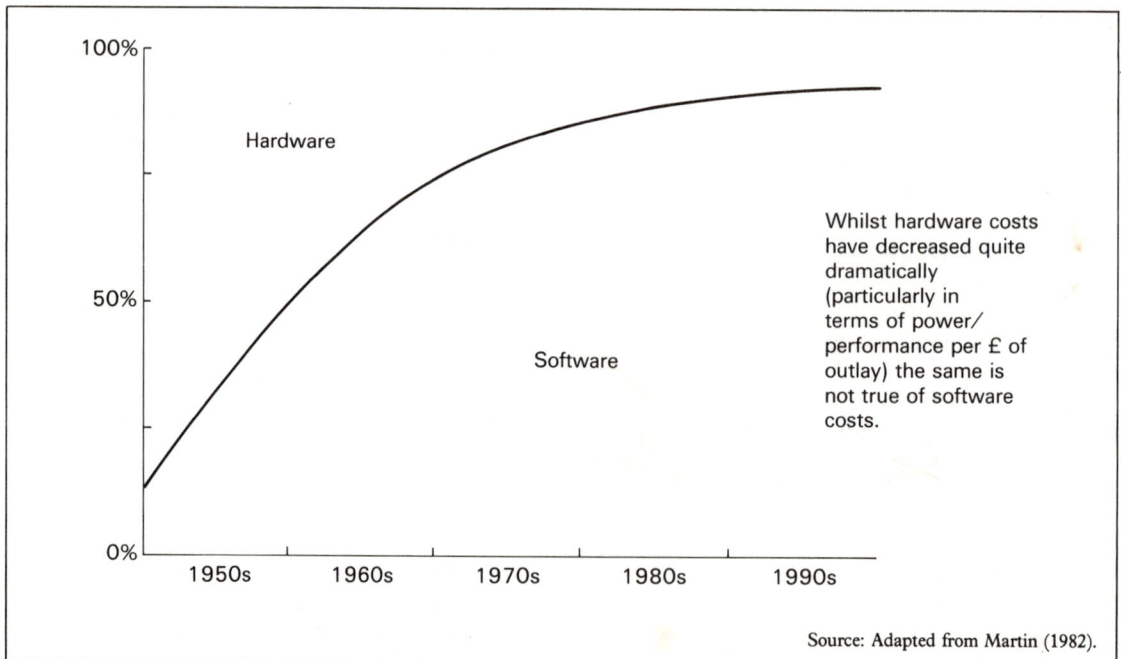

Whilst hardware costs have decreased quite dramatically (particularly in terms of power/performance per £ of outlay) the same is not true of software costs.

Source: Adapted from Martin (1982).

Figure 2.1   *Computer hardware v. software costs*

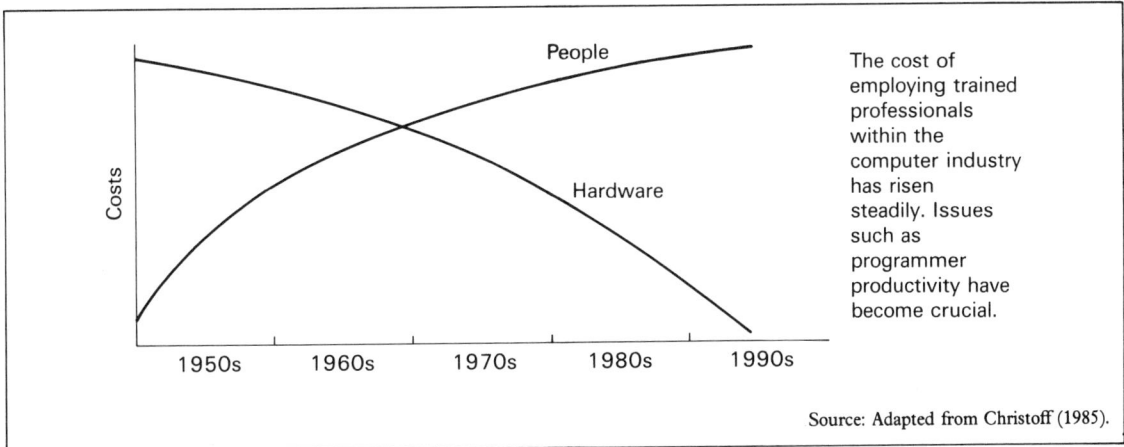

Figure 2.2 *Computer hardware v. people costs*

Other aspects of the problems with such trends and developments are:

★ They may have not been foreseen and hence fully catered for, e.g. significant advances in the computer's speed and power.
★ They may have gone in a different direction than expected, e.g. the move towards knowledge-based or expert systems.
★ They may require new methods/techniques/skills which have to be learned, e.g. the use of structured methodologies.

These trends and developments, along with the inadequacies of 3GLs discussed in Chapter 1, have created several major problem areas for the DP industry.

2.1.2 Problems

These problem areas are discussed below.

A. The application backlog

The 'application backlog' is now well-documented (e.g. in Martin, 1985). It refers to the inability of information systems developers to keep abreast of requests for applications. This backlog has been quoted as being as much as two to five years (e.g. Martin (1985) and

Grindley (1986), although references to this backlog are frequent in the literature on 4GLs). That is, if a user wants an application developed, they could wait up to five years before the request is even considered. Because of this kind of delay many users do not even bother to ask. These 'hidden' requests constitute the 'invisible (or ghost) backlog'. Some would claim that they could effectively increase the application backlog by a factor of six, if they ever came to light.

Applications 'sitting' in this backlog are all of different types/sizes. They could range from very large complex systems to simple *ad hoc* requests. These applications will require differing amounts of time, effort and manpower to complete. Figure 2.3 categorises various application types.

It is also important to appreciate that most systems are not just straightforward batch or transaction processing applications. Many will involve a mixture of processing types, e.g. on-line update of database, with batch processing of reports.

B. The 'traditional systems life-cycle'

The so-called 'traditional systems life-cycle' is shown in Figure 2.4 and for completeness the stages of this life-cycle are outlined in Table 2.1. This is rather a simplistic view. Other modified

Application types include	*new operational systems.* The large-scale applications within an organisation for their basic business activities. Such applications would include sales order processing, stock control, production control, etc.
	management systems. Traditionally MIS, i.e. management information systems, now also includes decision support systems (DSS). These are systems used to enhance the role of management within an organisation. May overlap with some departmental systems.
	departmental systems. The applications which previously existed on a card file in someone's desk drawer and could now be implemented via a spread-sheet or other similar tool. Previously these would not have been considered important enough for the DP department to be involved with. The need for such systems has spurred the personal computer, 'do-it-yourself approach'. Could include some management systems.
	maintenance. This could take the form of fixes, changes or enhancements. It is often said that something like 70 per cent or more of a DP department's time is spent on maintaining old systems, rather than in building new ones.

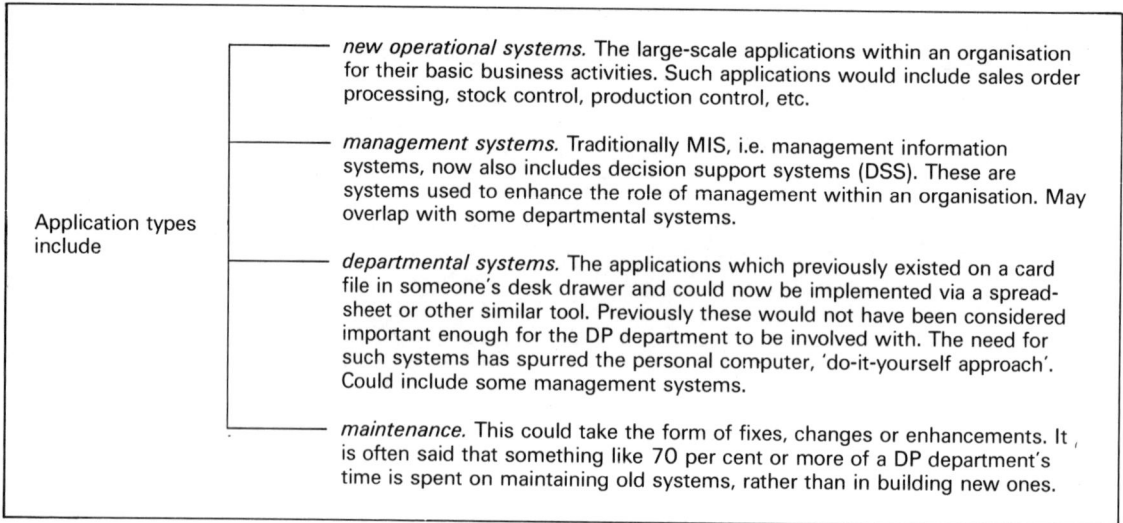

Figure 2.3 *Categories of applications*

Table 2.1 Stages in the life-cycle

Stages in life-cycle	*Description of stage*
1) Initial request	The user puts in a request for a system. This is often in vague terms and will need to be re-written by the developer.
2) Feasibility study	The feasibility study is an initial investigation into the existing system, if any, and the proposed alternatives. At this stage estimates of cost, effort, efficiency, effectiveness and reliability are made. The results are a feasibility study report and clearer understanding of the system goals and objectives. A decision to proceed must be made at this stage.
3) Systems analysis	During this phase the existing procedures are documented in detail. The user requirements must also be defined. This requirement specification is used to design the system. The boundaries of the system should also be defined.
4) Systems design	The design of the system is undertaken. Detailed specifications for the system are produced. Programming specifications are passed through to the next stage.
5) Programming	Programs are designed and coded from specifications.
6) Testing	Programs are tested for errors etc. Acceptance tests are carried out whereby the user accepts the system as working. Documentation is produced.
7) Implementation	System becomes operational.
8) Maintenance	Need for fixes, changes and enhancements. When maintenance becomes an impossible task or infeasible due to cost etc. the life-cycle may begin again.

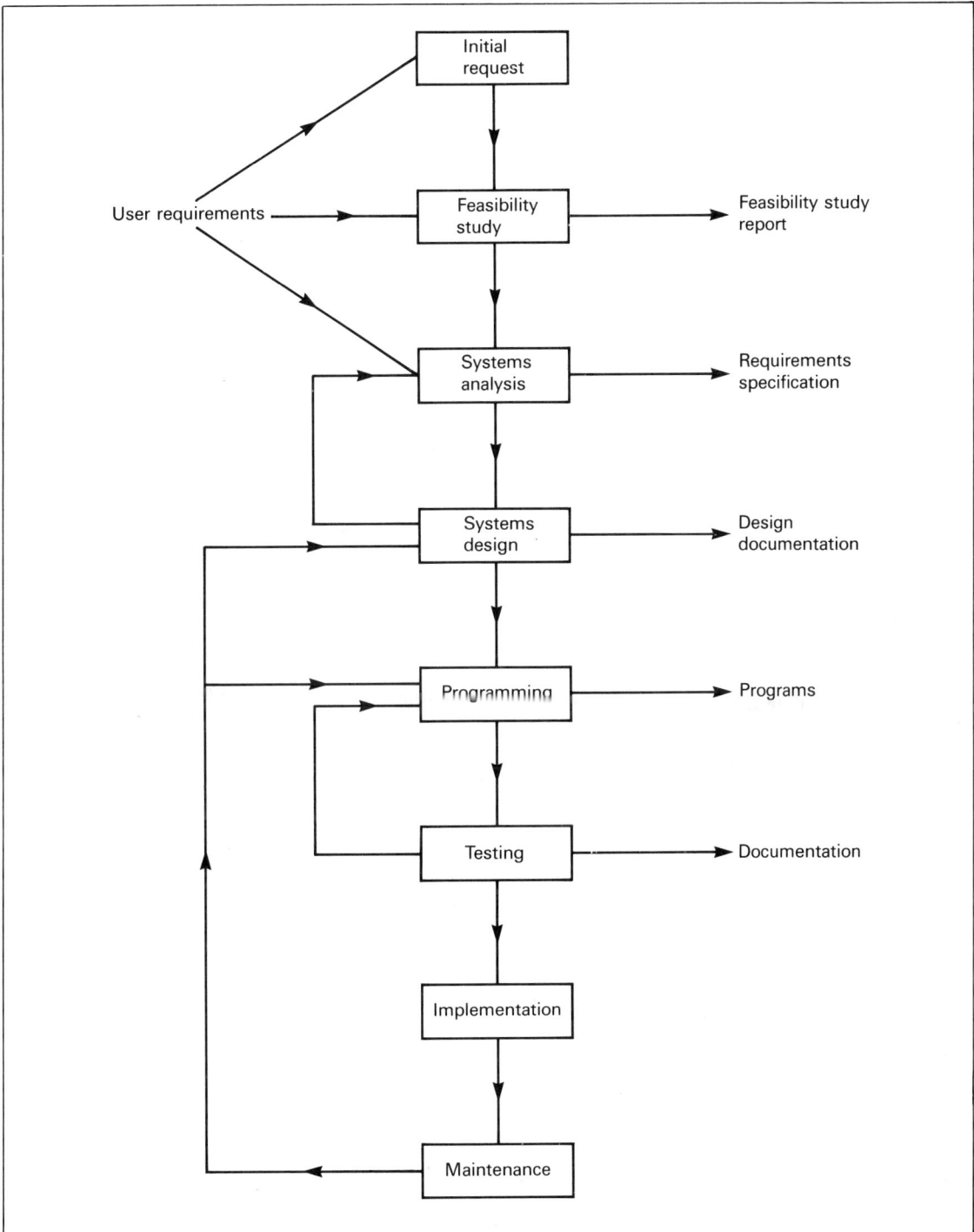

Figure 2.4   *The traditional systems life-cycle*

versions of this life-cycle exist, especially where techniques such as structured methods are used. Refer to Daniels and Yeates (1988) for one such modification.

This method of application development relies on a step-at-a-time approach and comprises a number of formal phases. Most of these phases have constraints fixed upon them, e.g. time, cost, etc., and culminate in a formal agreed milestone, many of which are in document form, e.g. feasibility study report, specification documents.

This approach has been criticised for its inflexibility, its serial nature and its reliance on pre-specification techniques (e.g. Lantz, 1986). That is, the system is designed around a pre-defined document (the requirements specification), which once agreed with the user and having been 'signed-off' does not change. This can happen when ideas are still not firmly fixed in the user's own mind or for applications where user requirements are difficult/impossible to define at the outset. All of this obviously leads to the types of problem under discussion, e.g. system not matching user's requirements exactly.

There are some obvious advantages to the traditional systems life-cycle or it would not be used. It does consist of well-defined stages and it does require a methodical approach. Used appropriately it produces results. However, it is obviously not working for all applications and could and should be enhanced by the use of other tools and techniques, e.g. more user involvement, structured methods. Where other approaches are more appropriate these should be considered as alternative development methods. For example, prototyping and iterative development are feasible alternatives. Prototyping and iterative development are explained in Chapter 6, where alternative development approaches are explored.

It must also be said in defence of the life-cycle that the inflexibility of the approach may stem from the way it is put into practice by the developers, rather than from the approach itself. For example, it is the developer who insists that the specification document is 'signed-off' by the user at a specific stage in the life-cycle.

C. User/DP communication

Communication between human beings is always a complex operation. When the people involved in the communication do not have a common language then failure is likely to follow. One of the criticisms levelled at DP professionals is their use of a special language which only they understand. DP professionals often think little better of users.

An article in the *Financial Times* (Gooding, 1986), begins, 'A programmer's definition of a user might be: "Someone who never knows what he wants until he's got something, and then wants something different." A user's definition of a programmer might equally be: "Someone to whom you explain exactly what you want and who then goes away and comes back months later with something totally different." ' A typical situation is illustrated in Figure 2.5.

The use of jargon by the professionals is judged to be deliberate. It somehow makes their jobs seem more important or difficult. Grindley (1986) calls this the culture of complexity. Whilst programming is perceived as a very complex operation requiring highly trained professionals, it will remain just that.

There is certainly a need for techniques/tools in the areas of analysis and design which can be used as a basis for the communication between users and DP professionals. Martin (1985), suggests action diagrams to fill this need.

The programmer who produces the final software has traditionally been completely isolated from the user. The analyst has acted as the 'go-between', translating the user's requirements into a formal specification from which the system is produced, so by the time the system gets to the production stage, parts of it are 'third-hand'. Other development methods such as prototyping brings the user closer to the professional(s) producing the system. They also allow greater involvement of the user in the development process and place the emphasis on communication between the participants.

D. Requirements specification

As we have already seen, the traditional

Figure 2.5   *User/DP communication*

approach to creating computer applications relies on pre-specification techniques. Specifications for these systems are usually in written English, supplemented by diagrammatic techniques such as flowcharts and dataflow diagrams. They may be huge, wordy documents which are not fully understood on either side. Inconsistencies and omissions may be over-looked and incorporated into the final system. Even the specifications for software passed from the analyst to the programmer, i.e. between professionals, are open to assumptions and mis-interpretation.

There is little or no allowance for changes of

mind or refinements of the specification when problems are better understood. Specification also becomes a problem when maintenance is carried out. Often changes made are not reflected in the specification documents. Hence these become out-of-date and inaccurate.

E. Development time and costs
There is little doubt that the activities within this traditional approach are often carried out too slowly, too rigidly and at too great a cost. Something like 60 per cent of systems (Patman, 1986) under development will go over budget on

both time and cost constraints. The reasons for this are two-fold:

★ Slippage in time estimates. This may be due to various factors including imprecise estimates and other important work such as urgent maintenance fixes which require the attention of key staff.
★ Unforeseen difficulties. Not all problems can be catered for in advance.

Many errors originate in the earliest stages of the development process (Figure 2.6), yet cost significantly more to fix as development progresses (Figure 2.7). By far the most expensive areas are the later stages of programming, testing and implementation. It is much more costly to rectify a mistake in analysis when it reaches the programming stage than at the analysis stage itself.

The emphasis on resources shifts therefore, from development to maintenance. In fact the proportion of resources spent on maintenance has changed dramatically (US figures):

1960s: 30% maintenance and 70% development
1980s: 80% maintenance and 20% development.

F. Traditional file processing

The traditional method of storing data for retrieval or modification is through the use of data files held on magnetic media such as disc or tape. Despite being a well-tried and tested method, there are several drawbacks to this approach, including:

★ Redundancy of data. Within organisations the same data items may be stored several times on different files, possibly across different applications. For example, customer details such as name, address and account number may be held both on an order file within the sales order processing function and on an accounts file.
★ Inconsistency of data. If information is stored in more than one place, it must all be updated at the same time if it is to remain consistent. This rarely happens. Inconsistency of data is a common cause of major errors within systems.
★ Low programmer productivity. For every new application, records and files must be designed, data definitions coded, procedures written, file storage and access methods chosen, etc. over and over again.
★ Maintenance. Data, record and file descriptions are usually embedded within the individual application programs. Any change requires a modification of the programs as well as changes to the data itself.

This is not necessarily an exhaustive list but it is these drawbacks which have led to the adoption of a different approach to data storage, i.e. databases, and which have contributed to the problems already identified. It is interesting to note that many 4GLs utilise database facilities either directly (they have integrated facilities, i.e. a database is an integral part of the 4GL), or

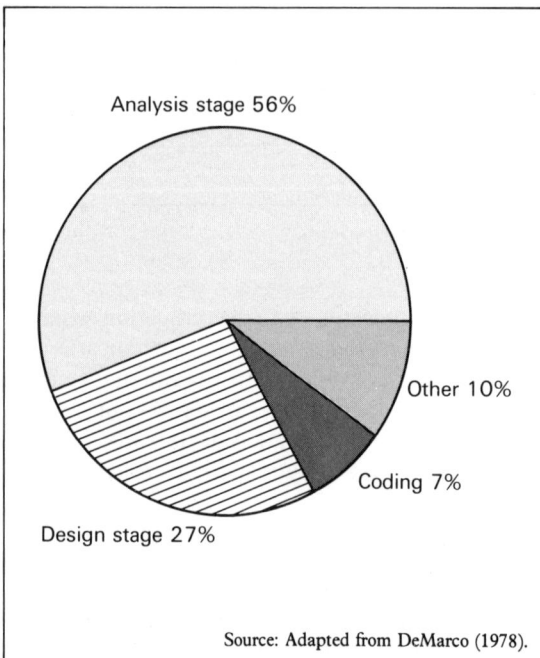

Analysis stage 56%

Other 10%

Coding 7%

Design stage 27%

Source: Adapted from DeMarco (1978).

Figure 2.6 *Distribution of bugs in the development process*

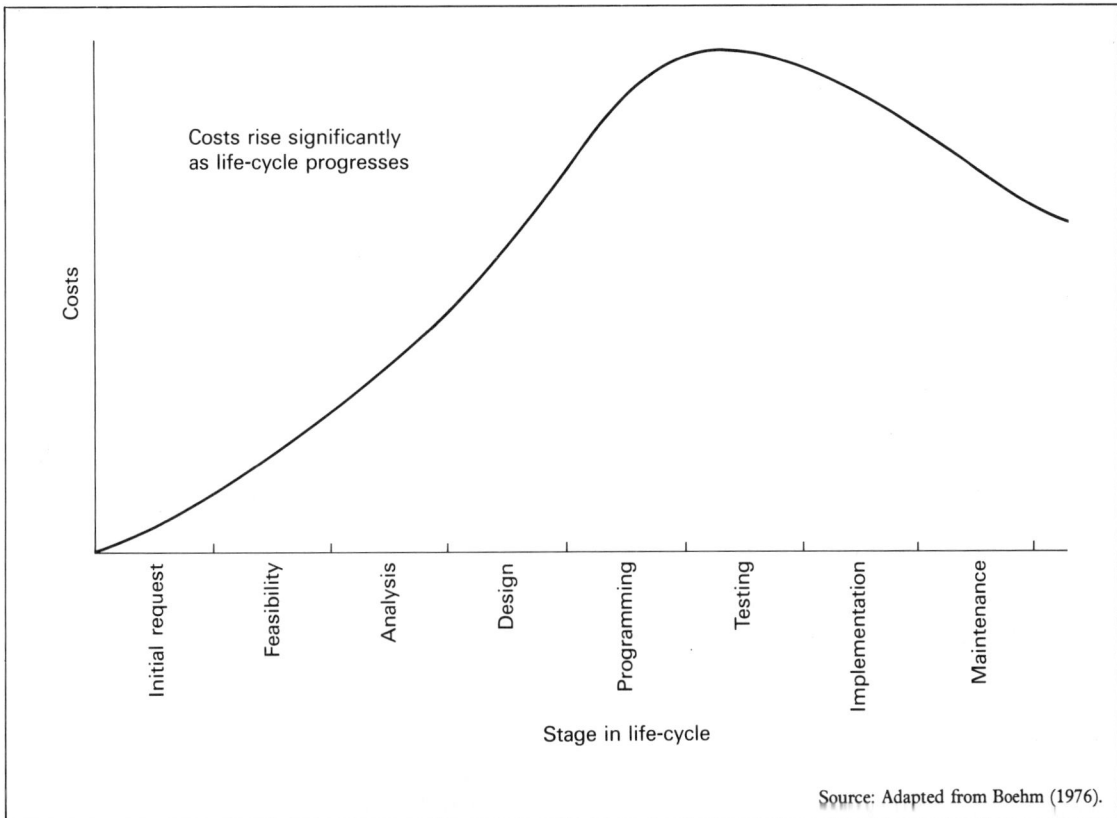

Figure 2.7 *Distribution of costs associated with life-cycle*

indirectly (they can access external database facilities). 4GL links to database facilities are discussed in Chapter 4. The ideas of integrated and non-integrated databases are also considered.

G. Systems do not fully match requirements

We have covered most of the reasons for this happening in previous points, e.g. the breakdown in user/professional communication and the problems with specification. Patman (1986) quotes a survey which suggests that less than 1 per cent of systems developed will be on time, be within budget and meet *all* user requirements. If these figures are accurate then the customer is not receiving what they want, when they want it, nor at the right cost.

H. Maintenance

Perhaps the most quoted statistic in computing is the one which says that 70 per cent of a DP department's time is spent in maintenance. There are four major points to be raised here:

1) Generally we are talking about software maintenance and in particular programmers maintaining code.

2) Maintenance of computer systems also involves other components:

★ hardware: changes in hardware, upgrades, etc.

★ people: updating of skills, techniques, etc.

★ miscellaneous: changes to forms, documents, etc.

3) Systems can and do run from Day 1 with little or no changes needed or can require a huge maintenance effort from the start.

4) There are plenty of statistics available. Here it is worth noting that:

   ★ $30 billion a year is spent on maintenance world-wide.
   ★ much of the maintenance being done is on COBOL code.
   ★ 2 per cent of the gross national product of the USA is spent on software maintenance and this is growing.
   ★ it is estimated that something in excess of £1 billion is spent on software maintenance in the UK each year.

These figures are quoted in Leonard, Pardoe and Wade (1988). Refer to this paper for a more comprehensive discussion on software maintenance and a full reference list. Maintenance is obviously a big problem, and in particular software maintenance requires attention.

It is therefore reasonable to ask why maintenance is such a problem? Table 2.2 lists the possible reasons.

It is usually accepted that software maintenance is an activity with three main components:

1) Corrective maintenance – the process of finding and correcting errors in software after it has been released for use, i.e. post-

implementation. These 'fixes' account for 17 per cent of all software maintenance.

2) Adaptive maintenance – changing software to adapt to some change in the hardware environment, e.g. the operating system. This accounts for about 18 per cent of software maintenance activities.

3) Perfective maintenance – enhancements to both the functionality (what it can do) and the efficiency (how well it does it) of the code being maintained. This accounts for all but a very small proportion of the remainder of the software maintenance task.

Figure 2.8 illustrates the division of these maintenance tasks. (Figures for this diagram are taken from Leonard, Pardoe and Wade (1988)). A fourth option is sometimes added:

4) Preventive maintenance – software is changed to improve its maintainability or to provide a better basis for enhancements to be made. This is offered as a possible solution to the problems and so will be considered as such later. It is also currently a rare activity in the maintenance process.

We could consider maintenance in further detail but will not as this is not intended to be a book on maintenance problems nor one on how to solve these problems by using relevant techniques. However the effect of 4GLs on the maintenance task is discussed again in Chapter 6.

Table 2.2   Software maintenance

Questions	Answers

Why does it occur?	★ Bugs in code
	★ Changes in legislation
	        technology
	        environment
	        procedures
	★ Additional requirements from users

Why is it a problem?	★ Old, unstructured code ★ Little or no documentation ★ Staff turnover ★ Maintenance can degrade code ★ Size of programs

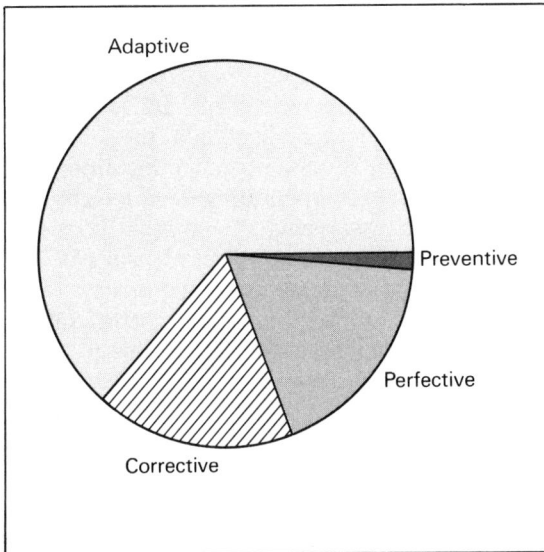

Figure 2.8   *The division of maintenance tasks*

I. The slow adoption of structured methods

We have already discussed the effects of allowing a mistake in the analysis stage of the systems life-cycle to go through to later stages of the development process and how this is the phase where the majority of errors originate. The idea behind structured analysis and design methods is that more emphasis is placed on 'getting it right' at the early stages so that this situation is avoided.

There are a number of structured approaches available, e.g. SSADM (Structured Systems Analysis and Design Methodology), SADT (Structured Analysis and Design Technique). (We shall return to a discussion of such techniques later in this chapter.) Despite the fact that these are not new approaches – they date back to the late 1970s – there is evidence to suggest that their adoption and usage has been a relatively slow process in some organisations. Also, where they have been put into use, some organisations have found that the expected benefits are not always achieved.

For example, Lee (1986) quotes the results of her survey, which showed that only 32 per cent of the sample organisations surveyed in the UK were actually using structured methods for systems development, with a further 15 per cent considering their adoption. This reinforces the idea that there is some resistance to the newer methodologies, with the tendency towards adherence to older ones.

Much the same can be said for structured programming techniques, although these methods have been around even longer (see Section 2.3.1).

J. 'Do-it-yourself approaches'

There is no doubt that end-user computing, i.e. where users develop applications for themselves, is increasing. This has been greeted by a variety of responses from the DP industry, ranging from scepticism ('users can't develop their own applications') to the provision of positive help and advice, e.g. the setting up of information centres within organisations. The role of such centres is considered in Chapter 7.

The danger is of course (and hence why we are considering it as both a problem and later as a solution) that, unless handled properly, end-user computing will not work. Instead of providing a solution to such problems as the application backlog, it could become an additional problem for the computing industry to sort out.

2.2 Reactions to the problems identified

Both users and DP professionals have responded to the problems discussed in order to find solutions, and in particular to the dilemma of the application backlog.

2.2.1 Responses from users

These have included the following:

★ To do without (the invisible backlog mentioned previously). They hence lose the potential benefits of a computerised system.

★ To adopt a 'do-it-yourself' approach. End-user computing involves users in developing applications for themselves, usually on microcomputers.

★ To carry on as before, waiting for their turn to come, possibly for several years.

2.2.2 Responses from DP

These include the following:

★ To increase existing resources, including personnel. However there is obviously a limit to how far this can go and a limit on the amount of skilled personnel available.

★ To exercise more management control over projects. Unfortunately even a well-managed project will probably not make all the required savings in time and cost. Inevitably there are factors contributing to such problems which are outside of this type of control.

★ To instigate a policy of 'buying-in' packaged software where this fits user requirements. This again does not have a particularly dramatic effect on the application backlog as this type of software is not always the best nor the most appropriate solution.

★ To use outside organisations to develop applications. This can be costly and organising maintenance is an additional headache.

★ To attempt to reduce the time needed to develop applications and time spent in maintenance activities.

This final response can itself involve several courses of action:

★ Reduce the cost of each step in the life-cycle by using appropriate tools, e.g. analyst/programmer workbenches which attempt to make some of the tasks undertaken by the analyst/programmer less time-consuming, e.g. the automatic production of various diagrams, like data flow diagrams. Tools such as this are considered in Chapter 9.

★ Reduce the need for or emphasis on one step in the life-cycle. This basically amounts to a modification of the traditional life-cycle by adopting other approaches to application development, such as prototyping.

★ Reduce the number of iterations back through the life-cycle, i.e. get it right quicker through the use of structured tools and closer liaison with the end-user.

★ Increase programmer productivity.

It is important to appreciate that these options could be combined through the use of 4GLs, particularly where these have been extended to link with other productivity tools (see Chapter 9). For the purpose of this chapter we need to consider other current solutions to the problems identified and the extent to which these solutions have worked. Some of the solutions are aimed at the analysis and design stages of the life-cycle, others at the programming stages and beyond.

2.3 Some current solutions to the DP problems

2.3.1 Structured programming techniques

As far back as the 1960s, the productivity of programmers was being questioned. This led to a re-think about the way in which programming is performed. In 1965 Professor Dijkstra suggested that the GOTO statement should be excluded from programming languages. In 1966 Boehm and Jacopini showed that any program with single entry and exit points could be expressed in terms of three basic constructs:

1) sequence or carrying out a process
2) iteration or looping
3) selection or decision-making.

This was the beginning of structured programming.

Structured programming techniques, e.g. Jackson Structured Programming (JSP) concentrate on design rather than programming. The aims of these software design methods are discussed in King and Pardoe (1985), but a brief summary is given here. The aims are to:

★ produce correct programs.
★ facilitate the control and handling of software tasks, particularly those of a large/complex nature.
★ provide workable, systematic and teachable techniques.

Jackson himself uses terms such as 'rational, non-inspirational, teachable and practical'. His method (JSP) looks initially at the logical data structures of the problem and leads from a program structure through to definition of tasks and finally the translation to a programming language (code). Figure 2.9 is an example of a logical data structure.

Unfortunately such methods do not provide a complete solution and we are still faced with problems:

★ Not getting requirements correct initially. We are now producing error-free, wrongly specified code.
★ Maintenance. There may be a positive effect on corrective and even adaptive maintenance, through the use of such techniques. Perfective maintenance will still be a major problem.

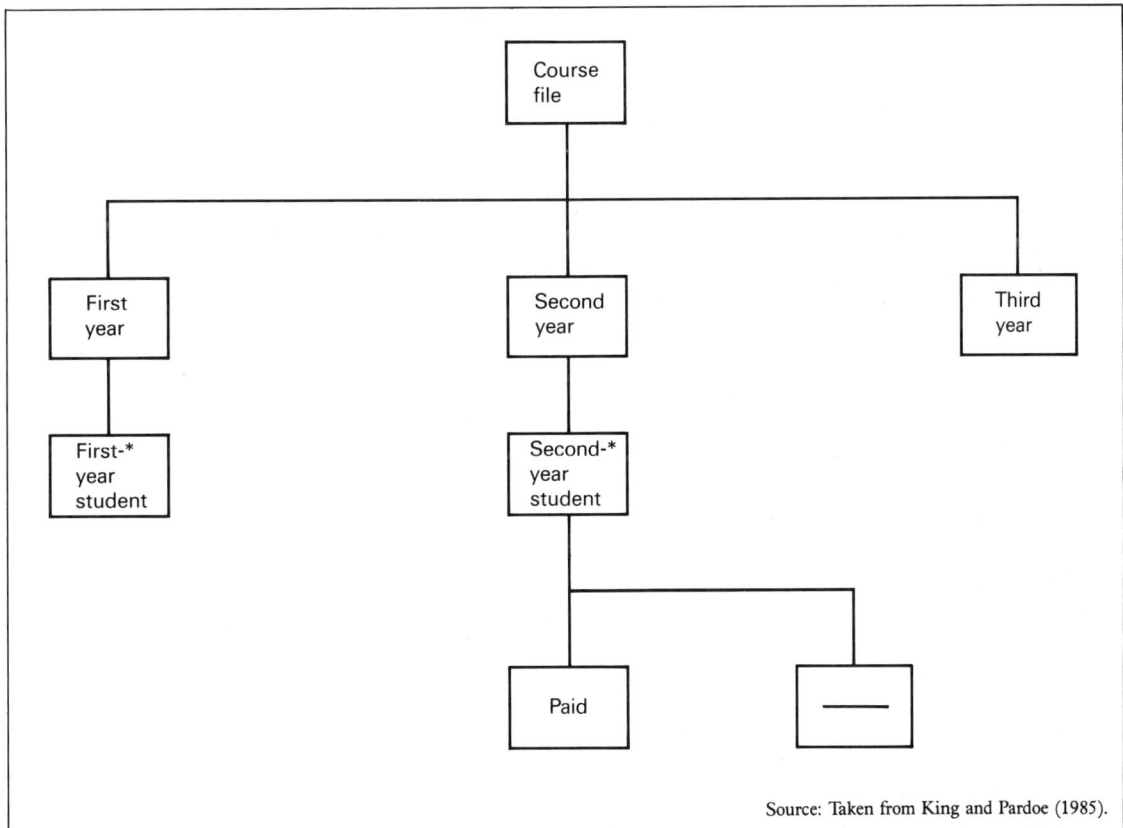

Source: Taken from King and Pardoe (1985).

Figure 2.9 *A logical data structure for a program to count the numbers of second-year students on a course who have paid their fees*

Most people accept the sound reasoning behind structured programming techniques but there are many organisations who for various reasons fail to put them into practice. For example there is evidence to show (Martin, 1982) that even with such techniques, programmer productivity is not increased by more than 25 per cent at most. The feeling is that the effort required to learn and use a structured methodology is not rewarded by sufficient benefits.

2.3.2 Structured analysis and design methods

As we have mentioned already, these methods began to appear at the end of the 1970s and concentrate on some of the problems not addressed by structured programming, e.g. poor systems design, which can undo all the benefits of structured programming techniques. A number of people have made significant contributions to this field, e.g. De Marco, Gane and Sarson, Warnier and Orr, Yourdon, etc. with various methods. Some emphasise data modelling and some function modelling. Basically they all concentrate on the idea that by spending more time on 'getting it right' in the early stages of development, less time will be spent 'putting it right' later on.

Many of the methods available share the diagrammatic technique of producing data flow diagrams (Figure 2.10). Data flow diagrams highlight the functions within a system (the processes) and the interfaces between them (data flows). They can be drawn and re-drawn and refined to various levels of detail.

The benefits of structured methods are:

★ They use a logical approach.
★ Diagrammatic techniques can be understood by users, i.e. an aid to communication.
★ They should provide consistent results.
★ They are easier to maintain.
★ They provide a framework for development.

It is obvious that despite their advantages, these methods are not a total solution to the problems raised. If they were, then in the ten or so years they have been available, they would have had a more dramatic effect in terms of benefits gained.

Martin (1985) suggests that part of the problem lies in the fact that these techniques are a move towards improving existing methods, i.e. they formalise the traditional systems life-cycle. To some extent they are trying to solve the wrong problem. What they should be offering is faster and more flexible techniques, instead of just an improvement to old ways.

Other problems lie with their disadvantages. Classic structured methods (Yourdon, 1986):

★ require a more disciplined approach.
★ need graphical skills.
★ require large amounts of data flow diagrams to be drawn and often re-drawn.
★ assume a straightforward system (e.g. not normally associated with real-time systems.)
★ require extensive time and effort for modelling the current system (referred to as 'analysis paralysis').
★ rely heavily on manual labour (unless automation is used).

However this is not to suggest that these methods are without value. The move towards the automation of the more tedious aspects, e.g. diagram production, is a further positive step resulting out of fourth generation techniques. Some products allow automation of the complete development process from analysis through to the production of COBOL code ready for compilation. Further improvements being introduced into structured methods include:

★ extension of the techniques to real-time systems through the use, for example, of state-transition diagrams,
★ evolution of data flow diagrams, e.g. to allow for real-time components: dashed line indicates signals or interrupts,
★ de-emphasis on the modelling of the existing system.

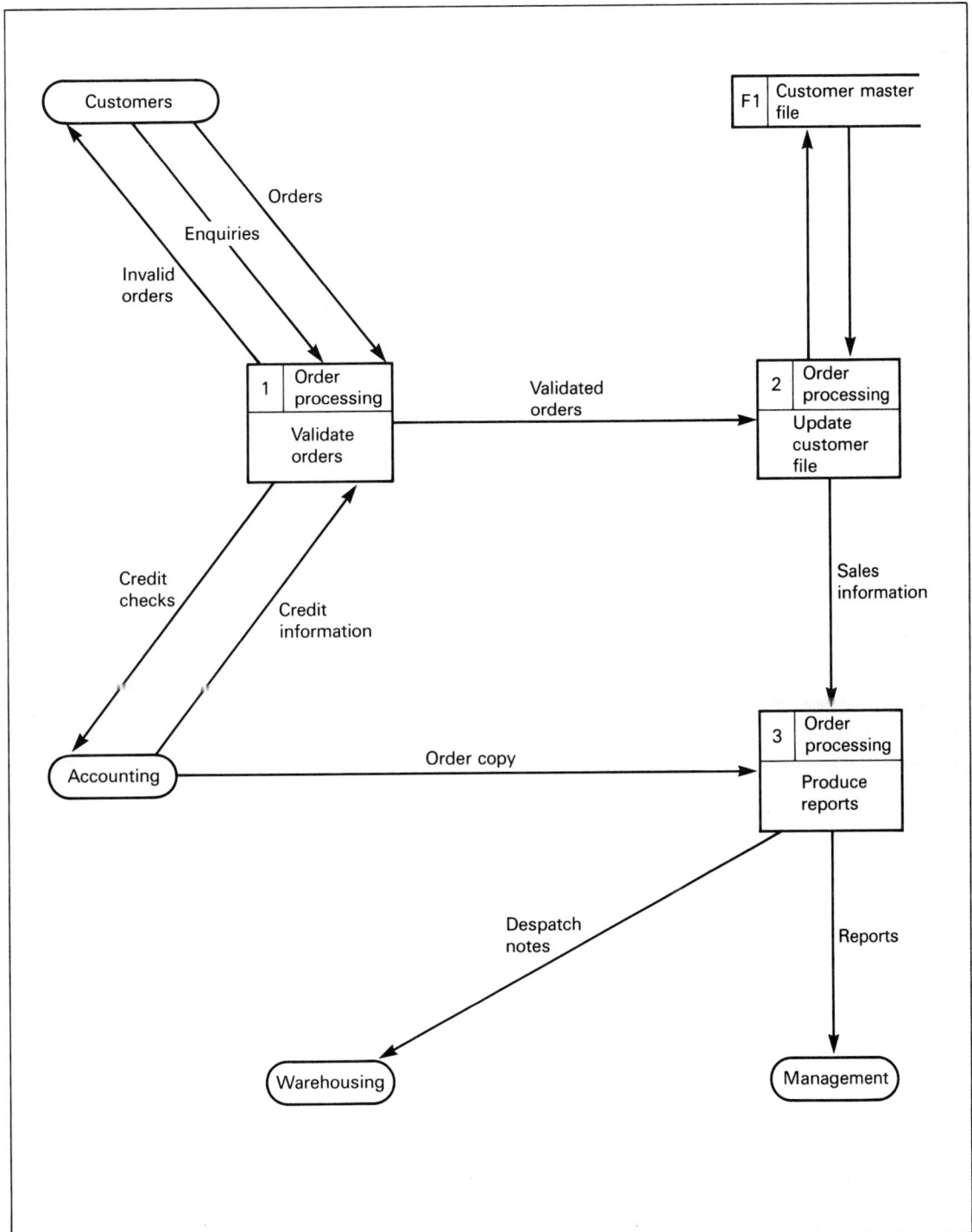

Figure 2.10 *A simple second-level DFD for an order-processing function*

2.3.3 Preventive maintenance

We discussed this earlier as the fourth dimension to the maintenance task. This was put forward as a possible solution to the maintenance problem. In order to improve the maintainability of the code, tools such as document enhancers, code formatters, code restructurers, and code documentors may be used.

The idea of preventive maintenance is of course to make the task easier and more bearable by tackling some of the problems identified earlier in Table 2.2 rather than make the maintenance problem go away. Unfortunately, at the moment preventive maintenance is not widely used.

2.3.4 Use of database systems

We have discussed the emphasis in organisations on data. The need is for speedy, flexible and convenient access to, and retrieval of, that data by the users of computer systems. This has meant a drift away from traditional file processing systems towards the alternative approach of the database. Justification for this approach involves:

- ★ the need to reduce long lead times and high development costs,
- ★ users' need to share data within organisations, often across functional/ departmental boundaries,
- ★ the need to improve the quality and consistency of the data provided,
- ★ the need to control access to data according to needs and privileges,
- ★ to help overcome the problems of frequently changing data.

We have already seen some of the drawbacks associated with file processing. On the other hand databases

- ★ control or eliminate redundancy.
- ★ enforce consistency (as a result of above).
- ★ reduce duplication of programmer effort.

- ★ provide data independence by separating the data from the applications programs. Hence changes to data do not necessarily result in maintenance of the application programs.

2.3.5 Formal methods

The use of formal methods seeks to place software development on mathematical foundations. It is largely aimed at two crucial areas, specification and verification. An important objective is that the software produced can be proven to be correct, i.e. verified to match the specification exactly. This increases confidence in the reliability of the software produced and should also reduce the need for testing and corrective maintenance. The language of specification must be a formal language with associated formal semantics and verification techniques.

A number of methods, tools and languages have emerged, including OBJ (an algebraic approach), Vienna Development Method (VDM) (a model-based approach) and Z (another model-based approach, with an associated language based on set theory and first-order predicate logic). See Ratcliff (1987) for an introduction to formal methods.

Although a lot of work is being done in the area of formal methods in academic and research organisations, it is often said that as yet such methods are a long way from the everyday realities of software development.

2.3.6 Other solutions

There are other solutions as well. Prototyping, i.e. building a model of the system and involving the user actively in the design, and end-user computing have already been briefly mentioned. These solutions depend on the availability of the right tool. 4GLs have facilitated these methods. How is explained in later chapters.

2.3.7 Quality management

One extremely important area which should be
mentioned here is quality management, i.e. the
management of the activities which go together
to ensure that a product is built to an
appropriate and acceptable standard. Such
activities are labelled quality assurance (QA)
which is usually the responsibility of a corporate
QA group and the project team building the
software. Many suppliers of software now have
QA systems as part of their organisational
structure and a number of standards, both
national and international, may be adhered to,
e.g. AQUAP-1 and the related software
production AQUAP-13, published by the NATO
Defence Support Division (AQUAP standing for
Allied Quality Assurance Publication). (The
DTI/NCC Starts Guide (1987) and Ratcliff
(1987) both discuss quality assurance.)

It is a further move towards producing the
right software at the right cost. Whilst such
techniques are not a solution to the problems
identified, they should be an integral part of the
software development process.

2.4 Conclusions

The DP industry has problems, problems which
have arisen partly because of the traditional
approach to the development of applications and
the unavailability of the right tools to overcome
the deficiencies and partly because of the other
trends and developments discussed in this
chapter. Several useful, if not complete
solutions have been offered. The drawback to
such solutions is that applied separately they are
largely solving either the wrong problem or only
attack part of the problem. Hence only minor
inroads have been made into various areas of
concern. However, if applied through a common
vehicle, such as a 4GL, more progress should
and could be made. It is this integrated solution
which will concern us in later chapters.

2.5 Follow-up questions and activities

2.5.1 Questions

1) Describe five major changes which have
occurred in the computing industry over the
last ten years.

2) a) What do you understand by the term
'traditional systems life-cycle'? Illustrate
your answer by reference to a diagram
where appropriate.
   b) What are the disadvantages of this
approach to application development?

3) Explain fully the following terms:
   a) application backlog
   b) requirements specification
   c) culture of complexity
   d) redundancy of data

4) a) Why is software maintenance such a
huge problem for the computing
industry?
   b) Describe the three main components of
software maintenance.
   c) Preventive maintenance is at present a
lesser used technique in software
maintenance. What is preventive
maintenance?

5) a) List the problems currently being
experienced in the DP industry.
   b) Discuss three of the solutions being used
to tackle these problems.
   c) Why are these not complete solutions to
the problems identified?

2.5.2 Activities

6) a) Find out which structured analysis and
design methodology is currently being
used in your college/polytechnic/
organisation.
   b) Are there any software tools in use which
link with this methodology? If so what
are they?

c) What are the major tools and techniques of the methodology, e.g. data flow diagrams.

d) What advantages does this technique have over unstructured methods?

7) Many organisations now use structured programming techniques such as Jackson Structured Programming (JSP).

a) List the advantages you have found in using structured programming techniques over other methods of program development.

b) What would you say were the main disadvantages of using structured programming techniques?

Part Two

The fourth generation 'solution'

3 What are fourth generation languages?

Objectives

After you have studied this chapter you should be able to:

★ attempt to answer the question, 'What are 4GLs?'
★ understand that different types of 4GL exist, and be aware of the classifications associated with 4GLs.
★ explain, in simple terms, the differences between pure and hybrid 4GLs.
★ appreciate that the users of 4GLs range from end-user to analyst to programmer and why this is so.
★ understand the need to choose a 4GL very carefully according to the task in hand.

3.1 Towards a definition

It should be apparent from the previous chapters that the emergence of 4GLs can be associated with historic problems. There are various reasons for their evolution and use. 4GLs use results from the need for the following:

★ Fast interactive development tools to help make inroads on the application backlog.
★ Increased programmer productivity.
★ To break free from some of the unnecessary restrictions imposed by the traditional systems life-cycle.
★ An opportunity for programmers to use up-to-date tools and techniques.
★ Reduction of the costs of producing software.
★ Involvement of end-users in the application development process.

Clearly there is a need for change within the traditional DP environment and 4GLs are contributing to that process of change.

The products which have and continue to emerge under the heading 'fourth generation' have been many and various, often with a minimum of commonality. Such products include:

★ query languages
★ report generators
★ application builders
★ very high level languages
★ decision support tools
★ database-oriented tools

as well as others. The inclusion of some of these products on the list, query languages for example, amongst other 4GLs is often disputed, as writers look for common threads on which to base their definitions.

It is precisely this apparent lack of commonality which has caused many people to claim that 4GLs are simply 'media hype' or that the term is just a buzz-word used to sell any product aimed at ease-of-use or improved productivity. Such claims should be dismissed. 4GLs obviously offer something different from the previous three generations.

Finding an objective definition of 4GLs is not easy. Suppliers of 4GLs offer definitions (one each), but they largely amount to a list of facilities offered by each product. They are quick to dismiss competing products as 'not true 4GLs' without ever expanding on what that means. With some several hundred products on the market claiming to be 'fourth generation', it is not surprising that definition is difficult.

Unfortunately even the experts writing about the subject seem to be unable to come to any real consensus of opinion. Some writers focus on the increased productivity opportunities. Martin (1985) feels that this is a crucial issue and talks about 4GL systems having one-fifth or one-tenth the number of lines of code that the same system written in COBOL would have. Similar claims are made by product vendors and manufacturers. Others feel the move away from writing procedures in high-level code to be more central. Christoff (1985) talks about expressing ideas in a 'less wordy, results-oriented language'. Still other definitions concentrate on end-user appeal and ease-of-use, but in the end none of the definitions are totally in agreement nor precise enough to be definitive.

The term 4GL itself has been attributed to Nigel Read and Douglas Harmon in an article in *Datamation* (Read and Harmon, 1981). Prior to this, these types of products were often called 'high-productivity tools' and included application program generators (APGs) which use a type of procedural code to produce 3GL output such as COBOL and PL/1, and report generators which produce report output. The term application generator is still used for some of the products we might call 4GLs.

Many of the ideas around which 4GLs evolved came to the fore between (about) 1967 and 1974. At this time it was seen that the management of program control could be specified algorithmically, hence allowing the software to control the program flow. This of course is intended to free the programmer from anything except specifying what is to be achieved – the idea behind non-procedural languages. Hence some of the products currently being offered as 4GLs have in fact been around since the mid-1970s, although it wasn't until the late 1970s and early 1980s that they began to become more generally available.

3.2 Procedural and non-procedural languages

There is no doubt that this non-procedural element is central to 4GLs. Some people felt that the arrival of 4GLs should have heralded the end of the procedural language. The goal, of course, is that people (and not just trained professionals) will communicate with computers in natural language. 'Programming' will be in simple, English-like commands which specify the desired result rather than the actions required to achieve that result. The machine will do the rest.

However, only a few 4GLs can claim to be totally non-procedural (called 'pure' 4GLs – see Section 3.5.1 in this chapter). Most offer non-procedural facilities but procedural methods are also employed in order to overcome the restrictions of the non-procedural elements. The non-procedural components may themselves be 'pure', but the combination produces a hybrid tool, i.e. a mixture of non-procedural and procedural facilities.

Some people dispute the description of 4GLs as non-procedural languages. Read and Harmon themselves felt that the term non-procedural language was too limited. They felt that the term 4GL described something which is a 'full-bore comprehensive programming language which is a quantum leap over COBOL'. Others have accepted the idea of the non-procedural language as a full definition. Grindley (1986), for example, talks about 4GLs as non-procedural languages.

One thing that must be made clear is that 4GLs are not a 'stop-gap' between the third generation and the techniques of the fifth. There is certainly a point at which the fourth and fifth generations complement each other. For example, some 4GLs now link to expert or knowledge-based systems (see Chapter 9). The idea of natural language interfaces, also adopted by some 4GLs, is associated with the fifth generation rather than the fourth. However 4GLs have evolved in order to solve different problems.

3.3 The problems of definition

The debate over the 'true' definition of a 4GL is on-going. 4GLs employ a variety of techniques to do a variety of tasks. 3GLs such as COBOL can create all or a large percentage of the applications needed in a DP environment. Having said that, we must not forget that there is always a large number of 'back-up' tools employed, e.g. compilers, pre-processors, debuggers, etc. Not all 4GLs can be used to develop all applications, nor are meant to be for that purpose.

The term full-function 4GL is a useful means of describing 4GLs which could be used as a direct replacement for COBOL, i.e. one which can build any application which previously might have been built in COBOL. However, used in the right situation, a 4GL with a limited set of functions aimed at a specific task may be equally useful, e.g. a spreadsheet tool.

Perhaps we are no nearer to a definition than before. That does not really matter. The following now becomes clear from our discussion of 4GLs:

★ There is more than one type or classification of 4GL. This makes definition difficult. It is probably better to use the classification to describe the 4GL than to accept a less than complete or satisfactory definition until such time that standards are agreed. We shall return to these classifications later.

★ Nevertheless there are a number of common threads across the range of languages. These threads will occur again in our discussions and are summarised in Figure 3.1.

★ Different products are coming onto the market and disappearing all the time. A 'settling down process' has yet to occur.

3.4 Is the term language appropriate?

In Chapter 1, we discovered that as well as the term 4GL others such as fourth generation tool (4GT) and fourth generation system (4GS) are also used to mean much the same thing. One of the reasons for this is the debate over whether use of the term 'language' is appropriate.

We would all accept that the purpose of any language is communication. Traditionally the term 'programming language' is used to describe those languages which people (generally programmers) use to communicate with a computer, ranging from machine language (code) to the so-called high-level languages of the third generation.

However there is a dislike amongst some academics and other professionals (Professor Dijkstra, the pioneering Dutch programmer, for example) of the term programming language. They feel that languages such as COBOL and FORTRAN are best described by the term 'notation'. The reasoning behind this is the naturally vague and informal quality of language, which is in complete contrast to the precise and formal nature of programming. Despite this objection the term programming language is very commonly used.

The description 'language' is generally accepted when applied to FORTRAN, for example. It is as acceptable to apply it to spreadsheets and database manipulation languages which may well be classed as 4GLs? Perhaps not, but many people use the command set of these 'languages' to communicate with their computers. To get round this problem the term 'dedicated' or 'specialist' language is often used to distinguish them from more general purpose languages.

The other problem is that programming languages are traditionally used by programmers, and we all know that programmers use some 'mystical mumbo-jumbo' to communicate with their machines, or at least that is how it

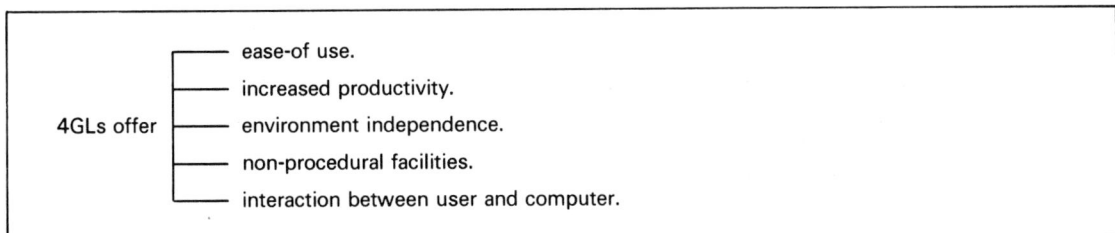

```
                  ┌──── ease-of use.
                  ├──── increased productivity.
   4GLs offer     ├──── environment independence.
                  ├──── non-procedural facilities.
                  └──── interaction between user and computer.
```

Figure 3.1 *Common themes in 4GL discussions*

seems to many non-DP people. Even the idea that a language like BASIC would be used by non-professionals to achieve results for themselves is largely misplaced. Most busy managers, for example, have not got the time for, and anyway would not remember the IF . . . THENs and FOR . . . NEXTs required to write programs.

Those 4GLs aimed at end-users will have to offer true ease-of-use methods. Some 4GLs are indeed programming languages and are often referred to as very high-level languages (e.g. Martin, 1985), by virtue of offering more powerful constructs than the 3GLs. This in itself is a disputed term (see the chapter by Kit Grindley in Martland *et al.* (1986)). Those people who see 4GLs as specification, rather than programming languages argue against them being described in this way. However the procedural language element does exist and it does require programming skill.

Perhaps 4GLs could be described as a set of tools (or 'goodies' as one writer put it), only one of which may be a language as we understand it. Many of the tools may be non-procedural in nature and could include components such as those listed in Table 3.1.

It is understandable that some organisations prefer to talk about 4GLs as 4GSs. The National Computing Centre (NCC) has defined a 4GS as an 'integrated set of software engineering tools which have evolved to provide an environment for the support of the produc-tion and development of interactive processing applications, and for *ad hoc* access to an applications database. . . . Fourth Generation Tool (4GT) may be defined as a subset of a 4GS.'

In some ways this is just beginning to happen. Most current 4GLs do not offer the facilities that such a 4GS would demand. The idea is to provide a complete application development and support environment which would rely on both fourth and fifth generation techniques. Consider for example the use of IPSEs (Integrated Project Support Environments) and CASE (Computer-Aided Software Engineering) tools, which aim to provide an automated development environment. (Refer to Chapter 9 for a further discussion of IPSE and CASE tools.) This is the way application development is moving. Cortex's CORVISION, for example, allows automation of the complete life-cycle, by providing a CASE environment as well as a 4GL component.

The fact that different phrases have been 'coined' to mean much the same thing is of little significance outside of the environment in which they are used. In other words, if everyone around you uses the term 4GL then you probably will too. It basically comes back to the same problems that were encountered when trying to pin down a reasonable definition of a 4GL, i.e.

★ 4GLs are still evolving.

Table 3.1   Possible or desirable components of a 4GL

★ A database management system (DBMS)

★ A data dictionary

★ A query language

★ A report generator

★ Screen definition facilities or screen painter

★ Graphics facilities

★ Decision support and/or spreadsheet and/or statistical facilities

★ An application development facility (employing either a 3GL or a 4GL)

★ Other facilities, e.g. PC to mainframe links, on-line help facilities, etc.

★ There is a diversity of products offered under the same general heading.
★ No standards have as yet been imposed.

However the fourth generation is not just concerned with the use of a language. It is not enough for organisations to consider a 4GL in isolation from the environment in which it is used. The languages of the third generation 'stood alone', as it were. Many 4GLs cannot be separated from their basic infrastructure or supporting elements, such as the data dictionary, database, etc. They may provide links to word processing and electronic mail facilities as well. In the end the whole approach to development is different. The emphasis is now on prototyping, data management and end-user participation.

3.5 Classifications of 4GLs

We have already determined that there are several 'types' of 4GL. In this section we shall consider the various classifications associated with 4GLs. These classifications are summarised in Table 3.2. They are also discussed in the major texts on 4GLs, such as Grindley (1986), Martin (1985, 1986), and Unicom Seminar Proceedings (1988).

3.5.1 Pure v. hybrid 4GLs

A. The pure product

It is felt that there are several 'ancestors' of the 4GL, which helps to explain where we are in today's technology. One of these is the idea of the translating process, where an easier-to-use language is automatically translated into the more obscure language of the computer. The successful development of second and third generation languages owes much to the continuing improvement of these translators (assemblers, compilers, etc.). It has also opened up the way for the fourth generation.

The second 'ancestor' is the idea of the 'packaged solution'. Generally these capture a general purpose solution to a particular processing problem and allow users to supply the details or parameters which are specific to their own needs or problems.

This is one of the approaches adopted in the fourth generation. The 4GL is a pre-coded system, i.e. software written in a particular procedural language. All the facilities offered by the 4GL are decided by the designer of the product itself. The 4GL offers a set of precoded 'templates', the templates on offer determining the range of tasks the 4GL can perform, e.g. database enquiry, report generation. This is not particularly difficult to understand if you

Table 3.2 Classifications of 4GLs

Classification of Product	Opposing Classification
Pure – totally non-procedural in nature	Hybrid – mixture of non-procedural and procedural facilities
End-user – aimed at the non-professional, often computer-literate user	Professional – for programmers or analysts or the analyst/programmer
Information centre – aimed at the end-user and the analyst	Development centre – specifically aimed at the professional
Dedicated – aimed towards a specialist use, e.g. decision-support	General purpose – similar general usage you may expect from a language like COBOL
Decision support – not to be used in the mainstream data processing tasks, also dedicated	Mainstream DP – used for the bread and butter operations
On-line – on-line interaction between user of tool and the tool itself, via a terminal	Off-line – some early 4GLs required forms to be filled in off-line, using manual methods

consider the template as a tool used to provide a pattern or guide for a previously mapped-out design. Some 4GLs allow the user to provide their own templates.

Any 'programming' we think of was carried out when the templates were coded. The user is required to provide the parameters for their particular problem – referred to as a problem statement – in a notation specific to the product being used. For example, the user may be required to provide descriptions of the data items within their problem, or of the associations between those data items. This is specification rather than programming.

The templates contain the computer strategy, which is worked out in advance. The appropriate template will be called up for the job in hand. The problem statement is transformed into a procedural solution by means of a generator. The statement of what is required has become one of how to carry it out, through the process of 'transformation'. The user makes no use of a procedural language as no 'programming' as such is required. They only employ non-procedural techniques. This is the essence of the non-procedural or 'pure' 4GL and this process is illustrated in Figure 3.2.

It is worth remembering that although specification with non-procedural facilities may simply require the user to provide a list of parameters, chose options from a menu or use a fill-in-forms dialogue, many people feel that the syntax involved in some non-procedural 'specification' is still very close to 'programming' in the normal sense of the word.

A typical routine to print out a report might involve this type of non-procedural syntax:

```
FILE SALESMAN
LIST NAME COMMISSION
WHERE AREA EQ 1
END
```

Contrast this with the code required to produce the same result with COBOL, say. Obviously there is no comparison. But judge for yourself how far removed it is from programming-like techniques.

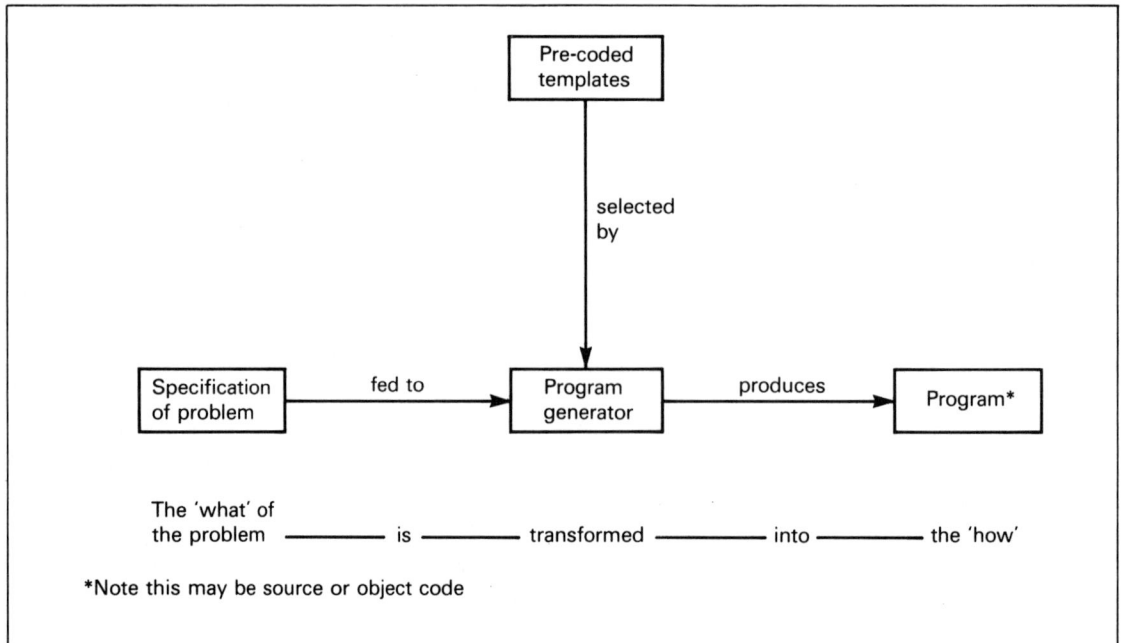

Figure 3.2   *The non-procedural approach to program development*

It helps to remember that the term non-procedural is often used to refer to the 'level' of the language being used. The level of languages tends to be comparative anyway, depending on the current 'state-of-the-art'. The second generation assembly languages seemed a giant step away from machine code but are nothing like 3GLs in terms of being high-level. The higher the 'level' the further away we get from the details of the machine and how the results are to be obtained. Some possible non-procedural elements of a 4GL are shown in Figure 3.3.

There are obvious advantages to this non-procedural approach:

★ The complexities of procedural programming are eliminated. This involves a reduction in the programming skills required and makes it possible for non-professionals to use the facilities available.
★ The development speed is increased.
★ The templates have been fully tested so that correct results should be obtained first time.
★ Any changes in the problem statement may be made by generating a fresh solution (hence changing the role of maintenance – refer to Chapter 6).

Why then are most 4GLs not pure products? Some people claim 4GLs to be more of an academic concept than a reality, whilst others see spreadsheets as the only true 'pure' 4GLs. Grindley (1986) discusses the pure 4GL. Unfortunately there are limitations to this approach, the major one being that for the 4GL

to cope with every problem it would have to provide a template to cover all options. This is obviously not feasible and hence the types of problem which can be solved are restricted by the templates provided by the 4GL.

It is not difficult to see why pure 4GLs are not general-purpose or full function tools. It's a bit like buying a house only to find that when you need to expand you cannot build an extension. The only solutions available to you are to stay within the boundaries of your original home or to buy a more suitable (general-purpose) house.

Having said this, some 4GLs could be said to be predominantly non-procedural. They offer a comprehensive range of non-procedural components that may be attractive to an end-user backed up by more complex tools for the professional. Several of the leading 4GLs are predominantly non-procedural. For example, FOCUS offers a mostly non-procedural environment, including its FOCUS language. For the reasons discussed above, however, even though they come close, such 4GLs are still not pure products.

B. The hybrid product

One way around the problem is to adopt a different approach. Hence the 'hybrid' 4GL extends the template approach offered by the pure 4GL by also allowing the use of procedural statements via its own built-in 4GL or an interface to a 3GL such as COBOL. The procedural component allows the 4GL to become (more) general-purpose. The templates still offer the attractiveness of the non-

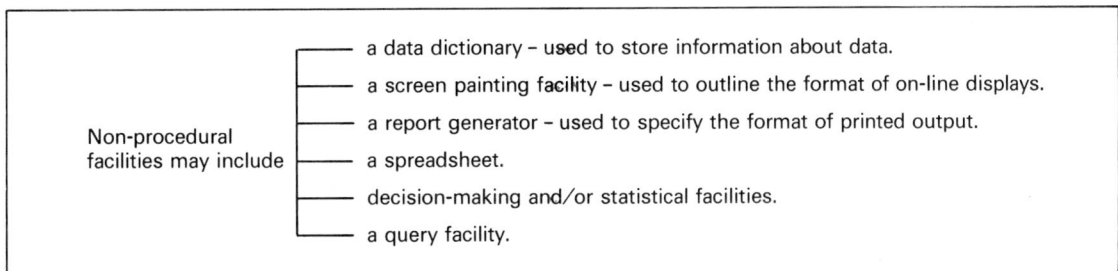

Non-procedural facilities may include
—— a data dictionary – used to store information about data.
—— a screen painting facility – used to outline the format of on-line displays.
—— a report generator – used to specify the format of printed output.
—— a spreadsheet.
—— decision-making and/or statistical facilities.
—— a query facility.

Figure 3.3 *Possible non-procedural elements of a 4GL*

procedural approach but the user of the product no longer has to stay within the boundaries of the templates offered. Now they can build their extension!

A hybrid 4GL overcomes the major limitations of the pure 4GL. The process of transformation is still used but the translation process is now needed for the procedural language.

The provision of an 'escape feature', i.e. the ability to call up routines written in COBOL, say, would seem to make this an attractive option to installations still embedded in the COBOL programming environment and who now want to make use of these tools without losing their 'life-blood'. However, there are drawbacks to the provision of such features. Skill with the procedural language is now required. This may prevent a systems analyst, for example, completing the task. It could result in a (long) wait for a COBOL programmer, thus causing a hold-up in the project and making maintenance a problem once again. Wherever possible it is desirable that the user of the 4GL can also use the language of escape.

Most 4GLs fall into this category, mixing non-procedural techniques with more conventional procedural methods. Often the non-procedural aspects are aimed at the end-user and other facilities at the professional application developer. For example, MIMER

offers easy-to-use report generation facilities in the form of MIMER/RGFORM and a query-by-forms facility, MIMER/QF, both of which are suited to the end-user. Some of its other tools are deliberately aimed at the professional developer and call for the use of more conventional techniques.

Table 3.3 summarises the main differences between the two types of product in this category.

3.5.2 End-user v. professional 4GLs

One of the reasons given for the emergence of 4GLs is the need to involve end-users in the application building process or to allow them to carry out those procedures of interest to them effectively, such as retrieving information from a database. Database enquiry or query languages, report generators and spreadsheets are not new. Each of these is now classed as a 4GL, basically because the emphasis is on the non-procedural. These kinds of products are suitable for the end-user who, in general, would not be expected to come to terms with the intricacies of a procedural programming language.

The term end-user is sometimes misleading. Basically it means the person the application is aimed at. Some end-users will already be highly computer-literate, while others will be reluctant to become involved with a computer at all. With

Table 3.3   Differences between pure and hybrid products

Type of 4GL	Facilities offered	Problem solution	Production of solution	Usage	User-type
Pure	Non-procedural	Specification of problem statement	Problem statement transformed to procedural solution by generator	Dedicated or specialist tools	End-users or analysts (possibly programmers)
Hybrid	Non-procedural and procedural	As above and coding in procedural language	As above and translation of procedural code	Often general purpose but may be dedicated	End-users,* analysts and programmers *Possibly a sub-set of tools

4GLs the end-user may also be the person who produces the specification, implements and uses the system and also the results, i.e. end-users are not just users of the system, they also become users of the 4GL itself.

Some suppliers and manufacturers of 4GLs claim spectacular results for end-users using their products. Claims such as 'end-users with no previous experience in such matters can build applications in a fraction of the time it takes a programmer using COBOL' and 'within 30 minutes the end-user is producing useful work with our product'. Many DP professionals are sceptical about end-users being involved in anything but trivial tasks, despite claims that end-users are stepping over the application backlog and producing their own applications. End-users may be able to use spreadsheets and query languages or operate word-processing and electronic mail facilities, but building applica-tions . . .? Not possible – or is it?

The answer to that question is yes and no. Many 4GLs are just not suitable for end-users (and this includes some query languages and report generators). Others have been produced with the non-professional in mind, concentrat-ing on providing non-procedural facilities and offering ease-of-use techniques. The term 'user-friendly' springs to mind but has come to mean so little. Perhaps a better term is good 'human-factoring'. If end-users cannot in general use programming languages such as COBOL or even BASIC then it stands to reason that 4GLs aimed at end-users must not employ the same methods.

There are many ways that a 4GL can offer good human-factoring. Some of these ways appear in Table 3.4 (see Martin (1985) for a wider discussion of this topic). In fact the list can become very long and it is not appropriate to cover every aspect here. Many of the items included are obvious, almost common sense you might think, yet many manufacturers of software products do not incorporate them to their fullest potential. End-user 4GLs should make the best possible use of human-factoring

Table 3.4   How can the 4GL appeal to an end-user?

★ End-users should be able to get started with the product as easily as possible. They will not want to plough through two 300-page manuals to get started. Many 4GLs offer an initial tutorial option, e.g. PROGRESS.

★ The dialogue (between computer and user) should avoid the need for programming language-like syntax. Non-procedural techniques should be used where possible. A user will prefer to fill in forms or select from menus, at least initially, than get involved in complex syntax or mnemonics. Most 4GLs recognise this fact.

★ There should be a simple method for the user to navigate around the system. Recovery from mistakes should be an easy process. Pressing a wrong key should not be a disastrous error.

★ Error messages and help facilities are very important. Users find messages such as ERROR REDO FROM START off-putting and unhelpful. Help should be comprehensive, on-line and easily accessible from any part of the software. POWERHOUSE for example allows simple access to two levels of help.

★ Methods aimed at the novice user can often become quite irritating to the more experienced one. Different techniques should be available in terms of comprehensiveness, speed, etc. RAMIS for example offers an 'expert path' to more experienced users. This eliminates the need to go through all the menus offered to the novice user.

★ There are many proven methods for improving the interface between the human and the computer. Cutting down on the number of key-strokes through touch screens, a mouse, icons and the use of graphics, windows, etc. – in fact anything which improves the interaction between the user and computer – should be employed.

★ Defaults, i.e. the situation where a value is chosen for the user, unless an alternative is specified, are also useful.

techniques. It is often the human-factoring techniques which distinguish an end-user tool from one that is not suitable for the end-user.

However it is still more than just a question of giving end-users the right tool and leaving them happily to build applications. Many end-uses will never be in the position of being able or of wanting to do this. (Many of the products they use are not meant to be for this purpose.) We said before that there are many different types of end-user, as diverse as the products we have been discussing. Some can claim the title only by virtue of using computer systems indirectly through someone else, e.g. a passenger booking an airline ticket. Others are direct users, but this can involve anything from using the results off a computer print-out to having a terminal or personal computer to work with. Even direct users are not all about to build applications for themselves. Some will, through non-procedural facilities. A small percentage may be successful with procedural methods.

We must not forget that many 4GLs are sets of tools. Originally, the query language, the report generator, etc. may have existed as separate entities. Some manufacturers have brought these separate tools together and are offering them as a 4GL. Unfortunately this can mean that there is little or no relationship in syntax or dialogue across the tools. This is not true of all 4GLs, of course; there are those which are integrated and offer common syntax in all but the procedural language component (this is always going to be different). Other products are 'growing' all the time with respect to the functions they offer. This is not always a good thing. Whilst the original 4GL may have been restrictive in the options it offered, extensions often change the emphasis from ease-of-use to the need for formal programming skills.

All of these factors make it impossible to expect that most end-users will master all components of a 4GL. Some may cope well with database enquiry and report generation; others will need to master the decision-support end of things; while some may become proficient across the full range of facilities. All of these activities

need training and support. One of the growing ideas in computing is that of the information centre. Whereas the DP department of an organisation traditionally produced the applications for end-users (but in isolation), the information centre also has the responsibility of supporting and encouraging those end-users who make use of computing resources for themselves, and of co-ordinating their information needs (see Chapter 7).

Whilst there are other issues involved with end-user computing which we shall return to later, it can be seen that some 4GLs or subsets of the set of tools offered, are suitable for the end-user but that many others demand specialist skills outside their scope. The very high-level procedural languages of the fourth generation are programming languages and although some end-users may acquire the skills needed to use these languages, they are not meant to be end-user tools. However the choice is not as clear cut as, 'Is the 4GL aimed at the end-user or professional programmer?' One of the advantages claimed for 4GLs is that they allow the application building process to be fast. Hence prototyping becomes realistic. Together with the end-user the systems analyst can use the 4GL to produce the prototype. The analyst creates the application with the emphasis on end-user involvement. Some 4GLs are classed as end-user tools when in fact they are more suited to use by the analyst. Other 4GLs concentrate on facilitating the skills of the analyst rather than, say, the programmer, e.g. in specification, diagramming techniques, etc.

Now we have three categories of 4GLs, end-user, systems analyst and programmer. At the edges the categories are blurred. End-users may be able to use programming languages and subsets of the same 4GL may be used by all three categories. The analyst may also be the programmer in 4GL application development (refer to Chapter 6). The other problem is that some products, whilst claiming to be end-user tools, prove far too complex for the average end-user to make full use of them.

It is also worthwhile considering that the very features which makes a 4GL attractive to an end-user could make it useful to the pro-grammer. Entwined in complex procedural code, the programmer can lose sight of the task in hand. The use of 4GLs could help to overcome this problem. A 4GL which would meet the needs of both professionals and non-professionals may help to reduce software costs and rationalise skill requirements.

4GLs like ORACLE may allow the end-user to make good progress, even if it is not solely an end-user tool. In this situation the product will be used by both end-users and professionals. A different range of tools will probably be selected depending on who uses the product. ORACLE's fourth generation environment (the 4GL we have called ORACLE) offers a number of tools suited to the end-user, e.g. SQL*FORMS, SQL*PLUS and SQL*REPORT as well as tools more suited to the professional developer, e.g. the RDBMS, SQL*MENU, SQL*DESIGN DICTIONARY, etc. It also offers optional tools specifically aimed at the end-user, e.g. SQL*CALC, EASY*SQL, SQL*Graph.

Other products, such as GENER/OL, are aimed at the professional user and make no claims to be end-user tools. A few products are just end-user tools.

3.5.3 Information centre v. development centre 4GLs

Another category, similar to the previous one, is information v. development centre 4GLs. Basically the information centre 4GL has been designed with either the end-user or the analyst in mind. Its main concern is that of easy-to-use facilities, rather than the ability to build complex systems. The information centre 4GL will generally offer a predominantly non-procedural approach, relational database facilities and ease of learning. The development centre product on the other hand is aimed at the programmer. Its aims are to allow gains in productivity and at the same time ensure flexibility and performance.

3.5.4 Dedicated v. general purpose 4GLs

We have already discussed most of the issues concerned with this area but it is a classification of 4GL and it is worth reiterating the main points. Not all 4GLs are full function, general purpose tools. Many are unable to carry out the tasks that a 3GL would be used for. The provision of non-procedural facilities only inevitably imposes limitations.

However, despite claims by some suppliers of 4GLs to the contrary, many 4GLs were never meant to fulfil this role. They are specialist or dedicated tools, useful for the specific purpose or purposes for which they were designed. Even putting several of them together to provide a set of tools does not necessarily produce a general purpose product. Selection of the right tool for the right task is very important. Spreadsheets and decision support tools are dedicated 4GLs, whilst a product such as PROGRESS is general purpose.

3.5.5 Decision support v. mainstream data processing 4GLs

It is also worthwhile to make a distinction between those 4GLs which can be used for tasks usually associated with 'mainstream' data processing, e.g. allowing users to query a database or building applications, such as sales reporting, and those used in decision support tasks, e.g. modelling, or asking 'what if' questions, etc.

This classification cuts across others. A 4GL used for decision support may be a dedicated tool. However, decision support is a growing area and both fourth and fifth generation techniques are offering much to facilitate the building of decision support systems.

The term 'mainstream' data processing covers a multitude of ideas. Many 4GLs are suitable for building on-line transaction processing applications, given that this is the direction in which data processing has generally gone. Some 4GLs will handle batch processing systems. Applications may demand 'heavy-duty' systems, able to handle large volumes of transactions, whilst others need only cope with low transaction volumes. Many 4GLs are suited to commercial data processing rather than scientific applications.

More and more we keep coming back to the idea of choosing the right tool for the right task.

3.5.6 On-line v. off-line 4GLs

This category is included for completeness but in some ways is rather unnecessary as the latter of the two types of 4GL no longer exists. However, some of the early 4GLs required their users to fill in forms and/or coding sheets. These could be said to be off-line 4GLs. Generally speaking most 4GLs now operate on-line with the user and the software interacting at a terminal or personal computer. This has of course both become more possible and more desirable with the wider availability of computing power and the improvement in the terminals offered to users.

3.5.7 Tools under the 4GL 'umbrella'

This final classification really draws together those tools currently being called 4GLs. They may stand alone or be component parts of the complete set of tools. Again, many are to be found in more than one of our classifications.

A. Application builders
Before the term 4GL was widely adopted, there existed a number of software tools whose origin is to be found in the search for improved productivity in the DP environment. These were given various names, like 'application development tools', 'application program generators' (APGs) and 'high-productivity tools'. They included such items as application packages designed to meet a specific business need and file maintenance packages allowing the retrieval and updating of data from a single file type or single record type in a database environment.

Some of the tools originally marketed as APGs are still available, but now as 4GLs. This is not really surprising as both have the same

roots. APGs are a class of software tools used in addition to, or as an alternative for, other products concerned with DP applications. There is as much indecision over what constitutes an APG as there is over the term 4GL. Some people, for example, include report generators in this category whilst others exclude them by virtue of their restricted output. A report generator is usually a component of an APG (we shall deal with report generators separately).

It is useful, if only for clarity, to distinguish three types of APG, differentiated by the form of their output.

1) A code generator produces output in the form of a high-level language (or sometimes assembler) source program. The subsequent translation and/or execution is independent of the APG. The resulting program is a separate piece of stand-alone software, like that produced by hand coding. Code generators were typically intended for use by technical DP staff, as their usage demands an understanding of the environment in which they work. Hence they support a more traditional centralised DP environment.

2) An application generator produces output in the form of a complete application, such as payroll or accounts receivable, which is directly executable. The application generator usually incorporates a translator and also controls the execution of the generated application. This means that both the generator and the application must be present at run-time. Translation is either through an internal compilation facility or through interpretation of parameter tables at run-time. Extensive documentation and report generation facilities are usually provided.

3) A systems generator is also theoretically possible, which, although similar in character to the application generator, is for creating complete systems. Hence it must generate the required linkages between various application programs in the system. It may also accept existing

applications as input and incorporate them into the generated system. True system generators are not easy to find although some application generators offer similar capabilities.

Although it has happened in some cases, it is not enough to call APGs 4GLs and leave it at that (although a systems generator is getting close). If we accept that the true general purpose 4GL offers a complete environment, then an APG is only part of that environment. Hence the term APG must not be confused with the class of 4GL referred to as 'application builders'.

For a 4GL to be classed as an application builder it must offer the facilities to construct a complete system. Many such application builders will revolve around a data dictionary and offer the collection of tools we have mentioned previously. Generally the systems to be built will be transaction processing systems employing a database, but some batch process-ing products do exist. Most application builders require professional skills to complete the whole application (although the comments we made about end-users still hold true).

It might be reasonable to expect that most 4GLs, except those specifically claiming to offer a specialist function, would provide this general capability. However it is by no means mandatory or even likely that all 4GLs can fulfil this expectation.

B. Transaction processors
This is another group of 4GLs used by professionals to build transaction processing systems which 'add-on' to the user's existing database. Hence no database is offered as part of the tool set. Their aim is to allow for more efficient computer usage in high volume environments. They offer the benefit of allowing a cheaper alternative to changing completely existing systems.

C. Decision support tools
The boundaries of this category are somewhat blurred. Their range of users is wide with the emphasis on end-users in specific situations, e.g. managers, financial analysts and engineers.

Their purpose is to provide users with the ability to analyse data and ask 'what if' questions. They should facilitate the building of models and help the user display and manipulate data. Decision support tools may be anything from a simple spreadsheet to tools allowing complex analysis techniques. A database (of the relational type) is generally supported.

A decision support tool may be offered as part of a general purpose 4GL. More and more commonly, fifth generation techniques are being integrated into decision support products allowing the incorporation of a knowledge base as part of an expert system.

We have already made the distinction between decision support tools and those used for mainstream DP tasks.

D. Very high-level languages
We have said before that some 4GLs are very high-level procedural programming languages, offering more powerful constructs than their third generation counterparts. Many of these languages also offer non-procedural code facilities. Although the 3GLs have basic differences, they largely offer similar constructs and facilities. There is a greater diversity among the 4GLs than there is among the 3GLs. One must for the fourth generation is that languages allow database access and screen input and output. Constructs are built into the languages to facilitate these functions.

The amount of code necessary to produce many applications with 4GLs is less than that when COBOL, say, is used. Claims for how much less vary and will be discussed again (see Chapter 8).

The very high-level language may in fact be only one component of a 4GL which offers a set of tools for building applications. See Chapter 5 for a wider discussion on the language provision in 4GLs.

E. Query languages
Simple query facilities allowing the printing or display of records have been around for a long time, in fact since the early disc storage devices

became available. More complex query languages, sometimes called database manipulation languages, may allow for other functions, for example the insertion and deletion and updating of data as well as the retrieval of data items.

Some query languages are suitable for the end-user, as they attempt to keep to a minimum the knowledge required of the underlying data structures. The query language may be expressed in an English–like syntax. Other query languages are for use by professionals and demand a knowledge of the database structure.

Query languages may come as specialist tools complete with a (relational) database and data dictionary, or may be part of a general purpose 4GL environment. Query languages are discussed again in Chapter 4.

F. Report generators

Again, these tools are not new but have come to be expected as part of a general purpose 4GL. They allow for the production of reports using data extracted from a file or database. Some will allow arithmetic or logic to be performed on the data before display.

Some report generators are easy to use and employ English-like syntax, making them suitable as end-user tools. The specification of the report format is largely non-procedural. Report generators may be independent of a database or be an extension to a database query language. Report generators are looked at in Chapter 4, as one component of a 4GL.

G. Other tools

There are many tools under the fourth generation 'umbrella'. Most of them we have covered. However it is useful to look at just one or two others under this final heading.

Computable specification languages
One of the problems identified in the traditional life-cycle approach to producing applications was the program specification. These are often written in English and may be long and wordy. The final results are the programmer's interpretation of the specification. The problem

of course is the imprecision of such interpretation. Some formal ways of specification now exist, called specification languages, which tend to be built around mathematical methods. Some allow code to be generated directly from the specification through linkage to a code generator. These are known as computable specification languages.

Application packages
Application packages are not new. They offer a packaged solution to a particular problem (see Chapter 1). Their drawback is that they are difficult to modify or tailor to suit a user's specific needs. Fourth generation packages are written (at least in part) in a 4GL which is also made available for modifying the package.

3.6 Conclusions

Our discussion of 4GLs has taken us along some diverse, yet interesting paths. We have seen that one cannot simply define a 4GL; it is easier to say what a 4GL is not than what it is. However this discussion has led us to a number of conclusions:

★ There are several classifications of 4GL which provide more 'clues' than the many (attempted) definitions.
★ Many 4GLs are not general purpose tools, unlike the 3GLs. In the fourth generation those tools offering ease-of-use also offer limitations. In order to overcome these limitations, complexity follows. The 'trade-off' is very much between simplicity and scope.
★ Not all 4GLs are suitable as end-user tools. Many demand skills normally beyond that expected of most users.
★ It is extremely important to choose the right tool for the right task.

The roots of the 4GL are not academic, as was the case for many of the 3GLs. They have been created by entrepreneurs and software houses and now many people feel that academic interest and involvement could bring a degree of respectability that 4GLs do not already have.

For many years people have looked forward to a true successor to COBOL, since, as we have seen, there are problems associated with its use. However, although COBOL is not likely to disappear just yet, 4GLs are fulfilling a useful role by tackling some of those problems.

3.7 Follow-up questions and activities

3.7.1 Questions

1) Why are 4GLs now in common use?

2) Why is it difficult to 'pin down' an exact definition of the term 4GL?

3) What do 4GLs have to offer over and above the languages of the third generation?

4) Explain the following terms:
   a) pure 4GL
   b) hybrid 4GL
   c) dedicated 4GL
   d) general purpose 4GL
   e) full-function 4GL

5) a) Describe the facilities and techniques you would expect to find in an end-user 4GL.
   b) How might these differ from the 4GL aimed at the professional developer?

3.7.2 Activities

6) Find out about the 4GLs currently available in your college/polytechnic/organisation. If there is more than one product available, compare the sets of answers you get. This will help you to see how different, various of these products can be.
   a) Where is the 4GL used in the organisation?
   b) What tools does the 4GL offer?
   c) Is it a specialist or general purpose tool?
   d) Does it claim to be an end-user or professional tool (or both)? If professional, is it aimed at the analyst or the programmer?
   e) Is it a pure or hybrid 4GL?
   f) If hybrid, which features distinguish it as such?

7) The term 'fourth generation language' obviously means different things to different people. Some people accept and use a particular definition, while others feel that none are definitive. Collect together the various definitions of 4GLs you can find and discuss these with your colleagues, friends and classmates. Decide which definition you feel is more appropriate in the light of your experience with 4GLs. Give reasons for and against your choice. (You may be unhappy to accept any particular definition completely.)

4 What do 4GLs have to offer? Part 1 Databases, data dictionaries, query and reporting facilities

Objectives

After you have studied this chapter you should be able to:

- ★ understand that 4GLs offer a range of facilities.
- ★ list some of the typical facilities offered by 4GLs and in particular database related facilities.
- ★ briefly describe each of those facilities listed.

4.1 The typical facilities offered by a 4GL

Most 4GLs offer a set of tools. The tools offered depend solely on which product is under consideration. For example, a product which is just a query language or a report generator will not offer the range of tools necessary to build applications. However, what has tended to happen more and more is that 'stand alone' products have been integrated with various other tools to provide a more comprehensive product.

As we have mentioned before this has sometimes led to problems. For example, the integrated set of features may not be fully integrated, so that radically different notation and methods are required to use each tool in the set. True integration should ensure that learning to use one tool within a product provides a starting point for all the others.

Many 4GLs have recognised this fact and allow the same techniques to be used for a variety of tasks including, for example, screen and report definition. The approach adopted may be based on menu selection or similar techniques. Another feature of integration is allowing all tools to relate to and access the data dictionary provided, so that a common set of data definitions can be used throughout the application building process.

In Chapter 3 we saw that the sort of tools we might expect to find in various 4GLs would include the following:

- ★ a database management system (DBMS)
- ★ a data dictionary
- ★ a query language
- ★ a report generator
- ★ screen definition facilities or screen painter
- ★ graphics facilities
- ★ decision support and/or spreadsheet and/or statistical facilities
- ★ application development facilities, i.e. languages
- ★ other facilities, e.g. PC to mainframe links, on-line help facilities, etc.

In this chapter and in Chapter 5 we will consider various of these facilities; what they are and what they are likely to offer within the context of a 4GL. These discussions will be illustrated by relating them to particular 4GLs. This Chapter will focus on database and related tools whilst Chapter 5 will look at other, perhaps more diverse features of 4GLs. The database is an important but by no means standard part of the 4GL. It is discussed here in some depth because of the diversity of approaches adopted.

4.2 Database management systems (DBMSs)

The eight major functions a DBMS should provide are shown in Table 4.1. We will now discuss some of the components generally found in a DBMS.

4.2.1 Data dictionaries

The data dictionary is an important part of many DBMSs, allowing information about all the data within a system to be stored. Because of its importance, the data dictionary is treated separately in this chapter.

4.2.2 Data definition languages

The data definition language, or DDL, allows the designer of the database to specify the rules governing the data to be stored and retrieved, i.e. it allows the content and structure of the database to be defined via a set of commands or a vocabulary. A schema is a specification or description of a database using the DDL. DDLs differ between products but have some commonality between families of database types.

For example:

★ The hierarchical family – used to describe fields, segments, database records, and databases.
★ The network family – used to describe data items, records, sets, and user views.
★ The relational family – used to describe attributes, domains, relations and views.

4.2.3 Data manipulation languages

The data manipulation language, or DML, should provide those operations required by the application programs, e.g. creating, finding records, modifying data. Basically it is the interface between the DBMS and the application programs. The DML is often embedded in a host language such as COBOL or FORTRAN. In the relational model, the DML is in the form of relational algebra or calculus. Data manipulation may be achieved through the query language provided by the product. Martin (1976) discusses DDLs and DMLs in more depth.

4.2.4 Database query languages

Database query languages, or DQLs, allows users to query the database and extract the data

Table 4.1   The functions provided by a DBMS

★ A data dictionary/directory allowing for the storage of data about data.

★ Data storage, retrieval and updating mechanisms, allowing data to be stored, accessed and changed. This may or may not be through the use of a common language such as IBM's SQL (Structured Query Language).

★ Integrity provisions, e.g. edit checks to ensure the completeness and accuracy of the data.

★ Transaction integrity, i.e. if a transaction fails during processing, changes should not be made (aborted transaction). Changes should only be made (committed) if the transaction is successful. The boundaries of success and failure must be clearly defined.

★ Concurrency control: the DBMS must prevent or overcome the possible effects of concurrent access, i.e. simultaneous access to a record by more than one user.

★ Security mechanisms: protection against accidental or intentional misuse.

★ Recovery mechanisms: the restoration of the database or at least a return to a known condition when failure occurs.

★ Data communications interface.

they need. A wide variety of such languages exist and the approaches taken differ from product to product. Query languages are considered separately later in this chapter.

N.B. IBM's SQL (Structured Query Language) is a unified language which brings together all the functions of definition, manipulation and access. SQL and its derivations are employed by a variety of 4GL products which include a DBMS, e.g. ORACLE and INGRES among many others. In fact the increasing importance of SQL as a 'standard' query language has meant that many 4GL vendors previously not offering an SQL option are now doing so in later releases of their products. We shall consider this SQL option again later.

4.3 DBMSs within 4GLs

Many 4GLs are database oriented or offer database facilities. Some products, such as ORACLE and MIMER, have an integral database as part of the set of tools on offer. Some of the systems offering this facility may in fact be primarily database systems extended to include other facilities, such as program and report generators.

Other 4GLs, rather than providing an internal database facility, interface to standard DBMSs. The links obviously depend on which hardware the 4GL runs on. Standard DBMSs include IBM's DB2 and DEC's RdB. GENER/OL for example, is IBM oriented and offers links to standard database products, such as DB2. If the product runs across a range of hardware types, different interfaces will be offered, depending on the environment in which the 4GL is being used.

Systems offering an interface to external database facilities may also provide file environments. There are also 4GL vendors which offer their own DBMS as well as links to external products. Cincom's MANTIS offers users the option of linking to external products, such as DB2, but Cincom also offer their own

DMBSs, such as SUPRA, ULTRA and TOTAL DBMS. Different file types are also supported. For example, MANTIS supports VSAM files for IBM environments and VMS files for DEC VAX machines. This flexible, open architecture approach is an increasingly common feature amongst 4GL products.

Many 4GLs allow links to products such as INGRES and ORACLE, although these products themselves are usually classed as 4GLs. For example, FOCUS provides links with ORACLE and INGRES, whilst also supporting other DBMS types.

These links between different 4GL products are becoming more and more common, particularly with products designed for a specific range of hardware. Often this allows various 4GLs to sit alongside each other in a development environment or complement the facilities each product offers. For example, Pansophic now offers its products GENER/OL and EASYTRIEVE PLUS as a package, the former aimed at on-line systems and the latter at batch.

The reasons behind allowing a diversity of data storage capabilities within 4GLs include flexibility, the ability to access/use current files and to move between 3GLs and 4GLs.

Some 4GLs offer a file rather than a database environment. Generally, the provision of just a file environment should be considered less than adequate in the context of 4GLs. Some 4GLs which earlier offered only a file environment are now extending this to include database facilities. This may either be in the form of integrated facilities or the provision of external links.

We saw in Chapter 1 that databases may be modelled on a variety of data structures, the most common being relational, hierarchical and network, although inverted files or lists are also often included in this set. Many 4GLs offering database facilities have adopted the relational approach, e.g. ORACLE (the first commercial implementation of the relational database model), MIMER and PROGRESS, to name just three. However, very few so-called relational database products offer all the capabilities of the full relational model. Various degrees are defined

Relational database types	A semi-relational database. This only supports a tabular data structure and not the set-level operators.
	A minimally relational database. This supports tables and has the relational operators select, project and join.
	A relationally complete database. With tables and complete usage of relational algebra.
	Fully relational. This supports all aspects of the relational model.

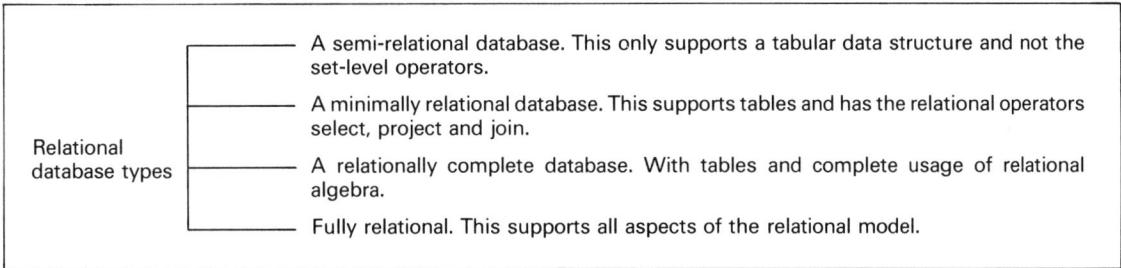

Figure 4.1 *Various degrees of the relational model*

in Figure 4.1. Refer to Date (1986) for further discussion.

Some 4GLs offer hybrid constructs which may be some combination of the relational, hierarchical network and inverted file structures. The FOCUS database employs a model called shared-relational structures which claims to draw on the strengths of the four common models, whilst eliminating or reducing their weaknesses. Other products offer a relational option but recognise that this is not the best way of dealing with records which display dependence. The hierarchical or network models may provide a second, alternative option which increases flexibility. The developer of an application may chose the optimum structure for their data. In general the relational model may be an attractive option for the end-user, whilst the professional may use the hierarchical or network options for increased efficiency.

There are various desirable features that the DBMS within the 4GL should provide. These are discussed below. There is obviously some overlap with the functions described in Table 4.1 but we need to appreciate what the 4GL may offer specifically.

4.3.1 A relational database

This offers various advantages:

★ Two dimensional tables which are easy to use, particularly for non-professionals.
★ Ease of representation. The logical database representations are relatively clear. Relations are also precise in meaning and

inconsistencies in database content or design are quickly revealed.
★ Security can be related to specific relations so that the data items can be isolated from particular users.
★ Ease of implementation. The physical storage of flat files is less complex than with other structures.
★ Data independence. If the database is in normalised form, with data independence in the software, the data can be restructured and the database can grow without, in most cases, the need to re-write application programs.

A number of 4GLs offer a relational database facility, as we have already seen; among them are ORACLE, MIMER and INGRES.

4.3.2 Alternative data structuring

Various data structures are not best supported by the relational model, and not all records display the one parent characteristic of the hierarchical option. Some people feel that having two options available allows the best of both worlds. In response to this, many 4GLs offer the relational and alternative models, e.g. hierarchical and network. The user can then choose the optimum data structure. It is particularly important for the professional user to have this option.

Several products offer this 'more than one option' facility, either by virtue of the internal DBMS, which might offer alternative data structures, or by providing an interface to different external database types, like MANTIS's interface to Cincom's own relational DBMS SUPRA and IBM's DB2, as well as other non-relational products, such as Applied Data Research Inc.'s DATACOMB/DB and Cincom's TOTAL.

4.3.3 Intelligence

The DBMS within the 4GL may display 'intelligence' or provide intelligent data types. Intelligence in this instance is difficult to define but the product may, for example, perform automatic range and integrity checks when the data is entered or automatic audit trails may be set up. Various procedures may also automatically trigger certain actions. (The word intelligence may seem inappropriate as we are largely describing automatic checking procedures, however, it is used in this context, e.g. Unicom Seminar Proceedings (1988).)

For example, in the UNIFACE system field and entity definitions may be declared, e.g. data type is 'string' or field length is fixed and equal to '45', or they may be given as processing specifications (Procs) which are triggered by events. For example, semantic validation such as existence checks, range checks, etc. may automatically be triggered when the user tries to modify a data value. The user will be warned if illegal or already existing values are used.

4.3.4 Data integrity

Data should be both accurate and consistent. Various integrity features may be included to ensure this is the case. Integrity checks include:

* Limits or range of acceptable values. The upper and lower values may be defined or a set of values given, e.g. M and F for gender.
* Masks, i.e. the picture of a data item.
* Referential integrity ensuring consistency between tables/files.

Such checks may of course be defined in the data dictionary. Other integrity features could include:

* Transaction integrity, i.e. transactions must not be committed unless complete. This requires that transaction boundaries, i.e. the logical beginning and end of the transaction, be carefully defined.
* Concurrency control. This is required to prevent, minimise or overcome the effects of more than one user accessing the same data simultaneously. Several measures may be taken:

    * Resource locking. When data is retrieved for updating it is automatically 'locked' so that other users cannot access it until the update is complete.
    * Prevention of 'deadly embrace' or deadlock which occurs when two users try to access the data locked by each other. User 1 locks record A. User 2 locks record B. User 1 tries to access record B and User 2 record A. Hence a deadlock situation is reached. This may be overcome by locking all records required in the updating process prior to commencement of the update. This is hardly practical as the full update path is rarely known in advance. Often it is better to allow the deadlock to occur but ensure that there is a back-out facility so that deadlock can be broken.
    * Optimistic case. This assumes that concurrency conflicts will happen very infrequently. If the conflict occurs, it is detected by the DBMS, which allows the cancelling and restart of one of the transactions.

Most 4GLs provide automatic integrity checks or allow them to be built into the data dictionary. For example, the PROGRESS data dictionary automatically validates data in any field.

4.3.5 Data security

This is obviously linked to data integrity and is a very important aspect of any 4GL that provides database facilities. Database security involves protecting the database against accidental loss, destruction or misuse. Possible security features within a 4GL are listed below.

★ Authorisation. Users should be identifiable through the use of passwords and user names.
★ Restriction of access. A user's access may be restricted to a particular file/table, a specific application or database. The developer of an application may be allowed to grant access to certain classes of individuals, e.g. departments, managers, etc.
★ Privileges. Users may be allowed different privileges, i.e. read, write or modify data and execute applications.
★ Encryption, i.e. coding or scrambling of data so that it cannot be read by humans. Passwords may be stored in encrypted form.
★ Recovery facilities. It is not possible to discuss security issues without mentioning recovery measures. These must be provided in case of operator error or hardware and software failures. Various facilities could be offered:

  ★ Back-ups of complete or partial database. This may involve regular and frequent dumping, say once a day.
  ★ Restart and recovery facilities, such as automatic restart, which may allow committed transactions to be re-applied to the database. The database is restored and processing recommences.
  ★ Checkpoints – where the DBMS temporarily suspends processing and checks files and journals for consistency. These checkpoints are hence known points in the processing where 'everything is fine'. In the event of failure these become points from which processing recommences.
  ★ Journal facilities, such as logging transactions, audit trails, etc.
  ★ Before and after imaging, and rollback/rollforward techniques. Before imaging involves copies of unmodified data

being taken before transactions are processed. In the event of failure, the system 'rollbacks' to an earlier consistent state and transactions can be reapplied to the unmodified blocks. With after-imaging, copies of the database blocks are held after transactions are complete. In the case of database loss or corruption, the after-images can be applied to a copy of the database, hence rolling forward the database to the point of failure.

4GLs take various approaches to the issues of integrity, security and recovery. The provision of such features is obviously very important. Some of the features provided by MIMER for database security include:

★ password protection
★ optimistic case concurrency control
★ transaction logging
★ facilities for automatic recovery and restart
★ facilities for database loading and dumping.

INGRES provides various security features, including:

★ data locking
★ reinstatement of data in the event of failure
★ security privileges
★ password protection
★ automatic enforcement of integrity and security rules.

4.3.6 Interfaces to external DBMSs

We have seen the relative advantages and disadvantages of both the internal DBMS and external links. If the 4GL offers the external links, it may be better suited to an organisation's corporate plans, as it allows all systems to use the same database product. 4GLs such as MANTIS and GENER/OL allow these external links.

4.3.7 Dynamic reorganisation

It is important that the database may be restructured without affecting the existing applications. For example, if the database is a relational model, the 4GL should allow columns and rows to be added to tables or further tables to be inserted. This is particularly important where the 4GL is used for prototyping. Here the first database is not usually the final one to be implemented. For example, PROGRESS allows changes to be made to files, fields and indexes without impact on existing applications. INGRES also allows dynamic modification of its database.

4.3.8 Query languages and reporting facilities

These are discussed in sections 4.5 and 4.6. They are an important aspect of the database-oriented 4GL. Many 4GLs offer SQL for queries. For example ORACLE, MIMER and INGRES all offer SQL, among many other products.

4.3.9 A data dictionary

We will discuss its importance later. It forms the foundation of many 4GLs and contributes to their overall effectiveness. Many 4GLs provide an internal data dictionary, e.g. PROGRESS and INGRES. The facility offered should preferably be an integrated, active data dictionary.

4.3.10 Alternate indexing

It may be important within a system to allow quick and efficient access to individual records within a table. This can best be achieved by having a secondary indexing capability. This provides direct access to any row within a table based on a field not defined in the primary index.

In INGRES, any number of indexes per table are allowed. MIMER also allows the designation of one or more columns within a table as secondary indexes. A similar facility is found in many other 4GLs.

4.4 Data dictionaries within 4GLs

With the growth of data within organisations has come the need to keep a catalogue of that data. The aim is to ensure consistency, accessibility and standardisation of information about data within a system. One way to achieve this is through the use of a data dictionary, sometimes called a directory, library or catalogue, and even an encyclopedia.

A data dictionary is defined as a central repository of data about data. The term metadata is used to mean data about data. Hence a data dictionary is a repository or store for metadata. Such data may include data definitions, relationships, security and integrity rules as well as screen and report layout information.

Data dictionaries are often central to 4GLs, particularly those which are database oriented. Other products do not offer a data dictionary specifically or at all. For example, they may not be found in non-database oriented products such as decision support tools and spreadsheets. Table 4.2 outlines the possible contents of such a data dictionary.

Whilst the internal structure of the data dictionary obviously differs from product to product, it should be transparent to the user in all cases. The key to efficient application generation is to hold the data structures within the data dictionary, so that the user has no need to define data or structures.

A data dictionary is one of the eight major functions that a comprehensive DBMS should provide. The DBMS should maintain a user-accessible data dictionary containing all the information about an organisation's data. It should also provide the database administrator with the main means of managing the information resource. The uses of a data dictionary are defined in Table 4.3.

Table 4.2   The possible contents of a 4GL data dictionary

Typical attributes	Example
Name	Emp__Sal
Alias	Employee salary
Type	Numeric
Column-heading	Salary
Format	X999999.99
Upper limit	£100,000.00
Lower limit	£5,000.00
Default value	None
Help	The salary of an employee within the organisation

Most 4GLs support common data types such as character and numeric. Some may extend the type facility to a usage facility which allows the definition of a much wider range of 'type', e.g. postal codes, time, money, etc.

Many dictionaries are themselves complex enough to be databases in their own right. Sometimes data dictionaries are referred to as a metadatabase. A data dictionary is generally a useful tool necessary for the documentation and control of both manual and computer systems and their usage of data. The data dictionary should also provide an interface to systems analysis and design, programming, testing and other development tools. If the dictionary is to be of benefit to a company, it should be up-to-date, accurate and complete. This is facilitated by on-line access to the dictionary. The data dictionary should be employed throughout the development period.

Whilst our primary concern is to consider data dictionaries which are part of 4GLs, this is not their only implementation. Figure 4.2 categorises data dictionary forms. A computer-based data dictionary consists of two basic parts:

★ The data dictionary/directory – the repository for the metadata we have described. The directory may be a separate component which contains information about where the data is stored.
★ The data dictionary manager – the software used to manage the data dictionary.

However, the terms are not really standard. Sometimes the word dictionary simply means the tool storing the data definitions only, directory being used for tools storing screen layouts, report formats, etc. and encyclopedia when logic as well as data is stored.

Table 4.3   Uses of a data dictionary

★ Documentation of data and relationships between data items

★ Standardisation of definitions

★ Control of
    ★ Change – impact analysis, to investigate the effect of proposed changes
    ★ Synonyms – giving two or more names for the same data items
    ★ Homonyms – giving a single name to two different items
    ★ Redundancy – multiple copies of the same data

★ Aid to analysis and design – provides the analyst with available data

★ Generation of metadata, e.g. data definitions for programs, data descriptions for DBMS

★ Provision of auditing information/assistance

★ Aid to all users, including analysts, programmers, end-users and management

Although unlike 4GLs in general, some work has been done towards data dictionary standardisation, both in the USA and internationally. Two groups in the USA, the National Bureau of Standards and the American National Standards Institute (ANSI), were at one time working separately on standards. In 1983 they merged to develop an IRDS, i.e. an Information Resource Dictionary System standard. This has now been adopted as the American national standard and has also been considered as an international standard, although its adoption internationally is unlikely just yet.

The move is towards a central standardised dictionary system which is available to all applications within a system, rather than each application developing their own dictionary. This is of course a good idea in many respects. It enforces standardisation throughout system components and automatic updating for all applications, hence ensuring consistency. However practical implementation may cause some difficulties. Problems might include:

★ Size. It becomes a huge maintenance task.
★ If all metadata is stored in the central data dictionary, applications may have to access unnecessary data to 'get at' their own. Good security also becomes a crucial issue.
★ Even allowing for the usual synonyms, organisations may have large numbers of versions of a particular data item, e.g. Product-Code, Prod-Code, Product Number, Item Code, Prod-Num, Product Num, etc. It may be difficult to rationalise such diversity.

Another method is to have a core dictionary which helps to enforce standardisation of definition and which is used by the other application dictionaries for cross-referencing.

Within the unstandardised world of 4GLs, data dictionaries offer different facilities, although there is common ground. Some 4GLs have an integrated data dictionary as one of the set of tools, e.g. PROGRESS and ORACLE. Other 4GLs offer links to external, standard data dictionaries, just as links are provided to external databases. There are also products with internal data dictionaries and external links. This last option allows the 4GL to access data already in the system.

Some 4GLs take the centralised data dictionary approach. This allows data definitions and other application components to be stored centrally in the data dictionary. Despite some of the problems mentioned earlier, it is considered advantageous in several different ways:

★ Documentation is centralised and standardised. The dictionary contains information about every application component.
★ Cross-referencing is automatic.
★ The data dictionary facilitates reporting.
★ Access can be restricted by allowing developers of a particular application to modify the components of that application but authority only to view the components of another application.

The approach to the implementation of data dictionaries within a 4GL obviously depends on the vendor. Generally data dictionaries may be:

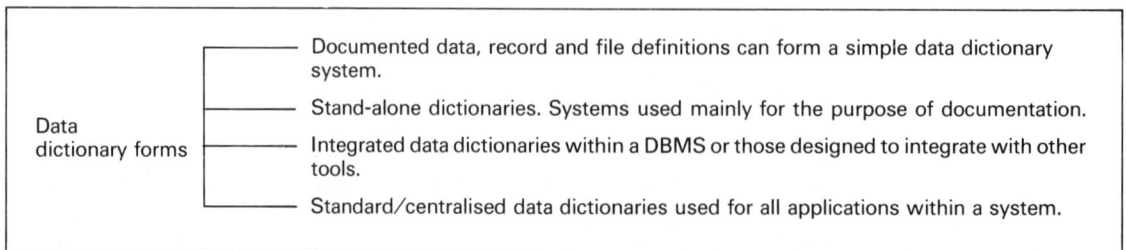

Data dictionary forms	
	Documented data, record and file definitions can form a simple data dictionary system.
	Stand-alone dictionaries. Systems used mainly for the purpose of documentation.
	Integrated data dictionaries within a DBMS or those designed to integrate with other tools.
	Standard/centralised data dictionaries used for all applications within a system.

Figure 4.2   *Data dictionary forms*

★ Passive, largely taking on a reference function. The passive data dictionary is not accessed by the various software components at run-time and hence cannot be updated at that time. The passive data dictionary tends to become a simple validation and checking repository for data and a source of documentation.
★ Active. The active data dictionary allows for the effective control of information by providing a single source of metadata which is accessible to all software components. MIMER, INGRES and many other 4GL products offer an active data dictionary.

A third category is the proactive data dictionary which is best described as a dictionary providing facilities for the generation of complete systems. This generation is achieved via the descriptions held in the dictionary. In their most sophisticated forms, proactive data dictionaries are front-end system generators.

The tendency in 4GLs is towards the active, integrated data dictionary form. The integrated data dictionary aids portability across a range of machines, as the dictionary is part of the tool set. For example, PROGRESS is portable across a wide range of machine types. If the 4GL runs on several machines then so does the data dictionary. The disadvantages of this approach are possible data duplication and accessibility. If the system already uses a data dictionary, then the provision of yet another dictionary means that there are now two sets of metadata to modify and maintain, with all the problems that this might cause. It is also unlikely that the integral dictionary can be accessed by languages other than the host language. Links to standard dictionaries reduces portability, as they are generally not available across a range of machines but tend to be specific to one machine family.

The INGRES data dictionary is fully integrated with its other application development tools, providing an on-line information resource and automatically enforcing security and integrity rules. As well as information about data structures and integrity and security rules, it also holds definitions of forms, reports, graphs, charts and applications.

Perhaps it is also worth reiterating the main benefits offered by incorporating a data dictionary within a 4GL. These benefits are listed below and include the following:

★ Data definitions are stored centrally.
★ Definitions may be 'inherited' by other components of the 4GL, hence preventing duplication and enhancing productivity.
★ Formatting and validation rules may be incorporated within the data dictionary.
★ Other parts of an application may also be stored, e.g. screens.

4.5 Query languages and 4GLs

Query facilities allow users of a DBMS to query the database and extract from it the data they require. Many are aimed at the non-professional user. Others require more skill and expertise to use them effectively. Query languages often have simple report formatting capabilities. Like many of the tools offered by a 4GL, query languages may be an integrated part of the tool set. Other query languages are stand-alone products.

Most query facilities operate interactively, on-line. There are a small number which offer off-line querying through forms. Some products will allow both access to and updating of data or even the creation of files. Query facilities will usually need to interact with the data dictionary if present. The approach to query facilities offered by the 4GL may be one of several types:

★ Query languages. These allow the user to retrieve data by specifying which records are required, rather than a process of record by record retrieval. They may employ relational calculus, hence giving the user a relational-like view of another database type. For example, Cincom's SPECTRA is a relational query system. These query languages allow fast access and results but usually involve a particular syntax or grammar which the user must learn.

★ Natural or English language. Some 4GLs, e.g. FOCUS, provide links to INTELLECT which is a query and reporting system using the English language. RAMIS offers ENGLISH amongst its range of tools. In both cases queries are asked through everyday English, hence eliminating the need to learn a specific query language and allowing easier and more flexible access to data. The drawback lies in the overheads in computer processing which may be required to translate the English statement.

Where high-volume and/or rapid response are the main requirements, it is often more efficient to employ other query methods. However this natural language approach has become quite popular. Data updating is not usually supported by this type of facility.

★ Query through form-filling. This is a different approach taken by some products. INGRES, for example, includes INGRES/QUERY, a query through forms facility.

Many 4GLs offer standard query language facilities such as SQL, e.g. ORACLE. Others offer several types of facility to accommodate different users. INGRES, for example, offers SQL, QUEL (another specialised query language like SQL) and the ability to query by forms. The forms-based query approach may be more suited to the end-user, whilst the professional user will employ the more complex query facilities.

SQL, or Structured Query Language, is the internationally accepted standard for use with relational databases. There is an official ANSI standard, but many products offer slightly varying forms of SQL. However most of these are compatible with the ANSI standard form. The objective of SQL is to provide a common application interface across different database types. There are only a few basic statements in SQL, but it is still a powerful language. SQL can be used for data definition, manipulation and control.

ORACLE was the first SQL-based relational DBMS. SQL is also found in MIMER, for example. MIMER offers interactive SQL (allowing statements to be edited directly on the screen, executed and saved in sequential files), embedded SQL (where SQL statements may be written directly into application programs coded in COBOL, FORTRAN, PL/1, Ada or C) and dynamic SQL (which lets the programmer construct applications which handle SQL statements submitted by the user at execution time).

4.6 Report generators and 4GLs

Reports are perhaps the most common method of providing information in a business environment. Reports may be anything from a one-page simple tabular format to a complex mixture of text and graphics. Many 4GLs offer a report generation facility or report writer, e.g. SQL*REPORT within ORACLE. Some 4GLs themselves are little more than a report writer or query facility and report writer.

Report generators provide a means of extracting data from files or databases and formatting it into reports. Some report generators will be stand-alone products, which are independent of database facilities or query languages. Others will be part of a set of tools, such as that provided by a 4GL. As we have seen, query facilities usually provide simple reporting facilities.

Report generators have been with us for a long time (notably products such as RPG) and were originally associated with the COBOL programming/batch processing environment. However, as they are often non-procedural in nature and may require little or no technical expertise to use, they have tended to become associated with the fourth generation. Now reporting facilities may be either batch or on-line. It is also worth noting that more complex report generating techniques may not be suited to non-professional or inexperienced users.

Within the 4GL, the reporting facility often accesses the data dictionary (if present) to extract automatically any relevant dictionary information, e.g. report titles and output pictures. There may also be an automatic formatting capability which is used as the default format for the reports. This default format often provides a simple tabular (rows and columns) style, which can usually be changed by the user of the 4GL so that more flexible and complex output can be achieved.

The development of reports within a 4GL may be possible in several different ways depending on the product being used. One product may also offer various different ways of producing reports. Ways of producing reports include:

★ Through the use of the non-procedural or procedural language within the 4GL, e.g. RAMIS offers a syntax-based language.

★ Through the use of menus, form-filling or similar simple techniques. For example, RAMIS also allows you to produce reports through menu assistance. MIMER offers MIMER/RGFORM, a tool for producing reports from a single table or view in the relational database.

★ Through the use of English Language statements. RAMIS's natural language facility allows the requests for reports to be presented in English, without the need for the user to learn other computer-based techniques.

Many 4GLs combine several options to provide a two or even three level facility. This may firstly allow the production of simple reports using only straightforward, non-procedural techniques. However, this facility will be extended so that more complex reports can be produced through the language capabilities of the 4GL or through query language facilities such as SQL. Non-professionals will usually employ the simpler options.

For example, RAMIS provides four reporting options: (1) through the use of natural language (English), (2) menu-assisted reporting, (3) through RAMIS's syntax-based language or (4) via a checklist (quick reporting). The reports produced may be enhanced through colour and graphics.

MIMER allows both the simpler MIMER/RGFORM mentioned previously and MIMER/RG for more complex reporting. MIMER/RG offers a non-procedural report specification language, RGL. RGL code can be generated from MIMER/RGFORM as a starting point for complex report definitions, and then modified and extended through text-editing.

The facilities offered by the reporting facility of a 4GL are not standard but there are often common features present. Some such features are listed in Table 4.4.

Table 4.4   Common features of a report generating facility

★ Report titling	★ Underlining
★ Page headings and footings	★ Annotation
★ Page numbering	★ Automatic column headings
★ Date generation	★ Automatic totalling/subtotalling
★ Sorting	★ Links to data dictionary
★ Choice of output facilities	★ Default features which can be overridden by users
★ Temporary fields to store the data derived from other fields, e.g. calculations	★ Display and review before printing facilities
★ Width/length of page control	★ Control of line/column spacing
★ Edit capabilities, e.g. zero suppression	★ Password protection
★ Data combined from several files/tables	★ Grouping of data
★ Printing of monetary values	

4.7 Conclusions

Many 4GLs offer database facilities, either through an integrated approach, i.e. the database is one of the tools offered by the 4GL, or by offering interfaces to other database products. Commonly the database is relational.

Another of the tools on offer is the data dictionary, which plays a central role in many 4GLs. Ideally this will be an integrated, active data dictionary. Again some 4GLs allow links to external data dictionaries.

Query and reporting facilities are usually offered with database oriented products. The approach to both querying a database and producing reports varies from product to product, with some products offering several options, each aimed at different user types. More and more 4GLs are now offering SQL as a query language option.

4.8 Follow-up questions and activities

4.8.1 Questions

1) List the database-related facilities you might expect to find in a typical database oriented 4GL.

2) a) What are the advantages of 4GLs offering links to external database or file facilities?
   b) Does the integrated database approach have any advantage over these external links?

3) What are the desirable features to be offered by a DBMS within a 4GL?

4) a) Why is the relational database model offered by many 4GL vendors?
   b) Are there any drawbacks to taking a completely relational approach? If so, what are they?

5) a) Describe the data integrity features that may be offered by a 4GL.
   b) What are the desirable database security features that should be offered by the database oriented 4GL?
   c) What approaches to recovery from failure are adopted by 4GLs?

6) a) What do you understand by the term data dictionary?
   b) What other terms are used to mean much the same thing as data dictionary?
   c) What advantages and disadvantages are offered by the 4GL providing (1) an integrated data dictionary and (2) links to external products?

7) What query and reporting facilities may be offered by a 4GL?

4.8.2 Activities

8) Look at the 4GLs on offer in your college/polytechnic/organisation. Is the product database oriented? If so
   a) What database facilities are offered?
   b) Does it offer a data dictionary?
   c) What query and reporting facilities are provided?

5 What do 4GLs have to offer? Part 2 Screen painting, graphics, statistical, language and other facilities

Objectives

After studying this chapter you should be able to:

★ understand that 4GLs offer a range of facilities.

★ list some of the typical facilities offered by a 4GL.

★ briefly describe those facilities listed.

★ appreciate why some 4GLs offer links to a 3GL.

★ explain the differences between the translation techniques of compilation and interpretation as employed by various 4GLs.

★ describe what is meant by the term 'fixed processing cycle' and how this relates to 4GLs.

5.1 Introduction

In the previous chapter we started to look at the wide range of facilities offered by 4GLs. This chapter continues with the same theme by considering other components such as screen painters, graphical and statistical tools and decision support provision. Each 4GL offers a slight variation on any set discussed. Hence we shall also look at various other components, perhaps less widely offered.

5.2 Other typical components of a 4GL

5.2.1 Screen definition facilities or screen painter

Whilst most 4GLs offer default screen facilities for users of applications, not all users have the same needs. 4GLs therefore offer means of producing customised screens through a screen generator or screen painter. This may allow the best interface to be produced for each user type or alternatively a standard interface for every application.

The term 'screen painter' is commonly used and generally means a tool allowing the developer of the application to 'paint' (i.e. outline) the screens interactively at the terminal. Many 4GLs offer screen generation facilities which go beyond screen painting. Screen painting may be achieved in several different ways. Some techniques for achieving screen painting are summarised in Figure 5.1.

Most 4GLs offer tools for screen production. INGRES/FORMS is a forms based tool which allows the developer of the application to choose facilities from menus, in order to produce screens. INGRES/FORMS is not restricted to INGRES applications and may be used as a means of producing standard interfaces for other applications. FOCUS provides FIDEL Screen Manager which allows automatic creation of basic screen-driven procedures. A screen painting facility is also built into the FOCUS TED Editor (full screen text editor). ORACLE'S SQL*FORMS incorporates screen painting as well as windows and query-by-example. Default forms can be painted as a starting point from which the developer can customise screens for their own application.

Screen painting techniques	A screen mapper. The developer lays out the format of the screen, differentiating between constant and variable data. Sequencing and access information may also be provided.
	A map editor allows the designer of screens to paint the screens in much the same way as the screen mapper. The software which supports the editor produces the communication control language statements needed to produce the screens.
	A communications control language. Screen specifications are made in a programming language, such as COBOL.

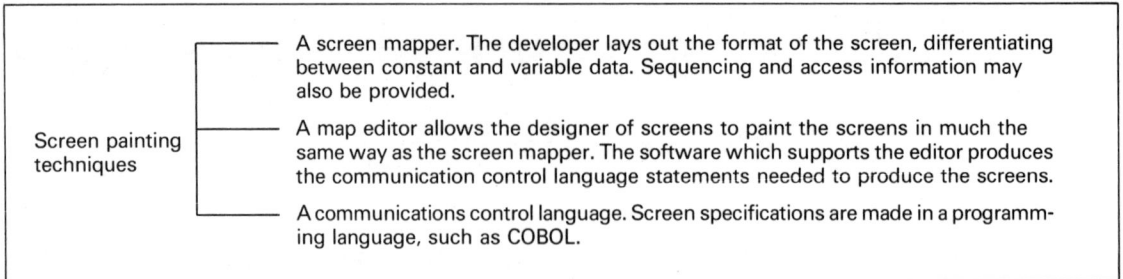

Figure 5.1   *Screen painting*

The process of producing screens should be on-line, interactive and provide comprehensive help facilities. Using menus is a sound approach and certainly screen definition should be a non-procedural component of the 4GL. There should also be links to the data dictionary, so that, for example, definitions from the dictionary can be automatically employed in screen painting and screens can be stored along with other information about applications (see Chapter 4). The screen painter usually permits freedom in placing titles, field descriptions and generated fields wherever necessary on the screen. Most field names will be tied to specific files/tables.

5.2.2 Graphics

The effective presentation of information is crucial in a business environment and graphics have become increasingly important in achieving this aim. Many 4GLs now provide graphics facilities, although this was not necessarily a feature of the early products. Some 4GLs provide graphics facilities as an integral part of the product. INGRES, for example, provides INGRES/VIGRAPH, which allows graphs/charts to be built into an application. Finished graphs can be saved within the integrated data dictionary. INGRES/VIGRAPH allows for the production of line graphs, scatter plots, bar charts and pie charts. Default text can be generated from the definitions in the data dictionary.

FOCUS also offers its own graphics component. The same language used for queries and reporting is also used for graphics. Defaults are used, allowing the developer to customise the graph for their own application. FOCUS offers bar charts, histograms, connected point plots, pie charts and scatter diagrams.

Other 4GLs offer graphics through an interface to external products. A third approach is for the 4GL itself to offer limited graphics but to allow the user to access external graphics packages for presentation quality graphics.

4GLs will often offer their graphics through the same means as other facilities, e.g. as in FOCUS. This, as we have mentioned previously, ensures an integrated approach, the user needing only to learn one technique in order to produce reasonable results with various components of the product.

4GLs offering a graphics facility will usually support a range of charts, commonly:

★ line graphs
★ scatter diagrams
★ pie charts
★ histograms
★ bar charts.

Pre-defined charts are often supplied, allowing the user to customise through colour, text, scaling, etc. The graphics generator may be linked to other tools within the 4GL, such as the report generator, statistical tools and analysis and design aids, the latter so that diagrammatic techniques like DFDs may be supported.

5.2.3 Decision support, spreadsheet and statistical facilities

One category of 4GL is the decision support tool. However, various products offer components which are decision support and/or financial and/or statistical tools. These are not facilities offered by all products, but increasingly the 4GL is trying to offer the complete business solution. It is probably best to consider two distinct categories, statistical tools and decision support tools.

A. Statistical tools

This may be as simple as the 4GL incorporating common statistical functions like mean and standard deviation or linking with a graphics tool to produce bar charts or histograms. Other 4GLs go beyond this by offering a separate statistical component. FOCUS provides FOCUS/STATISTICS, which is a menu-driven tool incorporating common statistical functions. This provides time series, correlation, regression, analysis of variance, factor analysis, discriminant analysis, exponential smoothing, etc. As in so many other of the features already considered, the 4GL may also provide links to an external package. For example, RAMIS has an interface to SAS (Statistical Analysis System).

B. Decision support and spreadsheet tools

These tools can range from two-dimensional spreadsheet packages, such as MULTIPLAN and Lotus 1-2-3, through to a multi-dimensional modelling facility or to a complex operational research package. It can be argued that a two-dimensional spreadsheet package is not a 4GL, particularly because of its limited nature. However, some such products do make this claim. Other people would say it is the only truly non-procedural tool available, i.e. the only pure product. More importantly some 4GLs incorporate such facilities within their range of tools.

For example, FOCUS offers the FOCCALC spreadsheet as an optional feature. FOCCALC allows data to be accessed from external files and databases as well as offering standard spreadsheet functions, such as goal seeking, depreciation and net present value (NPV) and arithmetic functions. The spreadsheet option also allows for graphical display.

ORACLE provides SQL*CALC, which is a spreadsheet compatible with Lotus 1-2-3. This allows selection and sorting of queries, results to be printed in reports, *ad hoc* queries, what-if projections and trend analysis, etc. ORACLE also provides an add-in for Lotus 1-2-3 which allows data from the ORACLE database to be selected, updated, inserted and deleted from a Lotus 1-2-3 spreadsheet.

RAMIS, along with other 4GLs, provides interfaces to standard/well-used spreadsheet packages, such as Lotus 1-2-3.

4GLs also offer various other similar facilities. FOCUS, for example, also has a financial modelling language (FML) which is used to create financial statements, such as balance sheets, budgets, etc. It also offers spreadsheet formatting and report production.

Various 4GLs are in fact solely decision support tools, although some will incorporate features such as a relational DBMS (or RDDMS), usually found in more general purpose tools. Decision support tools are dedicated tools and provide the capability to analyse data. They are not concerned with the 'bread-and-butter' operations that the majority of other 4GLs would be used for. Martin (1985) discusses decision support tools in some depth. Decision support tools may offer the features listed below.

* report generation
* DBMS
* graphics
* a language
* statistical features, e.g. mean, median, mode, standard deviation, variance, moving averages, exponential smoothing, regression, etc.
* operational research tools
* financial analysis and forecasting techniques
* what-if exploration
* modelling capabilities.

5.2.4 Language provision

Many of the components of 4GLs we have already considered have been non-procedural, requiring fill-in-the-forms or menu selection techniques. Even when the use of commands has been required for producing graphics, say, this has been at the List or Plot level rather than the full procedural code level. The provision of procedural facilities is important in overcoming the restrictions imposed by the totally non-procedural approach.

The provision of language facilities within 4GLs is again not standardised. Some cater for application generation, automatically tying together the various parts of the application. Other 4GLs produce 3GL code in languages such as FORTRAN, COBOL, C and PL/1. For example, COBOL, C, or FORTRAN code may be produced by MIMER and DELTA generates COBOL or PL/1. This code will then require translation. Another approach is for the 4GL to generate machine code directly.

Other 4GLs require that procedural code is produced via the language provided. Again the type of language provision is not standard and may range from a simple BASIC-type code to a very high-level language. Language provision is summarised in Figure 5.2. it is at the point where procedural code must be produced by the application developer that 4GLs cease to be end-user tools.

It is interesting that many 4GLs offer a link to the previous generation (or even the previous two). These products will allow code written in languages such as COBOL to interact with the application product via the 4GL. There are several reasons why this is the case:

★ To allow the application developer to utilise existing routines. Hence the product has more widespread appeal.
★ To overcome any deficiencies inherent within particular 4GLs. Some very complex applications cannot be produced via the 4GL route. This is of course not true for all products.
★ Most organisations have only slowly accepted 4GL usage. This link allows them to hold on to the familiar.
★ To increase efficiency, e.g. by utilising C routines or even compiled COBOL code.
★ Because of the very nature of the commitment to 3GL code in many organisations.

Some people take the view that applications can be developed via 4GLs but only built via a

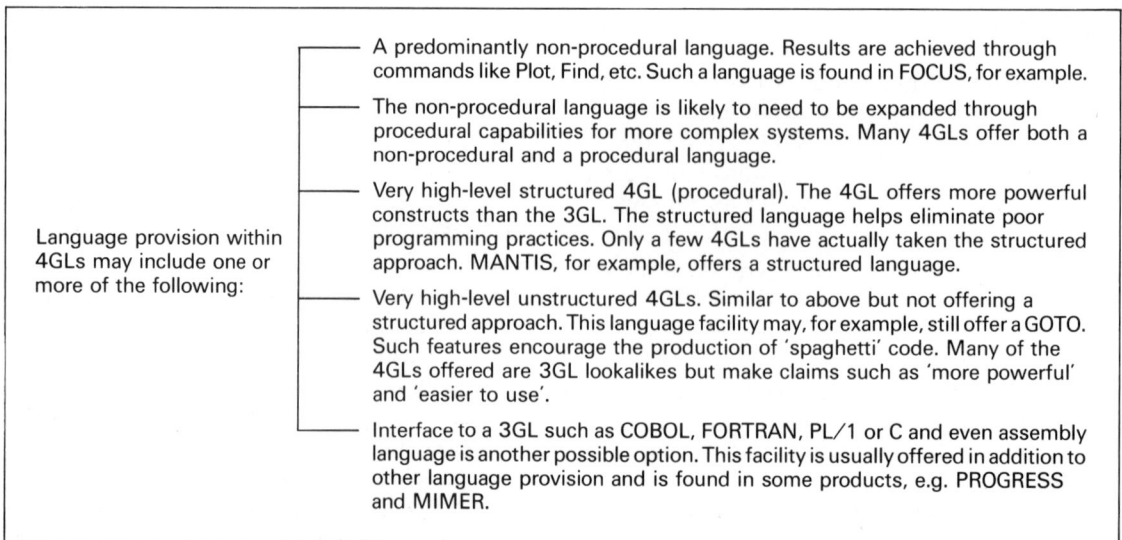

	A predominantly non-procedural language. Results are achieved through commands like Plot, Find, etc. Such a language is found in FOCUS, for example.
	The non-procedural language is likely to need to be expanded through procedural capabilities for more complex systems. Many 4GLs offer both a non-procedural and a procedural language.
Language provision within 4GLs may include one or more of the following:	Very high-level structured 4GL (procedural). The 4GL offers more powerful constructs than the 3GL. The structured language helps eliminate poor programming practices. Only a few 4GLs have actually taken the structured approach. MANTIS, for example, offers a structured language.
	Very high-level unstructured 4GLs. Similar to above but not offering a structured approach. This language facility may, for example, still offer a GOTO. Such features encourage the production of 'spaghetti' code. Many of the 4GLs offered are 3GL lookalikes but make claims such as 'more powerful' and 'easier to use'.
	Interface to a 3GL such as COBOL, FORTRAN, PL/1 or C and even assembly language is another possible option. This facility is usually offered in addition to other language provision and is found in some products, e.g. PROGRESS and MIMER.

Figure 5.2   *Language provision within 4GLs*

language like COBOL. The reasons for this view revolve around efficiency, particularly in respect of machine utilisation. We shall return to such problems in Chapter 8, when we consider both the advantages and disadvantages of using 4GLs.

Other 4GLs offer the same language that they, or, at least, components of themselves, are written in, e.g. PROGRESS, or provide tools written in themselves (e.g. FOCUS provides FOCAUDIT, a computer-assisted audit package written in FOCUS). This should allow for easier expansion and may eliminate the need for other languages, providing of course the language is 'full-function'. Despite this, interfaces to 3GLs are often still provided. This means that proficiency in the external language is required, as well as experience with the 4GL.

We considered earlier the idea of the 4GL offering similar techniques across a range of tools. Whilst this may be desirable, say for screen and report generation, if the same techniques were also employed in producing code, either report and screen generation become too complex or the language facility is severely restricted.

We have also mentioned the use of SQL in the previous chapter. More and more products are now offering SQL as the query language. As well as being used directly, this may also be embedded in a host language, such as COBOL. 4GL products may provide SQL for both inter-active and embedded use.

5.2.5 Other facilities

There are various other facilities a 4GL might provide. Because of the lack of standardisation, each product seems to offer at least one different feature not offered by its competitors. We cannot hope to consider every possible deviation. This section will look at those other features deemed to be of most importance or interest to our discussion.

A. On-line help
Help facilities are an extremely important feature of 4GLs, or in fact of any software tool claiming to provide ease of use. Such facilities

may vary in the type or level of help provided. In fact help may not be present at all. The user of the product may be left to learn about the tool from the manuals provided. Variations of on-line help include:

★ Demonstrations and tutorials. In order to get a user started with the system, the 4GL may provide an initial tutorial system which guides the user through the series of steps necessary to build part or all of the system. This is not on-line help in the true sense of the word, but provides a set of facilities over and above the ordinary manual. The user will be required to interact with the tutorial by providing data and/or responding to questions. PROGRESS, for example, provides a comprehensive tutorial facility to help the user learn how to develop applications with the product. Demonstrations tend only to show what features are available within the product and require less interaction on the user's part.

★ On-line manuals. Some on-line help facilities may be nearly as comprehensive as the features discussed in the written manual. Rather than expecting the user/developer to read through manuals, 'pages' of the manual are accessed on-line as required. To be successful, such a facility would have to be structured and easily accessible.

★ On-line help. Some 4GLs allow the user/developer to access help at any point in the development process. This is usually accomplished by pressing a key or typing the word help. Alternatively help may be a feature of the menu selection system. It is obviously preferable to allow users access to the help facility in a way which is similar to that used to access other features. Therefore if menu selection is the norm, then this should be the way the user obtains help.

The help provided may vary from a one-line help message about the feature in question to a more detailed explanation.

The one-line help message is often displayed at the bottom of the current development screen, whilst more detailed help may result in a different screen temporarily being displayed. Windows may also be used to display help messages. Many 4GLs allow the user to choose between the one-line help message and the more comprehensive facility. POWERHOUSE, for example, allows the user to select one-line help via the ? key and more comprehensive help by pressing the ? key twice.

In general the help facility should be useful to both the end-user and the developer. Most products will allow the developer of the system to specify application-specific help messages during the development of the application at run-time. For example, POWERHOUSE and PROGRESS both offer simple mechanisms for setting up application-specific help messages.

Another facility may be error message specific help. This provides help on the messages themselves and also the causes of particular error messages.

★ Computer-based training. Some products are now going even further than the demonstration/tutorial approach by offering a separate computer-based training package or component. This may be a PC-based package. For example, On-Line Software International offer PC/RAMLEARN, a computer-based training system for their RAMIS Information System. PC/RAMLEARN is to help users who want to learn RAMIS syntax-based reporting. Pansophic also offer a comprehensive computer-based training option for GENER/OL. Computer-based training is also offered for INGRES amongst other 4GLs. Computer-based training offers the advantages of allowing the learner to go at their own pace and go over things as often as they need without anyone 'looking over their shoulders'.

B. PC-mainframe links

Personal computers, or PCs, are proving to be popular for applications development. The number of PCs in many organisations has grown significantly in the last decade. It is usually not difficult for people to gain access to a PC. End-users in particular have become more familiar with PC environments as computer literacy has increased. However, in general many stand-alone PCs are not suited to full 4GL application development:

★ They lack memory/disc space. Often the resident software takes up much of the storage capacity even before the development proceeds. However, PC capacity is constantly increasing, the PC/workstation divide constantly narrowing and costs continue to fall.
★ Often corporate databases exist which the developer needs to access and use, rather than to develop their own. This can help to prevent unnecessary duplication of data.
★ Some products have no PC version currently available.

With 4GLs there are three possible uses for the PC:

★ A PC version of the software exists which is fully compatible with the mainframe version. The components developed on the PC can be integrated with those developed on the mainframe.
★ A PC version exists and the memory of the PC is sufficient or can be expanded to cope with the product. Even PC versions of 4GLs utilise large amounts of memory.
★ The PC can be connected to the mainframe. The developer can then access the resident database on the mainframe. Here the PC becomes a terminal emulator. The memory offered by the PC is transparently extended by use of disk space resident on the mainframe system (virtual storage).

Various developers offer PC versions of their products and in fact the numbers doing so have increased quite considerably over the last few years. PC versions include RAMIS/PC and PC/

FOCUS and INGRES's PC version. ORACLE is also available on PCs.

The 4GL may also offer links from other PC-based software to its tools. For example, INGRES/PCLINK allows links between software such as Lotus 1-2-3 and INGRES databases on a host system. PC/FOCUS offers FOCTALK, a micro-mainframe link for transferring files and PC/FOCUS requests to mainframe FOCUS.

N.B. Some companies offer stand-alone mainframe to micro linking software which allows the user of PC software to access data stored on the mainframe. Pansophic's CORPORATE TIE uses virtual storage concepts and works with software like Lotus 1-2-3 and their own PC-based EASYTRIEVE PLUS.PC. On-Line Software International provide FREE-LINK and OMNILINK, both micro–mainframe link products.

C. Distributed database handling

Many 4GLs can also handle distributed data-bases. For example, INGRES/STAR is a distributed data manager. INGRES/STAR will receive an SQL query from an application, break it down into sub-queries and route the sub-queries to the appropriate local data managers and gateways. Each local data manager executes its sub-query and the data is then returned to the application via INGRES/STAR. INGRES/STAR also includes an optimiser which picks the best route for satisfying a multi-site request. INGRES also provides INGRES Gateways which enables other types of databases and file systems to be included in a distributed database, and INGRES/NET, which is a transparent layer, providing network protocol support. Other 4GLs provide similar tools.

D. Text editor

Most 4GLs offer facilities to edit text inter-actively on the screen. FOCUS offers FOCUS TED, a full screen text editor, which allows for

the creation or editing of files either within or outside FOCUS. It offers a split screen capability allowing up to four files to be displayed at the same time. FOCUS TED incorporates a screen painting option. Similar tools are found in many other 4GLs.

E. Links to knowledge-based systems

Some 4GLs now allow their products to interface to an expert-or knowledge-based system. For example, Information Builders has recently released LEVEL5, an expert system shell developed in the USA by Level 5 Research which can be combined with the 4GL FOCUS. Other 4GLs, such as KnowledgeBUILD and GURU, also offer similar links to knowledge-based systems. Links such as these are looked at more closely in Chapter 9, where the combining of fourth and fifth generation techniques is considered.

F. Natural language interfaces

4GLs often offer a range of interfaces to the developer, aimed at different user types. One such interface may well be a natural language interface. The idea behind this natural language approach is to prevent the user from having to learn computer-based techniques or unnatural syntax. Drawbacks include the need for more keying operations and the overheads required to process statements. The use of a natural language interface is now adopted by several 4GLs, e.g. FOCUS uses the INTELLECT system to provide such a facility. This approach is considered again in Chapter 9.

G. CASE tool components

Computer-aided software engineering (CASE) tools allow for complete automation of the development process, from analysis through to the production of code. Some 4GLs are now expanding to include CASE tools components. The 4GL may be just one of the tools on offer, along with design and documentation facilities. CASE tools are discussed in more detail in Chapter 9.

5.3 Interpretation v. compilation

One other feature of 4GLs to be considered in this chapter is that of translation (see Chapter 1 for a full discussion of translation techniques).

One of the criticisms levelled at 4GLs in general is that they consume huge amounts of machine resources (see also Chapter 8). One of the problems lies in the 4GL approach to translation. 4GLs may either employ interpretation, compilation or generation techniques.

Interpretation allows more interaction between the system and the developer and allows the developer to see the effects of changes immediately. This is particularly useful in a prototyping environment, for example, where frequent refinements will take place during development. However, interpretation is much less efficient because each time the interpreter encounters a statement it translates it, no matter how many times it has translated it previously.

Compilers can be built to optimise the code they produce (called optimising compilers), hence resulting in more efficient code. Some 4GLs allow a combination of both interpretation and compilation techniques, interpretation at the prototyping stage for interactive debugging and compilation for more efficient production of code once the system is static.

Due to the generalisation incorporated into some generators, they tend to produce large amounts of inefficient code. They may also make excessive use of external subroutine calls which can make for a sluggish performance. This is not true in all cases and some 4GL vendors have specifically addressed the problems of inefficiency, which is a major criticism often levelled at these tools.

PROGRESS allows applications to be developed in an interactive, interpretive manner. As each block of instructions is completed, the GO key is pressed allowing the editor to check the syntax of each statement for errors. If no errors are found then PROGRESS compiles the code. The compiled procedures can be re-used without re-compilation unless modifications become necessary. Compiled procedures can be mixed with non-compiled code.

Other 4GLs generate code. The application generator is the core of the product KnowledgeBUILD. It transforms forms and reports produced via the forms or report painter options into BASIC, COBOL or FORTRAN applications. A compiler is thus required for each language generated.

The generator within the CORVISION system generates 4GL code. The 4GL within the system is BUILDER. The BUILDER code is automatically compiled into machine code so that no further translation is necessary.

5.4 Fixed processing cycles

Some 4GLs offer fixed processing cycles which combine all operations occurring in each application into a 'standard program'. This program can then be automatically included in the 4GL application. Fixed processing cycles work on the basis that, although each application built accesses different data and files, there are common processing activities, for example:

★ opening files
★ read/write operations
★ closing files, etc.

This means that standard functions will include:

★ input/output
★ updating
★ deletion
★ reporting
★ querying, etc.

The fixed processing cycle constrains the programmer and may produce less efficient programs than those produced by other means. They will vary greatly from one 4GL to another. Not all 4GLs choose to offer this option.

5.5 Conclusions

We have concerned ourselves in this and the previous chapter with the tools offered by 4GLs. There are many common components among the diversity of products on offer, such as screen and report generation tools, DBMSs, help facilities, etc. Other tools are specific to one or a group of products, e.g. 4GLs offering a PC version, with a PC–mainframe link. Further details of some of the 4GLs already described in this and the previous chapters can be found in Appendix A at the end of this book.

5.6 Follow-up questions and activities

5.6.1 Questions

1) List four of the features other than database oriented features which may be offered by a 4GL. Briefly describe those features you have listed.

2) a) In what ways may the 4GL offer links to 3GL code?
   b) What are the reasons for doing this?

3) a) What translation techniques may be employed by 4GLs?
   b) What are the main advantages and disadvantages of each technique?

4) What do you understand by the term fixed processing cycles?

5.6.2 Activities

5) Look at the 4GLs on offer in your college/polytechnic/organisation.
   a) Make a list of the facilities offered.
   b) Are there any facilities offered which are not discussed in either this or the previous chapter? If so make a note of what is being offered. Discuss these 'extra' features with your colleagues.
   c) Does the 4GL employ interpretation, compilation, generation or a mixture of translation techniques?
   d) Are there any CASE components offered?
   e) Does the product offer links with knowledge-based (expert system) techniques?
   f) Is a natural language interface offered?
   g) What help facilities are offered by the 4GL?

6 The effect of 4GLs on the traditional systems life-cycle

Objectives

After you have studied this chapter you should be able to:

★ appreciate the effect of 4GLs on the traditional systems life-cycle.
★ describe alternative approaches, more appropriate to 4GL system development.
★ explain what is meant by prototyping and the incremental, piecemeal approach to development.
★ understand the benefits and drawbacks of prototyping and how it can be achieved using 4GLs.
★ describe the approach needed for database design.
★ outline the changing role of maintenance and the place of standards in the 4GL environment.

6.1 The effects of 4GL use

In this chapter and in Chapter 7, the effects of 4GL use will be considered. This chapter will concentrate primarily on the effects on the traditional systems life-cycle approach when the language of development is a 4GL. Alternative development approaches are also explored. In Chapter 7, the emphasis is on the effects 4GLs are having on the organisation and its resources.

6.2 4GLs and traditional systems development

In Chapter 2, we considered the traditional systems life-cycle approach to the development of computer systems. We also discussed its contribution to the present situation in computing and to such problems as the application backlog. The basis of this approach is summarised in Table 6.1.

Despite its problems and disadvantages, the traditional systems life-cycle is widely accepted. The majority of third generation systems are developed using this, or a slightly modified approach. It has identifiable stages and clearly defined steps. It is built into the policy and standards of most DP departments and will continue to be used. The advent of other techniques, such as structured methods, has done little to change its basic form. The emphasis on various stages is altered but the stages remain much the same.

Some organisations retain this traditional approach when using 4GLs for development. All that basically happens is that the development language is replaced by a suitable 4GL. Whilst this saves time in the programming, testing and maintenance phases, other potential benefits are lost. 4GLs represent an opportunity to break free from this rigid approach, where it is appropriate to do so.

There is no doubt that there are differences

Table 6.1 Basis of the traditional approach to developing applications

★ Techniques largely devised in the batch processing environment of the 1960s
★ Manual design and programming techniques
★ The generation of large amounts of paperwork
★ The requirements specification, which is often incomplete/incorrect
★ Out-of-date standards
★ Maintenance to correct errors which have slipped through in the development stages
★ Large project teams, which tie up valuable human resources for long periods
★ A 'resigned acceptance' that projects cost too much and go on too long

between 3GLs and 4GLs. Successful development of applications with 4GLs requires alternative techniques from those used with 3GLs. It is therefore wrong to assume that the same life-cycle approach will be appropriate, although this may be the case for some systems. Various approaches to 4GL systems development are discussed in this chapter.

6.3 4GLs and other development approaches

Development of systems using 4GLs may be approached in several ways. Various methods are summarised in Figure 6.1.

With 4GL development the emphasis will be on:

★ Prototyping (which is discussed in detail later in this chapter).
★ User involvement. Users can become more involved in the development of systems and for a longer period of the development process because of the prototyping approach.
★ One person or small development teams The large project team approach largely becomes redundant. With small systems, all that may be required is one analyst/ programmer working with one or more users.
★ Faster systems development. The development period is likely to be shortened.

When a 4GL is the development language it is no longer valid to separate out systems analysis from programming, or development from maintenance. The traditional systems life-cycle boundaries become blurred. If prototyping is involved, analysis carries on as prototyping progresses, whilst at the same time programming may be an on-going process. New and changing requirements can be incorporated into the prototype, as users request them. They are not now revealed after implementation, when they become maintenance problems.

If, as seems to be the case, 4GL systems development requires an alternative approach, what is it to be? Many people believe that 4GL systems development is a totally *ad hoc* process. This is often used as a criticism by those people who like to 'knock' 4GLs. They see it as a 'get a request from a user, put together a prototype, tinker with it until the user is happy, and, hey presto, the application has been developed' approach. Even some people who regularly use 4GL systems will say, if asked, that it's just a question of 'getting on with it' (see Grindley, 1986).

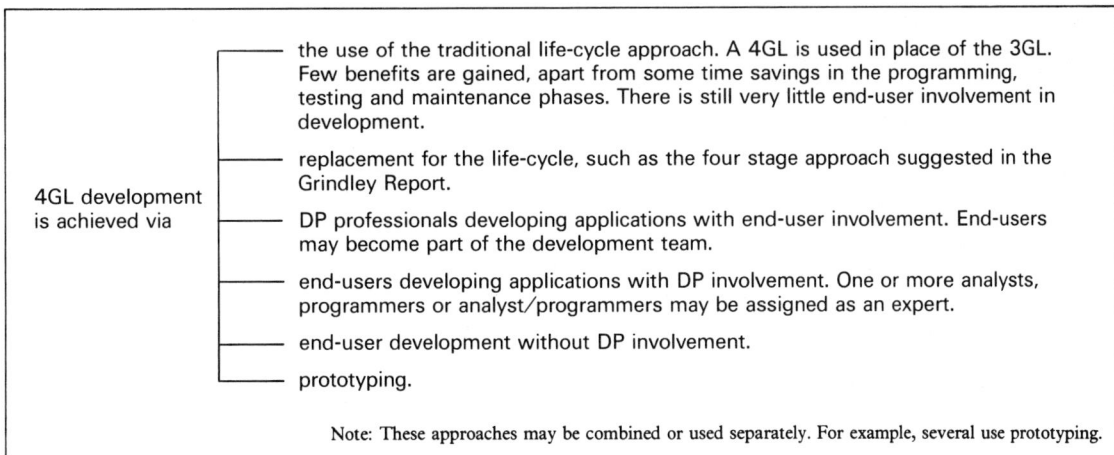

<table>
<tr><td rowspan="6">4GL development is achieved via</td><td>the use of the traditional life-cycle approach. A 4GL is used in place of the 3GL. Few benefits are gained, apart from some time savings in the programming, testing and maintenance phases. There is still very little end-user involvement in development.</td></tr>
<tr><td>replacement for the life-cycle, such as the four stage approach suggested in the Grindley Report.</td></tr>
<tr><td>DP professionals developing applications with end-user involvement. End-users may become part of the development team.</td></tr>
<tr><td>end-users developing applications with DP involvement. One or more analysts, programmers or analyst/programmers may be assigned as an expert.</td></tr>
<tr><td>end-user development without DP involvement.</td></tr>
<tr><td>prototyping.</td></tr>
</table>

Note: These approaches may be combined or used separately. For example, several use prototyping.

Figure 6.1 *Possible development approaches using 4GLs*

However, realistically it is not quite so simple. There still has to be a budget, justification for the application, objectives to work to and control. Constant refinement of a prototype, for example, may actually be a good idea. It may please the user to get closer and closer to their ideal, but at some point the refinements must be halted. Even with increased user involvement, the danger is that the end result becomes a moving target.

Organisations already committed to structured analysis and design techniques, for example, will not be anxious to abandon them. There are two schools of thought on this. One says that developing systems with 4GLs means that the developer can abandon the old ways. The other advocates the need for more, not less, control on the development process. Hence structured analysis and design should be used in conjunction with the 4GL.

There are three main points to consider here. Firstly, several 4GLs allow automatic production of DFDs and other design aids. Several of the producers of commercially available structured methods, e.g. LBMS have expanded them to fit in with 4GLs and prototyping. Some 4GLs can also link to other development tools. The trend towards a totally automated development environment is seen as the way forward. The advent of CASE tools, many of which offer a 4GL component, is the next step towards this. CASE tools are dealt with in more detail in Chapter 9.

Secondly, despite a move away from the traditional life-cycle there are activities which will not change radically. It is generally agreed that getting the requirements right helps to get the system right. Even when the main body of the requirements are hammered out through prototyping, there must be an attempt to capture the user's initial requirements. There is still a need for good analysis and design principles. As well as this, structured programming is always going to be preferable to spaghetti code.

Thirdly, as we have said before, the use of 4GLs does represent an opportunity to break away from the restraints of the old approaches.

Problems such as 'analysis paralysis' (see Chapter 2), should now be avoided.

The Grindley Report (1986) surveyed large numbers of 4GL users. One of the areas considered was the development approach adopted by these organisations. Although many developers seemed to perceive their approach as the 'just get on with it' method, a number of common processes emerged. From their findings, the report writers put forward an alternative to the traditional life-cycle approach, for 4GL systems development although it is probably too early in the lifetime of the 4GL to expect an accepted standard methodology. The Grindley Report advocated a four-stage approach as follows:

★ Stage 1. Data analysis and design
★ Stage 2. Budget preparation
★ Stage 3. Prototype production
★ Stage 4. Systems evolution

★ Stage 1, Data analysis and design. This stage covers such areas as
  ★ definition of the application area under consideration,
  ★ review of where the application stands in relation to the corporate objectives,
  ★ analysis of the data,
  ★ design of the database, or files. Also definition of the access paths to the data, and all data capture, maintenance and security strategies.

★ Stage 2, Budget preparation. This involves:
  ★ setting of system objectives,
  ★ determination of the period for which a budget should be agreed,
  ★ determination of the size of that budget,
  ★ deciding on the user objectives. These are the benefits to be derived from building the application.

★ Stage 3, Prototype production. This involves the establishment of the user's initial requirements which are then incorporated into the first prototype. The initial requirements may well be established by traditional analysis techniques.

★ Stage 4, System evolution. Here the prototype is refined. The prototype may become the system itself or the final system may be recoded in an alternative fourth, third or even second generation language.

One final word should be said about control. It is important that there is something by which to measure the success of any development activity. The 4GL approach requires less emphasis on staged activity, hence less obvious milestones are visible. It is crucial that careful objectives are set from the outset. If, for example, a user wishes to go beyond the agreed refinement cycles during the system evolution stage, it would be up to user management to meet any extra cost. 4GL system development is not an opportunity for everyone concerned to 'do their own thing'.

Note that prototyping and databases design themselves have associated techniques and/or methodologies. These are considered in greater detail separately in this chapter. Table 6.2 compares the 4GL approach with the stages of the traditional systems life-cycle.

6.4 Prototyping

Prototyping, like the term 4GL, tends to mean different things to different people. It is also not a new idea. Prototypes of ships, aeroplanes and cars, etc. have been built for many years. Such prototypes are usually first off and working forms of the real thing. Sometimes they may be scaled-down or model versions. Prototypes help to show up flaws in design which may need to be rectified before full-scale production commences. They may also be used to get commitment to the product before vast amounts of money are spent.

Prototyping in the computing sense is not much different. Lantz (1986) puts prototyping forward as a methodology, a methodology simply being a set of methods. Lantz's definition talks about prototyping as being based on building and using a model of the system for development of that system. The model is therefore the focal point for development throughout the analysis, design, construction, testing and installation stages of development.

Table 6.2 A comparison of the life-cycle with the 4GL approach

Stages in the life-cycle	*4GL development*
Initial investigation Feasibility study	4GL development does not tie up such large-scale resources at each stage. Often a one-person, or small development team is involved. Although progress still needs to be measured against objectives, there is less need for long-term planning. Justification for new applications should be at a company-wide level.
Systems analysis Systems design	Objectives become more important than requirements. Requirements do not get 'set in stone' before design takes place. More fluidity is allowed. Prototyping demands an initial agreement on requirements, followed up by further analysis, as the prototype is successively refined. Structured techniques can still be used effectively and documentation can progress as the prototype is evolved.
Programming Program testing	Programming is not a totally separate phase from systems analysis and design. Neither is it necessarily carried out by a separate set of professionals. If the prototype is discarded, and the system re-coded, this phase may re-emerge.
Implementation Maintenance	As we have seen with the traditional approach maintenance may begin almost immediately following implementation. With the 4GL, many of the refinements which would normally have been requested after implementation are made during the prototyping and refinement stages. Hence maintenance is not the same problem.

The word 'model' is crucial to the ideas behind prototyping. Generally speaking, it is the process of building and refining a working model of a computer system. The model, although not complete, is sufficient to demonstrate various parts of the system, such as input dialogues, reports and simple database operations.

Prototyping has become an important part of 4GL development. Prior to 4GLs and other interactive development tools, prototyping was not a feasible option. It would have taken an unrealistic amount of time and money to produce a prototype in a language such as COBOL, with few benefits. 4GLs lend themselves much better to the refinement cycle necessary for successful prototyping work. Changes are easier to implement. The non-procedural elements particularly accommodate 'fine tuning' of the system.

Despite this there are some (perhaps slightly cynical) people who believe that the systems developed via the life-cycle approach are themselves prototype systems. They are obviously not meant to be prototypes but tend to have been developed with flaws and omissions which need to be changed following installation. This leads to maintenance.

Although prototyping is seen by some as a methodology, there is no one way in which prototyping is currently used. A list of various prototyping terms and their definitions is given in Table 6.3.

6.4.1 Throwaway v. evolutionary prototyping

Piloting and modelling are examples of throwaway prototypes. Here the prototype is used to develop an understanding of the user's requirements or to test the feasibility of the proposals. The main reason given for the discarding of the prototype and rebuilding the system is machine efficiency. However, if the system is then rebuilt via a 3GL, say, from the appropriate stage in the life-cycle, costs are duplicated and maintenance once again becomes a problem.

Another problem may be that of getting management support to back throwaway prototypes. They may feel that this is difficult to justify when time and effort has already been invested. It is obviously important for management fully to understand prototyping and be committed to it.

The alternative is to use the same 4GL to prototype and to build the system. Incremental development allows the prototype to evolve into the completed application. There is no reason why the prototyping language should not also be

Table 6.3   Prototyping terminology

Piloting	This is the use of a prototype to test feasibility or to evaluate design proposals. It may be used for example to test the validity of some new design feature.
Modelling	Here the prototype is sometimes referred to as a 'mock-up'. It is used to develop an understanding of the user's requirements.
Throwaway prototyping	Both piloting and modelling are examples of throwaway prototyping. In both cases the system is usually re-built using a different development language, e.g. a 3GL.
Evolutionary prototyping	Evolutionary prototyping involves incremental development of the system. A series of prototypes are built. Each prototype represents a step along the way to the final system, which finally evolves. The prototyping and development languages are the same. This approach is highly cyclical in nature.
Partial prototyping	The prototype is developed to demonstrate part of the system only. This may include one or more components such as reports, dialogues, database operations, etc.
Full prototyping	Here, all aspects of the system are demonstrated.

used for developing the system. Not all 4GLs are highly inefficient. There are benefits to be gained as well. Such benefits include savings in development time and costs. The complete system does not have to be re-built and the final system can be changed in exactly the same way that the prototype was refined. The alternative approaches to prototyping are shown in Figure 6.2.

6.4.2 The role of prototyping

Prototyping reduces the risks of producing a system which does not match user requirements, is too expensive or is unreliable, i.e. some of the problems encountered in the use of the traditional systems life-cycle.

Producing the wrong system can result from application risk, i.e. the user changes their mind or the project team does not know enough about the application being developed. It can also result from technical risk because it is very difficult to build the system with the chosen software. Prototyping can help to reduce both kinds of risk

6.4.3 What to prototype?

Prototyping is a useful and powerful method of producing systems, if used properly. This is particularly the case when a 4GL is employed for part or all of the development process, yet it is still not as widely accepted as it could be in the computing industry. There are probably several reasons for this. Most of these can be explained by considering the potential dis-advantages of the prototyping approach. These disadvantages appear in Table 6.4, along with the benefits of prototyping.

Not all systems lend themselves equally well to prototyping. Good candidates are:

★ those where requirements are ill-definable through standard methods.
★ interactive systems with extensive user dialogues.

Poor candidates would include:

★ batch processing systems
★ systems with little user interface.

There are people however, who hold that all systems can be prototyped, either partially or completely. However, large, complex systems with complex interrelationships between parts will benefit from the more traditional attempt at pre-specification and possibly a division of the roles between analyst and programmer (see Chapter 7), even where a 4GL is being used.

Generally there are no hard and fast rules. Where organisations are developing systems via several methods, i.e.

★ packaged solutions,
★ traditional life-cycle,
★ 4GLs and prototyping,

a decision has to be made as to which approach is applied to which application. Some basic rules of thumb will be necessary. Organisations need to ask the following questions:

★ Is the system a solution to a common problem? There is little point in re-inventing the wheel if a packaged solution can be used. If the problem has specialised requirements then customised development is necessary, either through traditional methods or through prototyping.
★ Are the user requirements definable in a standard way? If so, then the traditional life-cycle approach may be used. If the users' requirements have little structure or definition, then prototyping should prove beneficial.
★ How crucial to the organisation is the system? If the system will have high impact on the organisation, then professional involvement is crucial, either through traditional means or via prototyping.

The choice between prototyping and traditional methods also has to be made. Currently, most organisations are choosing selectively those applications to be developed via 4GLs and those to be developed by more traditional means.

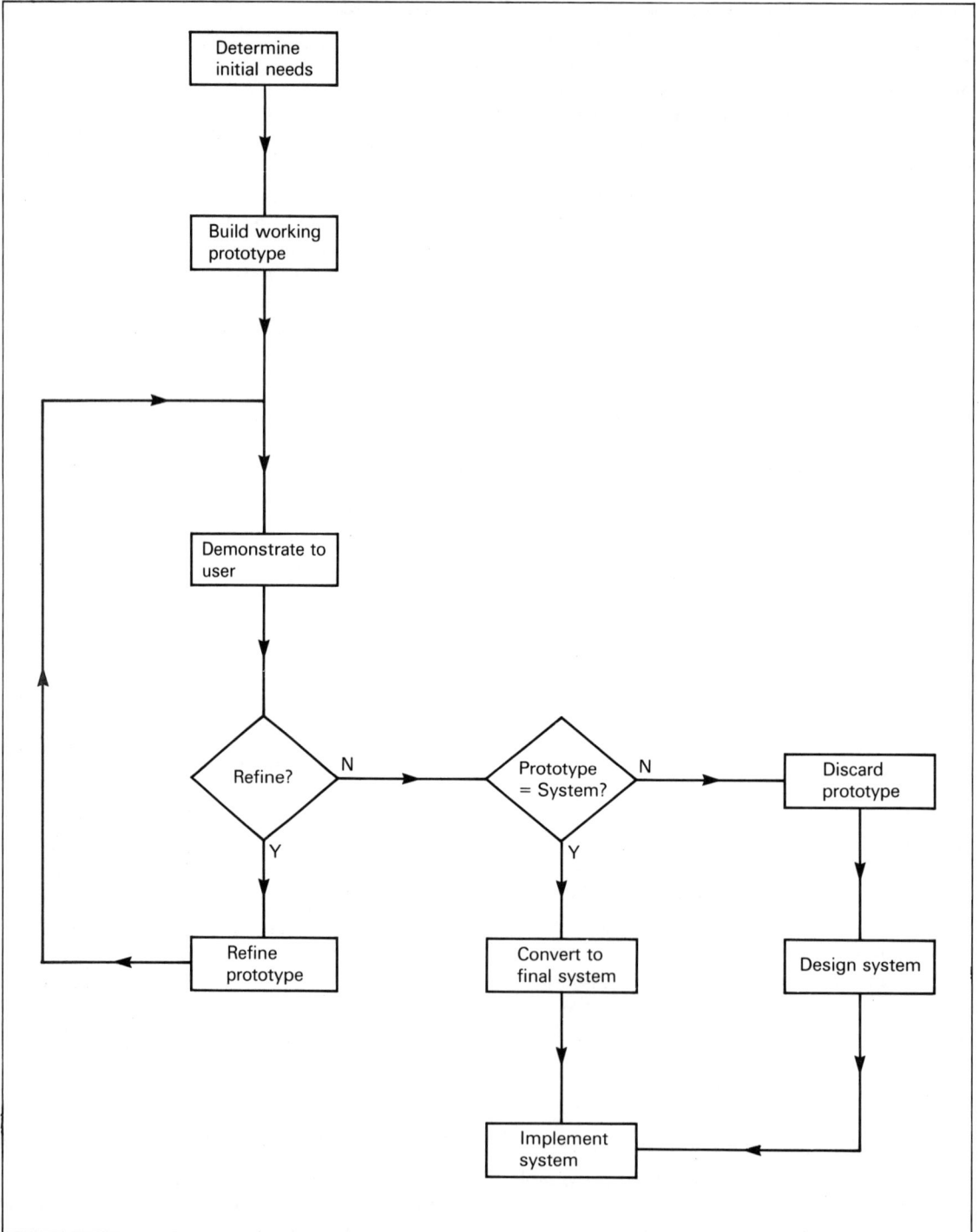

Figure 6.2   *Alternative approaches to prototyping*

Table 6.4 The advantages and disadvantages of the prototyping approach

Advantages

★ Encourages communication between professionals and end-users.
★ Allows greater end-user involvement in development.
★ Replaces a paper specification with a working model, hence giving the user a realistic view of what to expect. It also helps to diminish the problems of the 'I didn't realise it could do that, can it also do this?' syndrome.
★ Helps tighten up both end-users and developers thoughts on the system.
★ Allows changes to be made. The specification is not frozen.
★ Breaks down user resistance/fear of the system.
★ Confirms that the system can be produced.
★ Can speed up the application development process and reduce costs.
★ Allows rapid 'default' system component building, e.g. default screens and reports.
★ Helps to produce the right system, first time and reduce maintenance problems.
★ Aids training. The prototype can be used as an interim training vehicle.
★ Diminishes risk.

Disadvantages

★ Needs acceptance as a method. Some people still see it as an art.
★ Produces systems which may be less efficient than those produced via traditional means.
★ Requires co-operation between users and professionals and associated management.
★ Requires commitment from management.
★ Requires control.
★ Has greater visibility in terms of resources consumed.

6.4.4 4GLs and prototyping

What components of the 4GL are needed for prototyping? One of the most important aspects of prototyping is the ability to make rapid changes to the model. Obviously, the non-procedural facilities of the 4GL are particularly suited to this purpose, e.g. the screen painter, report writer, etc. Changes here require a change in specification rather than a change in coding. Whilst no one 4GL is best suited for prototyping, nor one set of tools, various components are of use. These would include the following tools:

★ A data dictionary – preferably both integrated and active. It is beneficial for this to become a single repository of all the information needed about the system. The data dictionary aids understanding of the data.
★ An interactive screen painting facility. This should be easy to use and capable of quickly producing screens. Changes should be simple to implement.
★ A report generating facility. This should be a non-procedural facility which allows prototype reports to be produced.
★ A query language capable of handling the required enquiries.
★ A DBMS capable of handling the necessary data and file structures. A relational DBMS may be particularly useful in the prototyping situation.
★ A high-level 4GL. This should preferably support structured programming and allow for fast, interactive coding and maintenance.

Such a set of tools facilitates

★ building the prototype rapidly.
★ making changes quickly.
★ interactive testing.
★ moving data between parts of the system.

One extremely important aspect of proto-typing is testing. Whilst the prototype may perform very well during the development phases, it is likely that it has yet to experience the effect of coping with a full load. If the prototype is to evolve into the system (evolutionary prototyping), both users and developers must be convinced of its performance under 'normal' conditions. For example, the prototype might be developed and used by a small number of people. Inefficiencies in the 4GL used to prototype will not show up at this stage. If the system is to be accessed by a much larger number of users, then realistic testing should take place. Sometimes at this stage developers feel the need to re-code at least part of the system in a 3GL.

6.5 Database design

As mentioned earlier, database design has its own set of associated steps. A general model for database design is suggested in Teorey and Fry (1982). Again, this has four major steps:

★ requirements formulation and analysis
★ conceptual design
★ implementation design
★ physical design.

The first stage is to identify the data required. Like all analysis activities, the user's requirements are the major input to this phase. Database design takes a data-oriented rather than a process-oriented approach. At this stage the data dictionary will be built so that identified data may also be described.

During conceptual design the user require-ments have to be brought together into a global design. The conceptual data model or schema describes entities, attributes and relationships. Various techniques could be used to do this, such as entity–relationship diagrams, normalised relations, etc. At this stage, the conceptual data model is independent of any specific data. The next stage requires that the conceptual data model is mapped on to an internal model

(hierarchical, network, relational). The internal model must be processed by a particular DBMS. This phase is an intermediate step between logical and physical design. Finally comes the physical design stage. All aspects of physical design are covered, i.e. design of record formats, access methods, security, integrity and recovery.

Database design is a specialist task and requires professional involvement. The particular model used, i.e. hierarchical, network or relational may depend on

★ the task in hand and hence the data involved.
★ the available software.

6.6 Changes in the role of maintenance

We have seen already that maintenance is a huge problem for the computing industry. 4GLs tackle the maintenance problem in the following ways:

★ By facilitating techniques such as proto-typing. Hence users get the systems they want and request fewer (immediate) changes.
★ The non-procedural elements of the 4GL allow changes to be made with relative ease.

However, many 4GLs require the writing of procedural code. As yet there is little evidence to suggest that overall the amount of maintenance associated with 4GL systems will necessarily decrease in comparison with 3GL systems. A recent survey in Datalink stated that two-thirds of the 4GL sites surveyed spend less than one-quarter of their time on maintenance. This is quite low in comparison with many 3GL sites, but it still leaves one-third of the sites spending quite some time, in fact as much as half, in maintenance tasks.

Other aspects of maintenance change with 4GL use. These changes are outlined in Table 6.5.

Table 6.5   Changes to the role of maintenance with 4GL systems

★ The complexity of the maintenance task. Often the 4GL is less difficult to change if non-procedural. Regeneration of code may also be possible. However difficulties may re-emerge where the 4GL is predominantly procedural or where it provides links to 3GL code.

★ The timing of the maintenance. There is less likelihood of immediate changes being necessary through users changing their minds or becoming aware of possible add-ons to the system. This is basically a change in the role of perfective maintenance.

★ The nature of the maintenance task. In general users will have had greater involvement in the building of the 4GL system than they would have in the building of a 3GL system. The user may even have built the complete system. The maintainer's task here becomes more consultative/supportive. Yet again it is a situation where an expert's skills are required.

★ Areas of the maintenance task. 4GLs have tended to coincide with, if not actively encouraged, a proliferation of decentralised computer users. Users may be making changes locally to corporate databases. The maintenance and consistency of the data content becomes a problem along with those of access and security.

★ Maintenance needed due to frequent changes to the product itself. 4GLs are still evolving. Despite promises of upward compatibility, changes to products can affect old code. Changes to this code will then be necessary.

6.7 4GLs and standards

In the computing industry it is not difficult to come across standards, e.g. documentation standards, computing language standards. There are a large number of reasons for having standards. Standards are intended to:

★ improve efficiency
★ improve effectiveness
★ allow control and supervision
★ enable training
★ allow clear communication
★ encourage good practices
★ promote ideas
★ show what (ideally) should be done
★ satisfy legalities
★ assist in safety measures.

A summary of the areas where standards can be found are shown in Fig. 6.3.

With 4GLs the situation is different:

★ No language standards exist. Some standardisation has in fact 'crept in'. For example, where the 4GL uses a query language, this is often now SQL.
★ Documentation standards are often seen as being part of the traditional systems life-cycle approach. They are then considered inappropriate where this approach is no longer used.

However, the reasons for having standards are still valid under 4GL use. These standards may need to change to accommodate new methodologies but should not completely disappear. Organisational standards could at least be set to cover such areas as

★ documentation
★ database design
★ format/style of code/procedures produced. (Programming design methodologies are as yet little used with 4GLs, although this should change in a CASE environment.)
★ content of procedures
★ naming of procedures, data items, etc.
★ creation of data files.

```
┌─────────────────────────────────────────────────────────────────┐
│                  ┌─────── Hardware, e.g. IBM PC – Industry Standard PC.        │
│                  │              RS-232 – Standard Interface.                    │
│                  ├─────── Software, e.g. ANSI Standard Cobol.                   │
│  Standards for   │              Industry Standard Word-Processing and Spreadsheets. │
│                  ├─────── Documentation, e.g. documentation standards such as NCC Standards. │
│                  ├─────── Design methodologies, e.g. JSP, SSADM.               │
│                  └─────── Safety/security, e.g. Data Protection Act.           │
└─────────────────────────────────────────────────────────────────┘
```

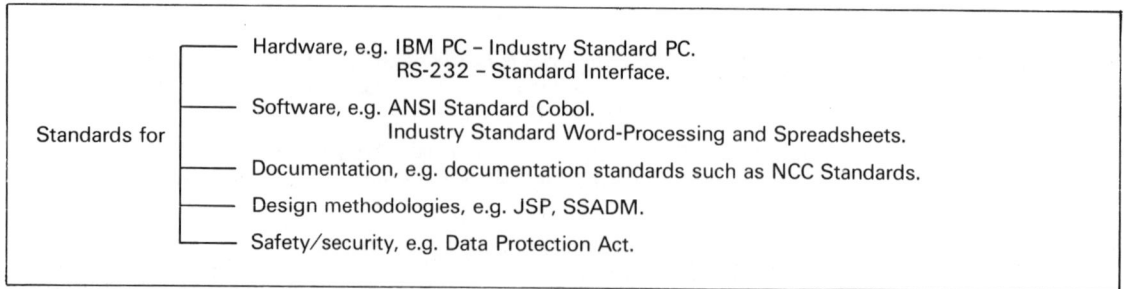

Figure 6.3   *Areas where standards can be found in the computer industry*

6.8 Conclusions

4GLs may be used within the framework of the traditional application development approach. However, in general this does not make full use of the techniques and facilities they offer. 4GLs provide the opportunity for more flexibility, although this does not mean that a totally *ad hoc* approach can be adopted. 4GL development should be within a framework, such as that put forward by the Grindley Report. Objectives must still be set and control exercised.

4GLs also facilitate prototyping, which has become an intrinsic part of the 4GL development approach. The advantages offered by prototyping lead many people to believe that all systems development should involve a prototyping component. This has of course been made possible by 4GL use.

Other changes involve maintenance which takes on a somewhat different role when 4GLs are involved. There is little evidence however to suggest that the amount of maintenance will decrease dramatically with 4GL use. It is probably a little early in the life of the 4GL to be completely definitive about 4GLs and the maintenance task.

One other area which must still be addressed is standards. 4GLs need standards which are not associated with the life-cycle approach.

6.9 Follow-up questions and activities

6.9.1 Questions

1) List the ways in which 4GLs can be used to develop applications.

2) How does the overall 4GL approach to application development differ from the traditional systems life-cycle approach?

3) a) What is meant by the term prototyping?
   b) Distinguish between throwaway and evolutionary prototyping.
   c) Outline the main advantages of the prototyping approach.
   d) What are its main disadvantages?

4) Which of the tools provided by a 4GL are beneficial to the prototyping process? Give reasons for your answers.

5) How has the use of 4GLs affected the maintenance process?

6) a) What advantages do the use of standards offer the computing industry?
   b) Indicate the main areas where standards are found in computing.
   c) What place have standards in a 4GL environment?

7 The effects of 4GL use on the organisation, its staff and resources

Objectives

After you have studied this chapter you should be able to:

* ★ appreciate how the use of 4GLs affects the organisation as a whole.
* ★ describe the changes which occur within the Data Processing department when 4GLs are used for application development.
* ★ list the effects of 4GLs on the resources of the Data Processing department including staff and hardware resources.
* ★ explain what is meant by end-user computing and how 4GLs have facilitated this approach.
* ★ describe the role of the Information Centre in supporting end-user computing.
* ★ explain the other effects of 4GLs including a change in management approach and training needs.

7.1 How do 4GLs affect the organisation?

In Chapter 6 we saw how using 4GLs affects the traditional approach to application development. Changes to the life-cycle are not the only changes that an organisation using 4GLs may expect to make. 4GL use can affect structure, working practices and job definitions. It is the purpose of this chapter to explore these changes.

7.2 4GLs and the organisation

The 4GL itself may have little direct effect on the organisation as a whole. The purchase and use of a 4GL is hardly headline news! However, there are several indirect effects which are important:

* ★ Organisations need to remain competitive. The provision of up-to-date information is a requirement in today's business environment. Computer systems can help to provide this information but they in turn need to be developed with reasonable speed. 4GLs help make this possible.
* ★ Organisations need to stay in touch with new technologies. It may be easier, for example, to recruit staff in an environment where up-to-date tools and techniques rather than outmoded languages and methods are employed.
* ★ There may be a need to restructure key departments, such as the DP department and to build bridges between end-users and professionals.
* ★ A corporate rather than a localised application development strategy may be necessary. It may be advantageous to the organisation to develop some computer applications rather than others.
* ★ There may be a change in organisational roles. This may not be wholly the result of 4GL use. Other factors, such as the move to database usage, will also have contributed. Jobs with names like Information Systems Director and Database Administrator will have sprung up as a result of this emphasis on information.
* ★ The need for additional services, such as an Information Centre, to help support changes in the application development process.
* ★ The need for additional resources (probably monetary) to increase hardware facilities or to fund re-training in new methods.

7.3 4GLs and the DP department

The DP department has been experiencing some major changes. Some of these changes are directly attributable to 4GL use, others are indirectly connected.

7.3.1 A change of name

The DP department of the 1960s and early 1970s assumed a traditional, centralised approach to computing. Its role was to provide other departments within the organisation with the benefits of computerisation. With the advent of smaller, cheaper computers distributed processing became widespread. Various departments within an organisation could now control their own computing power.

Inevitably, the role of the DP department has changed. The emphasis has shifted from the provision of operational systems, e.g. stock control, payroll, etc. to the provision of information. Many DP departments have experienced a change of name to reflect this new role. Titles such as Information Services or Management Information Services are now common.

7.3.2 A change of structure

The structure of a typical DP department of the 1960s is shown in Figure 7.1. This structure was developed out of the centralised computing approach and built upon the need to provide batch processing systems. Roles such as Database Administrator and Information Services Manager were neither needed, nor catered for. There was also no need to control end-user development, nor to provide end-user support. The changing role of the DP department has also been reflected in a changing structure. One such more up-to-date structure is shown in Figure 7.2.

7.3.3 A change in organisational role

DP managers have sometimes been guilty of building empires. For a long time it was their department and their staff who provided the computing facilities for the rest of the organisation. As the role of the DP department within the organisation has changed, this situation has also changed. End-users now build applications and buy hardware and software. Departmental computer groups have sprung up within finance, personnel, research and development, etc. These groups want to be responsible for their own computing needs. Some may have become disenchanted with the facilities provided by the DP department and the speed of that provision. 4GLs have coincided with and directly contributed to the increase in end-user computing.

Gradually the DP department has had to accept a change in their organisational role. This role is now one of giving advice and guidance and assisting in the co-ordination of the diverse needs of the groups within the organisation, as well as one of development. The DP department is no longer the only provider of computing services/facilities.

7.3.4 Change in development approach

As we saw in Chapter 6, 4GLs demand a different approach to development. The DP department have now to accept a different way of working. This may be difficult after years of the large project team, traditional life-cycle approach. Smaller project teams, and shorter development time-scales are the result of 4GL use. The emphasis is now on prototyping and closer liaison with users. A move has been made towards providing the required system, at the right cost. In general 4GLs have facilitated the changes shown in Figure 7.3.

7.3.5 Changing staff roles

The emphasis on information provision has led to the development of several new computing staff roles. New roles include the Data Administrator and the Database Administrator or Manager as well as others such as the Data Dictionary Manager. Other computing roles of the 1960s/70s identified in Figure 7.1 have also changed significantly. Data preparation used to be synonymous with punch card operation, whilst nowadays data preparation staff will be required to operate key-to-disc systems and VDUs, for example. The role of the operator has also changed, as computers have become more reliable and have less need of human inter-vention. The concept of the 'dark-room', where computer hardware and peripherals are left to operate in a sealed room without staff, has become more common. (Obviously staff must still be available when something goes wrong.)

The analyst/programmer division is also an example of the changing face of the DP

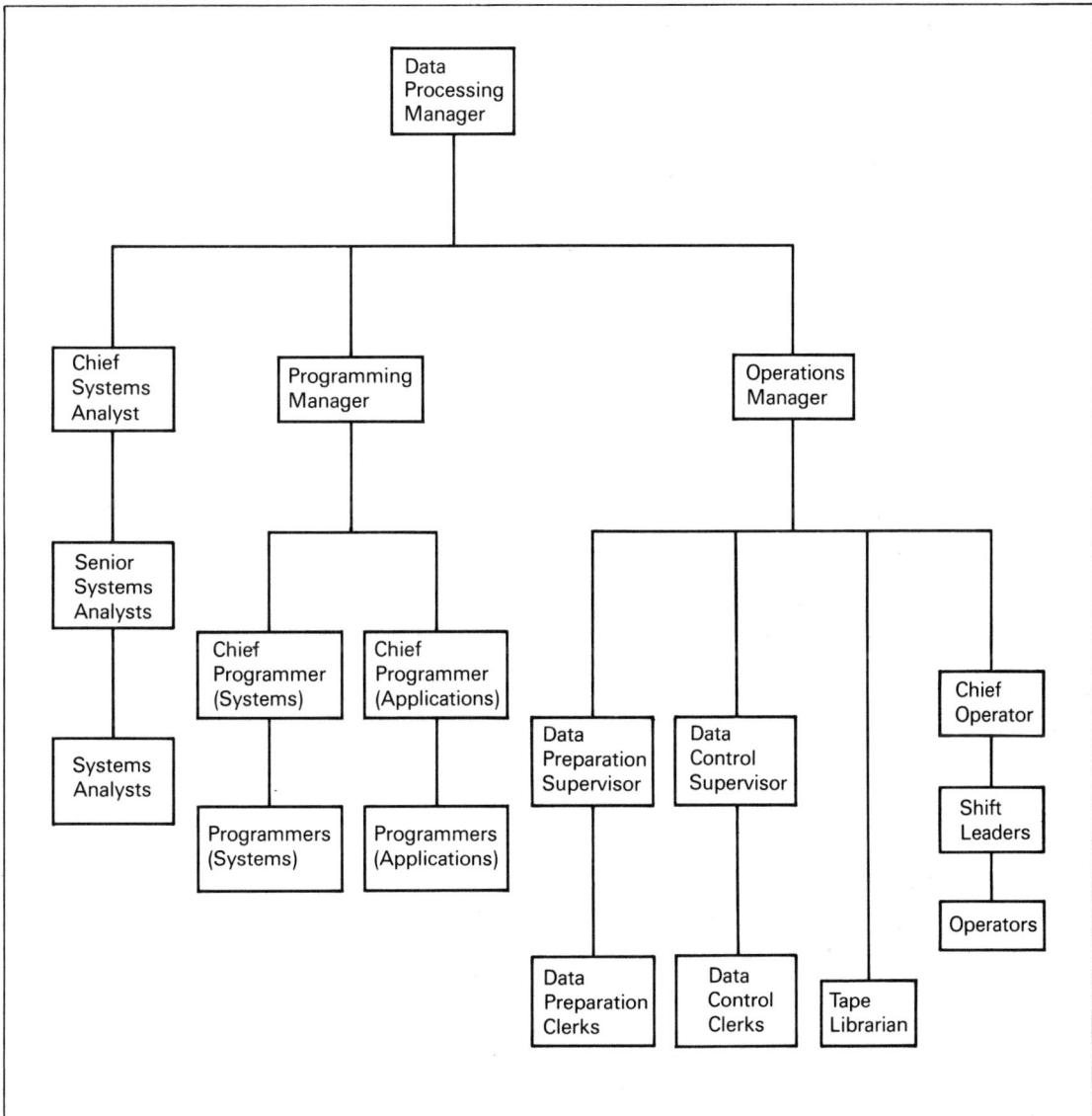

Figure 7.1   *The structure of a typical DP department of the 1960s/70s*

department. This is dealt with separately in the next section. Here we shall concentrate on new roles within the DP department.

A. The Data Administrator

Data administration is one of the newer roles in DP environments, made necessary by the advent of databases and the emphasis on the provision of information. The British Computer Society (BCS), Data Administration Working Party (DAWP), defines data administration as

> the corporate service which assists the provision of information systems by controlling and/or coordinating the definitions (format and characteristics) and usage of reliable and relevant data. Data that is internal to the organisation can be controlled, whilst data from external sources that is used by most organisations can only be coordinated.

The Data Administrator should (although it will differ from organisation to organisation)

★ identify company information requirements.

★ educate staff on the importance and value of data.

★ select data analysis techniques.

★ establish data definition standards.

★ control the use of the data dictionary.

★ sort out problems related to data and its use.

★ control data access and duplication.

★ look at privacy, security and integrity issues.

★ monitor usage of data and assess the impact of changes.

★ develop a policy for storing data on a long-term basis (archiving), possibly to satisfy legal requirements.

B. The Database Administrator

This role provides the technical support for the Data Administrator. The Database Administrator will be concerned with

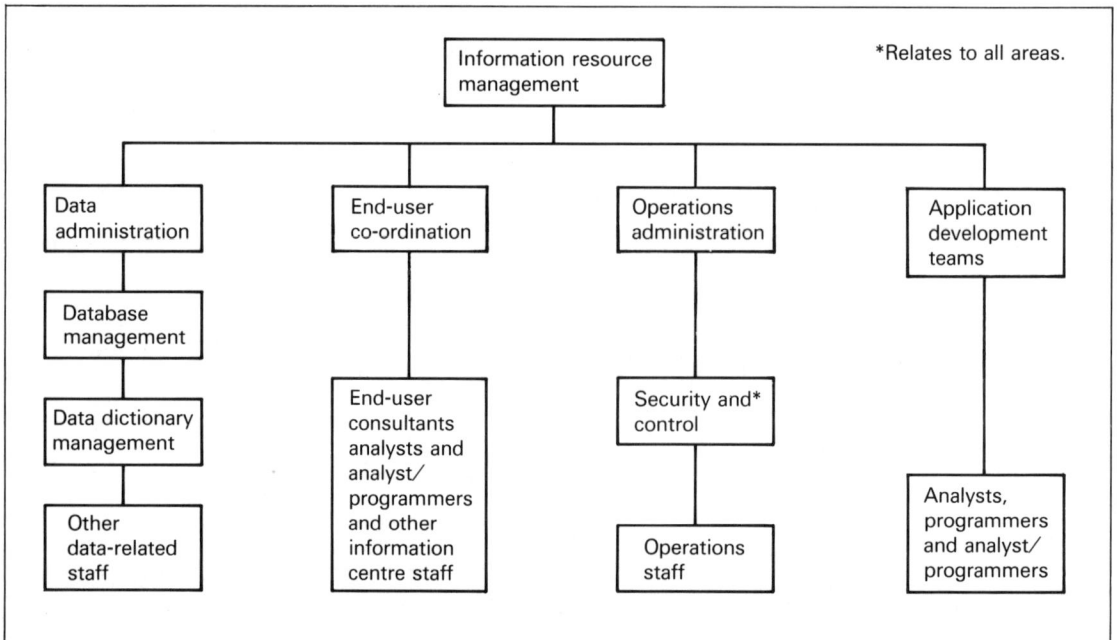

Figure 7.2   *A DP department structure for the 1980s/90s*

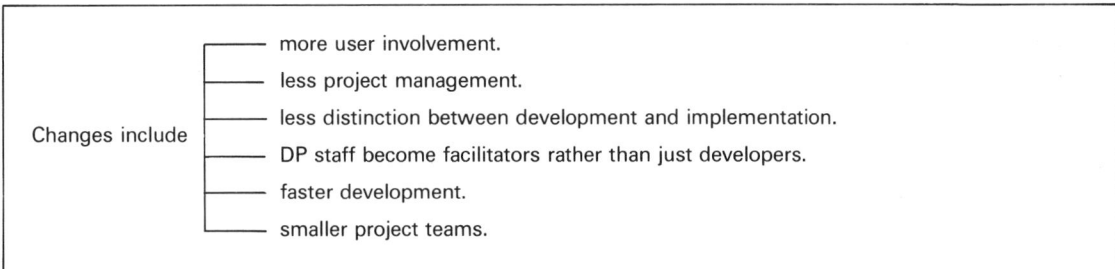

Figure 7.3 *Changes in development approach brought about by 4GL use*

★ the establishment of standards for data definition and representation.
★ database design and development.
★ organisation and definition of the logical use of data.
★ education and training on database technology and environment.
★ user support.
★ security, integrity and control.

Most 4GLs offer database environments. As we have seen, many offer an integrated database, whilst others offer links to external products. The trend is towards a relational DBMS, for the reasons outlined in Chapter 4. The Database Administrator will need to formulate policies on the use of database systems and to control the spread of individual databases.

7.4 4GLs and DP professionals

4GL use inevitably affects the professionals within the DP department. When 4GLs first began to appear in numbers the media tended to go overboard on their end-user appeal. Wild claims were made that professionals would soon become unnecessary in application development. There are several important points which need to be remembered in the face of such claims.

★ Not all organisations as yet use 4GLs, although most have at least one tool in use which could claim this title. In organisations as yet without 4GLs, the job of the DP professional has probably undergone little transformation.

★ 4GLs are not generally used in most organisations for all development work. At the moment 4GLs tend to be used quite selectively. Traditional application development and packaged solutions will continue to be provided.
★ Each organisation will decide how, and by whom, the 4GL is to be used. A small team of 4GL experts may be set up. Alternatively, all, or a large majority of the staff within the DP department, may be expected to become familiar with the 4GL and be involved with its use.
★ Even where end-users become reasonably proficient in various aspects of 4GL use, generally they will not be able to handle complex systems. Use of procedural code and the design of database structures, for example, require professional skill and ability. Hence there will still be a need for trained professional staff.

All these points aside, some changes have occurred and these are discussed below.

7.4.1 The analyst/programmer division

With the traditional method of developing applications, there is a clear demarcation line between the role of the analyst and the role of the programmer. The analyst needs interpersonal skills to be able to liaise and communicate with the end-user. The programmer needs technical skills to turn the analyst's specification into a working system. There is little need for the programmer to get involved with the user. Many programmers like this approach. They enjoy the challenge of solving a complex problem but do not want to get involved with end-users.

Where 4GLs are used, this analyst/programmer distinction is not as well-defined. The emphasis on prototyping requires that the developer remains involved with the user well beyond the initial determination of requirements. In fact, users may be part of the development team for the duration of the application development period.

If the development team is small or one-person, they will be required to take the process of development through to completion. Such developers become analyst/programmers and require the skills of both. This can cause various problems:

★ Analysts may have difficulty coping with the programming aspects of the task. Although various tools within the 4GL may offer ease-of-use, the procedural components inevitably demand a higher level of skill.
★ Analysts who have consciously made the move into analysis from programming may find themselves back in programming again.
★ There is more pressure placed on the analyst/programmer. Their involvement requires a higher profile than in the traditional development process, where the work is staged.
★ Programmers find there is little scope for programming ability alone. Other skills are also required.
★ Programmers may have to get used to new practices, such as less documentation, throwaway code, etc.
★ 4GLs and fixed programming cycles impose a way of programming that some programmers find restrictive and far from ideal. They may come to feel that their work is less interesting. Not all 4GLs of course adopt this approach.
★ People are often threatened by a change in existing practices. Antagonism may result,

while others may actually welcome the opportunity to learn new skills. There is some research evidence that shows that programmers in general do little to update their own programming skills unless specifically sent on company training courses.
★ Some activities may suffer, e.g. analysis/design activities, as there is no one specific person in overall control. The analyst/programmer has many diverse tasks to perform.

It helps to put this all into perspective if you consider that:

★ many analysts are trained programmers and hence the new skill requirements will not be too onerous.
★ few programmers would expect to stay in that position for life anyway. Most move on to do other jobs within the computing profession or change professions.

7.4.2 Operations and technical support staff

With 4GLs, operations and technical support staff will be needed. Their tasks will include:

★ installation of the 4GL.
★ monitoring the usage of the 4GL.
★ monitoring the performance of the 4GL.
★ fine-tuning the 4GL.
★ scheduling tasks.
★ maintaining the hardware.

This is a change of role for many operational and support staff. However, the implementation of a 4GL will be more successful if carried out in a controlled and systematic way.

7.4.3 Who uses the 4GL?

Another problem can arise for staff in the attitude taken within the department to who will use the 4GL(s). Organisations tend to take quite different approaches to this problem. Some have a special 4GL 'team', an approach with both advantages and disadvantages. On the positive side, this approach:

★ ensures that there is a 'hard core' of staff with expertise in the 4GL.

★ fits in with the idea that not all applications are being developed via 4GLs, so that many of the staff are needed for more important conventional development work.

On the other hand it could lead to:

★ an elitist approach, i.e. that the 4GL team is somehow special. (Although some people would not welcome the opportunity to be a part of the team.)

★ problems over training issues. The 4GL specialist may need to go on various training courses to become such a specialist. (This of course depends on the 4GL in question.) This agrees with the point made above, particularly if the training is restricted to a 'chosen' few.

Other organisations only allow programmers with at least one to two years' experience of a 3GL to use the 4GL. Usage here would not be restricted to just a few staff. Another attitude organisations have is that experience of and competence in a 3GL spoils you for 4GL use. Trying to apply 3GL techniques to 4GL programs is doubtless a mistake, but nevertheless competence in a procedural language provides skills likely to be necessary in the extensive use of a 4GL product (excluding facilities aimed at end-users).

7.4.4 Staff recruitment

Many people recruiting staff to use 4GLs feel that a background in business is almost, if not more important than pure technical skill. On the other hand, not all application development work within organisations is via 4GLs, so inevitably traditional programming skills are still required. In this respect, 4GLs are having little effect on the job market. However, it is true to say that in most job advertisements the phase 'two years' experience with COBOL required' is being replaced with 'two years' experience with COBOL and knowledge of a 4GL required'.

Sometimes a particular 4GL will be named, although there is a feeling that experience with one 4GL equips you to deal with others, on the basis that, having used a 4GL, you know both their limitations and their strengths.

There may of course be knock-on effects for graduates and diplomates. Those with a more varied background, for example, a computer studies course with a business orientation, will find the market-place very receptive to such skills. However, we must bear in mind that 4GLs are not the only direction for computing in the future. The use of formal methods in computing (see Chapter 2), means that computing may once again go back towards having a mathematical bias. Parallel processing and concurrency among other topics are also of interest to some mathematicians. Artificial intelligence (AI) involves the use of PROLOG (based on predicate logic) and LISP (a functional language). In the end, what we may see is more specialism in computing than we have witnessed in previous years.

It is still however safe to say, at least for the moment, that someone with sound experience of a leading 4GL would have no difficulty finding a reasonable position.

7.4.5 Relationship with the users

A positive effect of 4GLs and prototyping is a narrowing of the gap between DP professionals and the end-user. Not only will DP staff be required to work in closer proximity to the users, they will, as well as providing development staff as before, be required to perform other tasks for them including

★ giving advice on buying and using 4GLs and software packages.

★ providing training for users.

★ giving advice on buying and using personal computers.

★ providing software to facilitate end-user development, e.g. friendly front-ends, tools to download data from a database.

★ providing technical support for end-user development, e.g. database design.

Much of this will be done through the information centre. The structure and role of the information centre are described in detail later in this chapter.

7.5 4GLs and hardware resources

Some installations using 4GLs have reported the need to expand their computer hardware capacity at an accelerated rate during the first 2–3 years of use. This expansion may be at a rate of something like 60–80 per cent, rather than the 40 per cent increase which may already have been necessary over the last few years, due to the needs of a changing industry. Obviously capacity planning becomes much more of a crucial issue.

There is also a need for adequate basic equipment. 4GL programmers will spend more of their time at terminals than programmers writing code in 3GLs. Time spent at the terminal for 4GL programmers can amount to something like 80 per cent of their time, which is a 30–40 per cent increase over other programmers. Hence more dedicated terminals will be required. PCs will take on a more important role, both as terminal emulators and development machines. There will also be a need for more localised computing power for end-user computing.

In a 3GL environment, hardware loading is usually reasonably predictable. There are additional problems in a 4GL environment which means that this is usually not the case. Such problems include

★ Inefficiency of some 4GL products.
★ Increased productivity and faster systems development can lead to more systems being developed and more use being made of the hardware.
★ With 4GL applications, more programs tend to get developed. One program might be needed for screen development, another for reports etc. Although individual programs may be more trivial it still adds up to an increase in programming time, machine time and CPU utilisation.

★ Prototyping, whilst beneficial also makes high demands on machine resources.
★ 4GLs are generally associated with on-line rather than batch processing systems. On-line systems demand more resources and faster response times than batch systems.
★ There may be a greater use made of the programs developed because the system is on-line and they were developed for the end-user.
★ There is more uncontrolled use due to end-user computing and inefficient programming methods.
★ Changes to 4GL programs are easy to make and can result in many re-runs of the system.
★ Usage at peak times.

Some of the findings of the Grindley Report (1986) were:

★ Using 4GLs for transaction processing systems showed up lower efficiency losses over COBOL, for example, than when they were used for batch processing systems.
★ If database design was not optimised then the performance of the system was seriously affected.
★ Allowing users to have file create and update privileges greatly increased disc usage.
★ Little consideration has been given to running inefficient 4GL jobs at off-peak times.
★ Low volume applications appear less sensitive to efficiency problems than high volume work.

These findings are very important and have serious implications for any organisation considering the adoption of a 4GL.

7.6 4GLs and the end-user

7.6.1 End-user computing

In Chapter 3 we saw that end-users can claim this title by virtue of various levels of use of a computer system. Such use may be indirect, i.e. by people who inadvertently use a computer system through a separate need. For example, you go to book a holiday. The travel agent has a computerised system. You indirectly become a user of that system without even touching a computer. Other end-users make direct use of applications built by DP staff, like the order clerk who uses a computerised sales order processing system to process a customer's order.

Not so long ago, an end-user would have had little opportunity to become involved in application development beyond their contact with an analyst to determine requirements. Once the analyst had determined the user's needs, the 'visible' part of development disappeared. Many end-users would not see the result of their early involvement for a long time afterwards, when the system was finally implemented. The reasons for this are obvious.

★ Applications were built in languages, such as COBOL, which in general were only used by DP professionals.
★ There was a feeling that the development process required complex skills, not generally held by lay people. How could accountants, finance officers, etc. understand DP and its related technology?
★ End-users were there to use systems, not develop them.

Gradually things have changed. The problems we considered in Chapter 2, such as the application backlog and the rising costs of complex systems, have resulted in the demand for a different approach. End-users can now be more involved in application development. This has become possible for several reasons:

★ Efficient use of software packages needs expertise from both end-users and professionals. Selection of such a package for example, requires involvement from the user, who has most knowledge of the application.
★ The advent of end-user tools. Those 4GLs which provide end-user facilities allow users to develop simple applications for

themselves or to use query and reporting facilities.
★ There has been a growing awareness among end-users of what computer systems can do for them.
★ There has also been a general increase in computer literacy.

There are both advantages and disadvantages associated with allowing end-users to develop their own systems. Some of these are shown in Table 7.1. The right 4GLs are being used successfully by many end-users. Some will develop complete applications, others are more likely to use the non-procedural components, such as the screen painter, query languages or report writer. Some people have claimed that 4GLs are just end-user tools, but, as we have seen, this is not really the case.

7.6.2 Information centres

End-user computing has been recognised in many organisations and is being given support. This support is provided through the information centre, which aims to help end-users make the best possible use of information technology. We identified earlier that DP staff are having to work more closely with end-users and provide them with a range of services. The services provided by the information centre are discussed below.

A. Training
The information centre must be prepared to train users in the use of software (and hardware). Users need to develop the skills required successfully to employ software tools, which may be anything from a simple application package to an end-user 4GL for developing applications. The information centre must be prepared to disseminate information to all interested parties efficiently and effectively.

B. Advice on purchase of software and hardware
The information centre must not become an extension of the sales force of a particular

Table 7.1   The advantages and disadvantages of end-user computing

---

Advantages

★ An increase in the number of people producing systems.

★ Release of DP professionals from the smaller tasks, which may have gone to the 'back of the queue' anyway.

★ Provides a way of helping to reduce the application backlog.

★ Gives users more control over systems, particularly where they have the greatest knowledge.

★ Allows users to get the most out of various tools, e.g. 4GLs.

★ Gives end-users an insight into the computing task, which in turn may give them a better perspective on what is and is not possible. This can have knock-on effects in other application development tasks.

Disadvantages

★ The need for careful control. For example, users must not be allowed to duplicate data in a corporate database, or to update data, unless they have permission. There is a feeling that end-user computing encourages the setting up of personal databases and hence the duplication of data.

★ End-user computing still requires an input from professionals. For example, information centres need to be set up. This requires commitment from the professionals and again inevitably ties up their time.

★ It may cause a proliferation of tools within an organisation, e.g. several different 4GLs being purchased and used for similar purposes.

★ It can also cause a proliferation of PCs, some of which may lie virtually idle.

★ Users may not be sufficiently trained to do the tasks they set out to do. This can result in a number of half-finished or failed projects.

---

manufacturer. They should provide impartial and expert advice on a range of tools and hardware devices. Naive users are often tempted to buy obscure hardware and software because of price/sales jargon and through ignorance. The information centre should at least help to co-ordinate the purchase of computer tools and put users in touch with others with similar needs.

C. Development of tools to facilitate end-user computing

End-users sometimes need to carry out various tasks that are beyond the scope of their skills. Professionals can assist by providing tools to facilitate such tasks, e.g. downloading of data from databases. They may also provide on-line help and documentation facilities and other support tools.

D. Provision of expertise

Outside of end-user computing, the need for development staff will not radically change.

However even where end-users are developing their own applications, professional staff will still be required to provide the expertise needed in such tasks as database design. The information centre may provide consultants with this expertise.

E. Control and co-ordination of end-user computing

End-user computing needs careful control and co-ordination. It can result in duplication of data and a proliferation of trivial systems. Control of such problems will be in the hands of the Database Administrator as part of the general policy of data management and control. Other problems needing control include disk usage, access and scheduling.

F. Promotion of good practice

Professionals should at all times promote good practices, including comprehensive and clear documentation, security and integrity of data.

The Information Centre should be staffed by professionals who can communicate with end-users and who have a background in computing and business. This may lead to a situation where only a small number of suitable staff provide a service to the information centre. They may also have to spread themselves quite thinly across a large number of users and services.

7.7 4GLs and management

It is fairly obvious from our discussions that 4GL use needs careful control. 4GL use emphasises various management functions to a greater degree than with 3GL use. Tasks which need careful consideration are:

★ The choice of applications for 4GL development.
★ The extent of 4GL provision within an organisation.
★ The planning of hardware resources. Capacity planning needs to be considered very carefully.
★ Application development needs to be more flexible but still controlled.
★ Policies for 4GL adoption and use have to be formulated.
★ Control of the prototyping approach is crucial.

7.8 4GLs and training

The ease of use of 4GLs is often underestimated. No one could ask a programmer to write or maintain a large COBOL program without extensive training or expertise, yet it is often assumed that anyone with a reasonable amount of intelligence can learn and use a 4GL. This arises from the (mistaken) assumption that 4GLs are just end-user tools. Although to some extent this ease-of-use notion is true, 4GLs often offer more advanced features which require considerable skill. Organisations need to facilitate the use of 4GLs by provision of suitable training where necessary.

7.9 Conclusions

Adopting 4GLs involves much more than a change of language or tool for application development. Organisations need to consider the use of 4GLs within the development environment very carefully. Management needs to control and minimise the effects on staff and hardware resources. The DP department has undergone various changes in the last decade, changes that have been exacerbated by the introduction and use of 4GLs.

7.10 Follow-up questions and activities

7.10.1 Questions

1) Describe the ways in which 4GL use may affect the DP department within an organisation.

2) a) Name two new staff roles within the DP (or equivalent) department which were not part of the DP departmental structure of the 1960s/70s.
   b) What are the main reasons for the advent of these new roles?
   c) List the main job functions of the two new roles you have identified.

3) How has the use of 4GLs changed the role of (a) the systems analyst and (b) the programmer?

4) a) Explain why the use of 4GLs in an organisation may have adverse effects on hardware resources.
   b) What steps can be taken within an organisation to minimise these effects?

5) a) Why is it now possible/desirable for end-uses to be involved in the production of computer systems?
   b) Describe five advantages of end-user computing.
   c) Describe five disadvantages of end-user computing.

6) a) What do you understand by the term
      'information centre'?
   b) What are the main objectives of the
      information centre?
   c) How do these objectives differ from those
      of the more traditional DP department?

7.10.2 Activities

7) Find an analyst or programmer within your
   college/polytechnic/organisation (or another

organisation), who uses a 4GL for application development. Discuss with them the
effects of the use of the 4GL on their job
functions. Find out if it has changed their
job significantly and if so how?

8) Look at the information centre (or
   equivalent) in your college/polytechnic/
   organisation. List the facilities they have on
   offer. Compare these facilities with the ones
   discussed in this chapter. Make a list of
   those facilities not mentioned in this text.

8 The advantages and disadvantages of 4GLs

Objectives

After you have studied this chapter you should be able to:

★ appreciate that 4GLs can not solve all the problems of the computing industry discussed in previous chapters.
★ list the main advantages of 4GL use.
★ list the main disadvantages of 4GL use.
★ appreciate that, overall, the advantages of 4GL use outweigh the disadvantages.
★ describe how an organisation might best go about selecting a 4GL for use in the application development process.

8.1 Are 4GLs a panacea for all ills?

If we are to believe all the sales literature, 4GLs could cure all the problems of the computing industry. Yet it is not too difficult to find various discussions and articles which clearly spell out the disappointments and even disasters that some organisations have experienced with 4GLs (see Grindley, 1986), although we must remember there is bound to be difficulties during the settling-down process.

Many of these difficulties are caused by ignorance about what 4GLs are, their strengths and limitations. Several surveys, for example, have reported that many organisations purchase a 4GL by choosing the first product they look at (see e.g. Forage and Wilkes, 1985). Even if it happens to be a leading 4GL, this is not the way to select a major piece of software, particularly when that software could mean an important change for the organisation. Organisations need to consider the potential benefits and the drawbacks of 4GLs and allow for both. Organisations must have a definite strategy in mind when purchasing a 4GL for the first time. Unless clear objectives are set, disasters can

occur. It is not enough just to pick a product name from the sales literature.

The purpose of this chapter is to consider the advantages and disadvantages to be gained from the use of 4GLs and concludes that, when 4GLs are used properly, the advantages outweigh the disadvantages.

8.2 The advantages of 4GLs

4GLs can offer many benefits to those who use them. These benefits are summarised in Table 8.1. Each is considered below. Some of the issues have already been raised and discussed in some detail elsewhere in this text.

8.2.1 4GLs allow alternative methods of development

We have seen some of the problems caused by many years of developing systems via the traditional systems life-cycle. The increased demand for complex applications has not been matched by this approach. Few successful or complete alternatives have been offered. Structured analysis and design methodologies offer more precise methods of extracting requirements and of designing the system. Structured programming methodologies allow for the development of correct code. Neither have had a major impact on many of the problems we have identified. Other techniques, such as formal methods, have yet to be fully accepted at the commercial level. 4GLs allow the use of alternative development methods, such as prototyping. Where the life-cycle approach has ceased to be appropriate, these alternative methods should be used.

8.2.2 Enhancement of the traditional approach

Not everyone will wish to change their development approach, particularly where the changes

Table 8.1   The advantages offered by 4GLs

★ Alternative development approaches are possible.

★ The traditional life-cycle approach to development is enhanced.

★ Programmer productivity is increased.

★ Faster systems development is possible.

★ Systems developed are a closer match to user requirements.

★ Programs are easier to change, i.e. the maintenance process becomes less complex.

★ Personal (micro) computers can play a part in the development process.

★ They offer ease-of-use facilities.

★ Analysts, programmers and end-users can use up-to-date tools and techniques.

★ Program life is increased.

★ End-users have a greater involvement in the development process.

★ Portability is aided.

★ Improved documentation is facilitated.

★ Smaller development teams are required.

★ They improve requirements analysis.

★ End-users can develop applications for themselves.

are seen as radical. Many organisations are committed to the traditional methods of developing applications, although they may have made several modifications/improvements to the basic life-cycle over a number of years. Some organisations will also have adopted structured methods. Despite this most organisations will be amenable to making further changes, if such changes result in savings in either time or cost or both. 4GLs can be used to enhance, rather than replace, the life-cycle. The development language, traditionally a 3GL, is replaced by a 4GL, which results in savings at the programmer/testing/maintenance phases, although few other benefits are realised.

8.2.3 Increased programmer productivity

The need to improve productivity within the computing industry needs little explanation. Tools and techniques are required which help to do just this. These are needed to

★ help clear the backlog of applications.
★ restore confidence in the DP department.
★ reduce development and maintenance costs.
★ reduce the complexity of development.

Increased productivity is generally taken to mean more output and/or better quality for the same input (cost, time, etc.) as before. This can be achieved by greater control over people or processes and/or the use of high productivity tools.

There is little doubt that you can get further faster with a 4GL. However, claims such as hundred-fold productivity gains over 3GLs are more often than not exaggerated. Often like is not being compared with like.

Programmer productivity is at best a difficult thing to measure. With 3GLs, one measure is the number of lines of code produced by the programmer, although other more precise measures, such as function points, are also used (see Albrecht and Gafney, 1983). Measuring the number of lines of code a programmer produces says nothing about the following:

★ Quality. Are 1000 lines of structured code equivalent to 1000 lines of spaghetti code?
★ What a line actually is. Are comments counted, for example? What about the situation where two lines of code are joined by a colon to fit on one line?
★ Differences between languages.
★ Maintaining v. writing new code? How do we measure the productivity of a maintenance programmer who may spend up to 80 per cent of his/her time in maintenance?
★ Code which is re-written. Do we count first, second, third, versions, etc. or just the final product?
★ Modules which are used again and again.
★ The difference between code used for testing and production code. Is there a difference in productivity here?
★ Non-coding activities, e.g. documentation.

When the language being used is a 4GL, we have other problems as well. Much of the work done may be produced through non-procedural techniques rather than through the writing of procedural code. Even where code is actually written, one line of 4GL code may be a replacement for several lines of 3GL code. Lines of code produced hence becomes an unrealistic measure of productivity.

Having said this, the evidence does point to increased productivity with 4GLs. This may be more like a two-fold increase than the hundred-fold increase sometimes quoted, but much depends on the product in use and the type of application being developed. As products improve, it is likely that the productivity increases will also improve.

8.2.4 Faster systems development

If programmer productivity increases through the use of 4GLs, then reduced times for the development process may seem to be a natural and automatic conclusion. However, coding only plays a relatively small part in the development process (say 10–20 per cent of the total time required), so that, even if we have a ten-fold increase in programmer productivity, the resultant saving in development time will be much smaller. However, where 4GLs are used, making techniques like prototyping feasible, faster systems development is being achieved. Where the 4GL is the development language, the system is usually produced more quickly than when the development language is a 3GL, such as COBOL.

It would also be reasonable to expect that faster systems development would help to cut back the application backlog, discussed in Chapter 2. Unfortunately this does not always seem to be the case simply because some DP departments are finding that end-users are requesting more, not fewer systems. Many of these systems would have originally constituted the invisible backlog. Increased confidence in the DP department's ability to deliver systems has brought them out into the open.

8.2.5 Systems closer match user requirements

This is a direct result of 4GLs making the prototyping approach possible. Users are able to see what they are likely to get at the end of the development process, long before this stage is reached. They have time to make changes and request add-ons before the requirements are 'set in concrete'. In the end users are happier with the systems being developed.

8.2.6 Programs are easier to change

Complex programs written in 3GL code are often full of intricate interrelationships. Changes to one part of a program may have a knock-on effect for various other parts of that program. Even where a structured programming approach has been adopted, the maintenance programmer may find it difficult to foresee all such effects when changes to the original code are made. All too often programs are written in spaghetti code which adds to these problems. A nice definition of spaghetti code appears in the Grindley Report (1986). One of the organisations surveyed refers to spaghetti code as 'the creation of structures which are dangerous to fork over since something surprising usually happens on the other side of the plate'. In general it is easier to change programs written in a 4GL. The reasons for this are shown in Figure 8.1.

8.2.7 PC development of mainframe applications

We considered this particular feature of some 4GLs in Chapter 5. Generally speaking personal or micro computers:

★ are widely available in most organisations.
★ are familiar to a large number of people, particularly the end-user.
★ are often less utilised than mainframes.
★ can provide extra resources.

Several manufacturers of 4GLs have spotted the potential of offering a PC version of their product. This allows the PC to be utilised in the development of mainframe applications. The ways in which this can be achieved were also described in Chapter 5.

8.2.8 Ease-of-use

This is often put alongside increased programmer productivity and reduced development times as one of the main advantages of 4GL use. Many products claiming to be end-user tools make much of this ease-of-use criterion. Martin (1985) suggests the 'two day test' to help sort out end-user tools from more complex products. He says that if an end-user can carry out useful work with the product in two days it can be classed as an end-user tool.

There is no doubt that it is generally easier to get under way and make progress with virtually any 4GL than with a language such as COBOL or FORTRAN. However, it is often the non-procedural elements of the 4GL which offer true ease-of-use. Here the user of the tool will make progress very quickly. For example, setting up a data dictionary, defining screens and reports often seem quite trivial tasks with the 4GL. However, once the requirements become complex then inevitably the more complicated, procedural components of the 4GL are needed. It may become necessary to write code and programming skills will be required. Fitting the application together may actually take more time than producing the various parts!

Hence, while 4GLs do offer ease-of-use, it must not be mistaken for complete simplicity. Much depends on the product, the components of the product being used and the applications being developed. Some 4GLs do offer the same ease-of-use facilities throughout the whole of the product. Other vendors openly admit that the product is aimed at the skilled professional and the benefits to be gained are increased productivity and faster systems development.

There is a negative side to ease-of-use, that of lack of training. This is discussed later on in this chapter, as one of the disadvantages of 4GL use.

8.2.9 Up-to-date tools and techniques

This is one advantage which gets little acknowledgement. There are people who are quite happy to remain COBOL programmers all their working lives but there is evidence to show this is the exception rather than the norm.

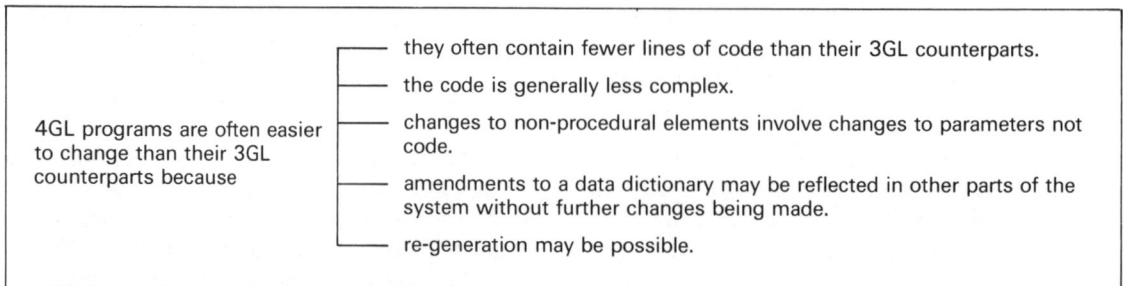

4GL programs are often easier to change than their 3GL counterparts because

— they often contain fewer lines of code than their 3GL counterparts.

— the code is generally less complex.

— changes to non-procedural elements involve changes to parameters not code.

— amendments to a data dictionary may be reflected in other parts of the system without further changes being made.

— re-generation may be possible.

Figure 8.1   *Why is it easier to change 4GL programs?*

People working in the computing industry have a right to up-to-date tools and techniques and it makes sense for organisations to provide them. It also makes sense for educational establishments to offer their students the same opportunity wherever possible.

Experience with a range of up-to-date tools such as 4GLs may help the analyst or programmer to:

★ ascertain where their strengths and weaknesses lie.
★ become familiar with different techniques for producing systems.
★ add another 'string to their bow' – useful when applying for promotion or other jobs.
★ get a psychological lift, which may well prevent their jobs from becoming tedious.

It may also be easier for organisations to attract staff if a range of up-to-date tools and techniques are being used.

8.2.10 Increased program life

Programs written in 3GL code often have a relatively short life from the point of view of having to undergo major changes or enhancements. We have already seen that in the traditional approach to application development the maintenance task may quickly follow implementation. The reason for this is that the systems produced are poorly matched against requirements or the user requests immediate changes following implementation. Some programs may also get through to the implementation stage still containing bugs. As we have seen, development with 4GLs allows the system to match more closely the original specification making maintenance less of an immediate problem. 4GLs and maintenance was discussed in Chapter 7. In the end the life-span of the 4GL program is increased because there is less need for modifications or fixes.

8.2.11 Closer development with end-users

We have seen throughout our discussions that one of the greatest benefits of 4GL use is the narrowing of the communication gap between the professional and the end-user. This has been brought about largely through prototyping, which requires more involvement from the end-user than other methods of systems development. This involvement requires input from a different type of professional, i.e. one who can not only work closely with the end-user but who can also understand the business requirements and possibly produce the complete system (the analyst/programmer). This involvement also helps to give the end-user a better insight into the computing task and the job of the professional. They are likely to develop a more realistic view of what can and what cannot be achieved.

It is to be hoped that this will eventually result in a better understanding between the DP professional and the end-user, and the development of a common, understandable means of communication.

8.2.12 Portability

One of the claims for the high-level languages of the third generation was portability, i.e. code in COBOL or FORTRAN or Pascal, once written, should run on at least one machine type other than the development machine without modifications. However, this has tended not to happen. Despite standardisation, different versions of 3GLs offer slightly differing facilities. This means that changes are usually needed if the code is to be used across different environments. In contrast to this, many 4GLs are portable across a range of machine types and operating systems. This offers several benefits to both organisations and individuals:

★ Organisations can port code from one environment to another, if, for example, they change their hardware or have several machine types.
★ Individuals can use a 4GL in one organisation, move to another organisation using different hardware and still utilise their previous skill with the same 4GL.

4GLs offer different templates rather than the need for different compilers. Inevitably, to achieve this portability, some sacrifices in terms of efficiency are made. Some 4GL vendors deliberately tie their software to one manufacturer's hardware. This has much to do with the origins of the product and the market they are aiming at.

8.2.13 Improved documentation

Many 4GLs are self-documenting. In fact some seem to produce a proliferation of hard-copy, much of which is of questionable use. However there are several benefits to the 4GL documentation approach. These include:

★ Systems can be documented as they are developed. The documentation does not have to be produced all in one go.
★ Changes to the system can automatically be documented, hence keeping documentation up-to-date.
★ Documentation can link to the data dictionary.

8.2.14 Smaller development teams

We saw in Chapter 6 that one of the overall effects of 4GL use is a change in development approach. This includes a change from the large project team approach to a smaller development team. One professional working with a group of end-users may be all that is required. Obviously much depends on the application being developed.

The smaller development team means that:

★ professionals work more closely with users.
★ fewer resources are tied up.
★ planning and control are simplified.

8.2.15 Improved requirements analysis

The reasons for this are those we have explored elsewhere in this text. 4GLs can improve the requirements analysis stage. This is achieved through:

★ a re-think of the traditional life-cycle approach
★ enablement of the bit-at-a-time approach
★ prototyping
★ enhanced communication
★ embedded methodologies.

Improvements at this stage obviously have a beneficial effect on other parts of the development process.

8.2.16 End-user computing

We have looked at end-user computing in some detail. It is obviously an advantage offered by 4GLs that some products allow end-users to become involved in building applications for themselves. Realistically, only a few will get this far, with many more using the non-procedural facilities offered by 4GLs.

8.3 Disadvantages of 4GLs

There are also several major disadvantages associated with 4GL use, some of which time and standardisation may well cure. Others are a feature of the tools themselves. Whilst these drawbacks should not inhibit organisations in the use of 4GLs, they need to be known and understood. These disadvantages are summarised in Table 8.2 and discussed below.

8.3.1 A diversity of products on offer

There are several hundred different products on the software market which claim to be 4GLs (or what we are calling 4GLs). As we have seen, this can mean a wide range of differing facilities for a large number of application types. New 4GLs are still appearing and earlier products disappearing. Some have undergone a change in name, many a change in the range of facilities on offer. As the market for CASE tools expands, some products which were previously called 4GLs are now called CASE tools. Some CASE products contain a 4GL as a component. The 4GL may have originally stood alone simply as a 4GL. (We shall return to CASE tools later.)

Table 8.2 The disadvantages of 4GLs

★ There is a diversity of products on offer.

★ The 'settling down' period is still on-going.

★ Impartial help and advice are not available to potential purchasers.

★ Problems of inefficiency.

★ The need for changes within an organisation (sometimes radical).

★ Unidentified training needs.

★ Earlier 4GLs (and some current products) were more suited to the development of small systems.

★ Satisfactory use may depend on the approach adopted.

★ There may be problems with interfacing to 3GL code.

★ Integration.

Any potential purchaser of a 4GL has a difficult task. How do they choose the right tool from such a wide range of products? Unfortunately, all too often the answer has been to select the first product they look at. This has sometimes resulted in the purchaser of the 4GL selecting a totally unsuitable tool and returning to more traditional means because of frustration and dissatisfaction with the 4GL. Other potential purchasers have rejected the 4GL route because of the complexity of choice. They take a 'better the devil you know' attitude.

This is obviously a problem. Not all the products currently being offered can hope to survive although several 4GLs have established themselves as leading products with a proven track record. With other 4GLs it is difficult to

be sure of long-term vendor support. This means that selection of the 4GL must be carried out in a systematic and controlled way. Several products offering the required facilities must be considered. Evaluation should be carried out against a set of predetermined criteria, like those shown in Table 8.3.

In addition demonstration/evaluation versions of the products should be looked at and facilities tried out. The background of the vendor and the product should also be considered. Areas requiring attention could include:

★ Age of the product? Older products may be established in the market-place but may not have been updated to include the latest facilities. For example, are they as efficient

Table 8.3 Possible selection criteria for a 4GL

★ Portability of the product or its suitability for the hardware being used.

★ Range of non-procedural facilities being offered.

★ Database facilities being offered.

★ Database security.

★ (Procedural) language being offered.

★ Can the data be imported/exported from external files or a database?

★ What documentation is supported?

★ What help facilities are available?

★ Are batch and/or on-line facilities available?

as newer products? Where products have been updated, are the newer facilities integrated with the original components?

★ How many people are using the 4GL? Many vendors will willingly supply this information.
★ Who are the major customers? Will vendors supply information about customers to whom, for example, requests for references can be addressed?
★ What type of application is the 4GL being successfully used to develop?
★ What user support is available?
★ What are the origins of the company? Is it well-established and knowledgeable in this field?
★ Is there any on-going development of the product? This often indicates continuing support.

A report by CCTA entitled 'Application Generator Assessment, Evaluation and Selection' (July 1986) was originally developed for use by government departments but is available and applicable to a wider audience in the selection of a 4GL. Other similar reports exist, for example, the comprehensive Grindley Report (1986).

The CCTA report suggests shortlisting three products which appear to meet a potential purchaser's original requirements. This is not particularly difficult to do if vendor information is compared and use made of the many magazines and journals published which list the facilities offered by various 4GLs. See, for example, the 4GL review in *Datamation* (October 1988). The shortlisted products should then be looked at in some detail through descriptions, reference manuals, evaluation versions, etc. before a final choice is made. This might finally be achieved by weighting various factors according to their importance to the organisation and producing a numeric score. Cost will also play a part.

8.3.2 Settling down period

4GLs are obviously still undergoing a settling down period, although this is not quite as true

as it was a year or two ago. This can cause problems for several reasons:

★ Frequent changes/upgrades to the product. Although compatibility with older versions is usually promised, this has sometimes not proven to be the case. Old code may need changing to work with upgraded software.
★ Changes are made in line with user requests/requirements. At the beginning of a product's life vendors sometimes try to incorporate too many such requests, the result being frequent changes. This can get out of hand unless controlled.
★ Products may become out of date as newer products appear with more up-to-date features.
★ Sometimes the later versions of products are not as satisfactory to the user as the one they originally purchased. For example, the incorporation of more sophisticated features may detract from ease-of-use.

Such problems have and will contribute to the dissatisfaction experienced by some 4GL purchasers.

8.3.3 Lack of impartial help/advice

Connected to the previous disadvantages is the problem of the 'hype' surrounding 4GLs, much of it intended to sway prospective users into buying various products. The independent surveys can help to clarify what features each product has to offer and provide a starting point for selection and evaluation, but little more. Some of the reports and books on offer about 4GLs, whilst comprehensive, tend to be very expensive and outside the pocket of the ordinary interested party or student who might need to be aware of the technology on offer.

Generally little academic interest and involvement surrounds 4GLs. They tend to be associated with rumour, myth and often confusion. Statements like the following are rife.

★ 4GLs are end-user tools.

★ Increase your productivity by 100 per cent.
★ 4GLs are dead. I know, I invented them.

(Apparently the last statement is attributable to James Martin, who wrote some of the first books about 4GLs.) Sometimes the 'buzz-words' change long before the problems are actually solved. Some organisations have yet to commit themselves to 4GLs whilst many others have only just started to reap the benefits and appreciate the drawbacks of 4GL use.

8.3.4 Inefficiency

One of the biggest single reported problems with 4GLs is their inefficient use of hardware resources. It is certainly not a problem attributable to all products, but many would fall or have in the past fallen into this category. This problem manifests itself through poor response times and higher utilisation of hardware resources.

We considered the effects on hardware resources in Chapter 7. Response times will vary dramatically from one product to another and across types of application. Many 4GL manufacturers have specifically addressed this problem. We know, for example, that interpretation can seriously slow down performance and hence is usually only offered as well as compilation facilities.

This whole area of performance is a bit like programmer productivity. A whole host of measures can be used to study system performance: CPU time, channel use, paging, memory service units, etc. Benchmark testing can be carried out. Comparisons with other fourth and third generation products can be performed. In the end management will probably only be concerned with the user's perception of the service they receive and with cost.

Some of the ways that performance can be improved include:

★ optimising file/database design,
★ controlling the size of files,
★ controlling the number of simultaneous users.

Many organisations feel that the increased need for hardware resources is a small price to pay for the benefits 4GL use has to offer. In any case they will argue that machine time is cheaper than programmer time.

8.3.5 Changes within an organisation

In Chapter 6 and in Chapter 7 we discussed some of the changes brought about within an organisation by the use of one or more 4GLs. Some of these changes are fairly radical, particularly as the computing industry has held on so long to out-of-date tools and techniques. Such changes need commitment from management within the organisation. Without this commitment use of the 4GL will inevitably fail, as it can without commitment from DP staff.

Some organisations are reluctant to tackle the changes necessary to make the transition from 3GL to 4GL use. They have so much effort, money and code invested in 3GL use that they find it very difficult to break away completely. This is of course why so many 4GLs offer links to 3GL facilities. Often, where there is full and immediate commitment to 4GL use within an organisation, there has been no previous history of 3GL application development.

Some organisations also have difficulty recruiting professionals with sufficient knowledge/experience of 4GL use. This gives them added incentive to hold on to the old methods and ways.

8.3.6 Training needs

We identified earlier that ease-of-use was one of the major advantages of 4GLs. However, we also identified a negative aspect to ease-of-use, that of lack of training. Whilst some 4GLs are not sufficiently complex to warrant training beyond perhaps the manufacturer's manual and the on-line training provided, others are much more sophisticated tools which require quite comprehensive training support. The ease-of-use label can mean that this very necessary training sometimes gets overlooked.

From my experience of 4GLs I have learned you can get quite far on your own very quickly with most products but there comes a stage with the more complex tools in the 4GL where progress is slow unless further help is given. Most professionals will require some training with the more complex facilities offered. However, on the positive side, competency with one product helps in tackling a different 4GL.

There also may be problems when the product is extended to offer new features. Further training might be required for these new components.

8.3.7 Small systems

One of the drawbacks often claimed for 4GLs is that they are only suited to small, stand-alone systems. Whilst this was true for some of the earlier products, and in fact remains true now for other products, this is not a criticism which can be levelled at all 4GLs. Many 4GLs are being successfully used to replace systems previously built in a language such as COBOL and deal with complexity equally well. Again, it very much comes back to selecting the right tool for the right task and being aware of both the benefits and the limitations of 4GLs.

8.3.8 Approach adopted

The success that an organisation has with a 4GL can often depend on the approach it adopts to its selection and use. The *ad hoc* approach of buying a 4GL without proper evaluation of the facilities it offers is doomed from the beginning. If the right tool is not selected then dissatisfaction will inevitably follow. Organisations must set objectives from the outset of considering 4GL use and they must be prepared to change their existing practices. Setting objectives will aid in the clarification of expectations and in setting long-term goals. Changes to existing methods should be phased rather than implemented all at once.

8.3.9 3GL code interface

Many 4GLs offer links to 3GL code. Some will generate code directly in COBOL or PL/1, for example. We have previously considered the reasons for doing this. However, some users of 4GL products have identified problems when trying to interface to existing 3GL code. This means that, instead of benefiting the organisation for the reasons identified earlier, the 4GL is causing extra maintenance problems. Again, not all 4GLs will cause this particular problem.

8.3.10 Integration

Most 4GLs are sets of tools. Some 4GLs are built on early products extended to include various facilities that the manufacturers felt the new package should offer. This was then labelled a 4GL. One of the problems in the past has been a lack of integration. For example, the add-ons have required radically different techniques from the other parts of the product. However, many 4GL vendors are conscious of this and have addressed themselves to the problems of integration. Again, proper evaluation of a product should help to identify this problem.

8.4 Conclusions

Despite the claims of many 4GL manufacturers and vendors, 4GLs cannot solve all the problems of the computing industry. In fact we have identified almost as many potential disadvantages as advantages. However, some of these disadvantages can be avoided if the 4GL is chosen in a systematic and considered way. In the end, the advantages will outweigh the disadvantages. Some of the disadvantages identified are also being tackled by 4GL vendors. Other problems may be ironed out as 4GLs develop and finally settle down.

8.5 Follow-up questions and activities

8.5.1 Questions

1) a) List eight major advantages offered by 4GL use.
   b) Briefly describe these advantages.

2) a) List eight major disadvantages of 4GL use.
   b) Briefly describe these disadvantages.

3) How can organisations minimise some of the disadvantages of 4GL use?

4) Describe how an organisation can best go about selecting a 4GL for use in the application development process.

8.5.2 Activities

5) Consider your own experience of 4GL use. Which of the advantages and disadvantages listed in this chapter apply to the product(s) you have used? Are there any others you could add to either list?

Part Three

The future

9 Where do we go from here?

Objectives

After you have studied this chapter, you should be able to:

* appreciate that no complete solutions to the problems of the computing industry have been found.
* review some of the partial solutions that are on offer.
* understand how the development of 4GLs may proceed in the future.
* explain the terms analyst workbench, IPSE and CASE tool.
* describe the role of 4GLs in CASE tools.
* list the components of a CASE tool.
* briefly explain what is meant by artificial intelligence (AI).
* appreciate the role of AI techniques in business and industry.
* describe how 4GLs interface with AI (or fifth generation) techniques.

9.1 The future for 4GLs

In Chapter 1 we looked at the past. If one considers what has gone before 4GLs, it becomes clear why they have evolved as major productivity tools for building a wide range of applications. Older methods are not keeping up with other developments in the technology. This, and the need to increase productivity and deliver systems faster, calls for new tools and techniques.

We have established during the course of this book that 4GLs are playing a valuable role in the application development process. They are not, as many people perceive them, simply a stop-gap measure until something else comes along. They are however still evolving and no one can predict where that evolution will take them. What we do know is that the problems we identified in Chapter 1, i.e.

* problems of specification,
* project planning and control,
* lengthy time-scales,
* bugs in software, etc.

are the same problems that were identified twenty years ago and which are still being tackled today. Things have improved and some partial solutions have been found. These solutions are reviewed in Table 9.1. This of course means that further development must take place. In this chapter we shall look briefly at what those developments might be.

9.1.1 Full acceptance of a new approach

Many organisations have come to use 4GLs (see Datalink Survey, 1988) over the last few years (at most a decade). We saw in Chapters 6, 7 and 8 that 4GLs have several major effects on those organisations which choose to use them. Most of these effects are beneficial rather than harmful. However, very few organisations have committed themselves fully to using 4GLs. These tools usually sit alongside their 3GL counterparts, often rather uneasily. Where full commitment to 4GLs is found, there tends to be no history of previous 3GL use. The reasons for this are obvious and include the following:

* The 'better the devil you know' syndrome. Some organisations are loath to face the risks of full 4GL use. Some may already have had bad experiences with 4GLs.
* The methods currently being used have been in existence for about 30 years. It will take quite some while for them to disappear or even be changed.
* Many organisations are so committed to 3GL use that a changeover would only add to the problems they already have in such areas as backlogs, maintenance, etc.
* Some organisations will build new applications with the 4GL but are committed to maintaining older applications written in 3GL code.
* Drawbacks such as increased need for hardware resources.
* The need for staff with 4GL expertise.

The alternative is to send staff on training courses which may tie up valuable human resources.

In many organisations there is room in the future for further commitment to 4GL use from all concerned, i.e. management, DP staff and end-users. There is a need for further standardisation and integration with other tools. One possible method of integration may be in the CASE tool approach (refer to Section C).

9.1.2 Automated development approaches

The idea of automating parts of the development cycle is not new. Various tools exist which produce, for example, diagrams and code. In the past these tools have tended to be aimed either at the front-end of the development process, e.g. analysis and design (analyst workbenches), or at the back-end, application generation, e.g. 4GLs. In the following sections we shall consider some of the tools aimed at automating part or all of the development life-cycle.

A. Analyst workbenches
The analyst workbench is part of the trend towards further automation of the development process. It provides a front-end approach and may be thought of as a simple form of the computer-aided design (CAD) tools which have been available for quite some time in engineer-ing. In its simplest form the workbench is an electronic drawing board which allows the automatic production of diagrams, such as DFDs. However, more importantly, such tools should also incorporate a dictionary to hold information about the entities on the diagrams and the relationships between them. The work-bench usually consists of a PC plus software, although other hardware may also be supported.

B. IPSEs
The idea of the IPSE (Integrated Project Support Environment) is to integrate the tools required to support the whole software develop-ment cycle. It should be neither development method nor language specific. At the heart of the IPSE would be the database containing the requirements specifications, designs and code, for a complete project. A standard tools interface would allow the passing of data between various parts of the IPSE, which would also include tools such as a dictionary, query language, etc. (see DTI/NCC Starts Guide for a full discussion).

Also relevant is the programming support environment, or PSE, which could be considered as a subset of the IPSE. The PSE is concerned only with the coding, testing and software and systems integration phases of the development cycle.

C. CASE Tools
Computer-aided software engineering, or CASE, tools are designed to automate the complete

Table 9.1   Review of the current partial and developing solutions to the major problems of the computer industry

★ Formal methods for specification and verification of software. Yet to be fully accepted commercially. More work will inevitably be done in this area.

★ Packaged solutions, seen by some as one possible way forward in computing.

★ Alternative development approaches, e.g. iterative refinement, prototyping, etc.

★ A move away from the rigidity of the traditional systems life-cycle.

★ 4GLs, to facilitate various of the solutions offered.

★ Automated development approaches including 4GLs, IPSE and CASE tools.

★ Structured methodologies.

★ Other types of language, e.g. functional languages, object-oriented languages.

★ Utilisation of other techniques, e.g. AI techniques.

development cycle from analysis through to the automatic generation of the necessary code. The phrase CASE tool seems to have picked up where the IPSE has (almost) left off, but the aims are virtually the same. As we have seen other approaches tackle various parts of the life-cycle but none the complete problem. Structured analysis and design methodologies, 4GLs, prototyping, amongst other techniques, for all their worth have only offered partial solutions. The next step is to improve the whole development process. The components of a CASE tool are not dissimilar to those offered by a 4GL. The CASE tool must, like the 4GL, cater for the prototyping approach. The basic CASE tool components are shown in Figure 9.1.

Riddle and Fairley (1980) define three categories of software development tools:

★ Cognitive tools, which help in the analysis and design of solutions to problems, e.g. design methodologies.
★ Notational tools, which allow ideas to be expressed and communicated, e.g. DFDs.
★ Augmentive tools, which support tasks that might otherwise prove laborious or impracticable for the developer, e.g. computable specification software.

By themselves, not all of these tools will be software. The pencil and paper approach might still be used. The integrated solution should incorporate all categories of tools and automate their use.

The benefits offered by a fully automated approach are:

★ Increased productivity.
★ Removal of the more tedious or labour-intensive parts of the development process.
★ Improvements in quality and reliability of the systems produced.
★ The development process is speeded up.
★ Support for development methodologies.
★ Documentation is provided.

The basic idea behind the CASE tool is shown in Figure 9.2.

D. 4GLs and CASE tools

One component of a CASE tool may be a 4GL, and in fact several 4GL vendors have built on their success with 4GLs to enter the CASE market. One such tool is Cortex's CORVISION, although many other CASE tools are now emerging. CORVISION incorporates a complete set of visual design tools which communicate with an application generator. The generator produces a fully documented application which is directly executable. CORVISION runs on DEC Vax computers under VMS. It uses techniques such as windows and icons and also incorporates an integrated 4GL. (Cortex have built upon their original successful 4GL, Application Factory.) The major components of CORVISION include:

★ Design tools:
    ★ Entity diagrammer, allowing entity

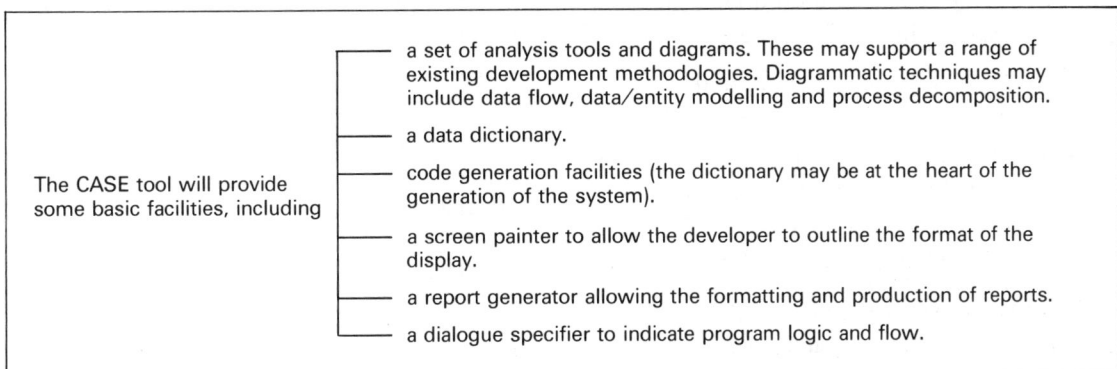

The CASE tool will provide some basic facilities, including

— a set of analysis tools and diagrams. These may support a range of existing development methodologies. Diagrammatic techniques may include data flow, data/entity modelling and process decomposition.

— a data dictionary.

— code generation facilities (the dictionary may be at the heart of the generation of the system).

— a screen painter to allow the developer to outline the format of the display.

— a report generator allowing the formatting and production of reports.

— a dialogue specifier to indicate program logic and flow.

Figure 9.1 *The components of a CASE tool*

Design	Specification	Generation	Operation
Design components, often in diagrammatic form ⟶	Specification techniques ⟶	Automatic generation of code and of documentation ⟶	Application is ready for operation

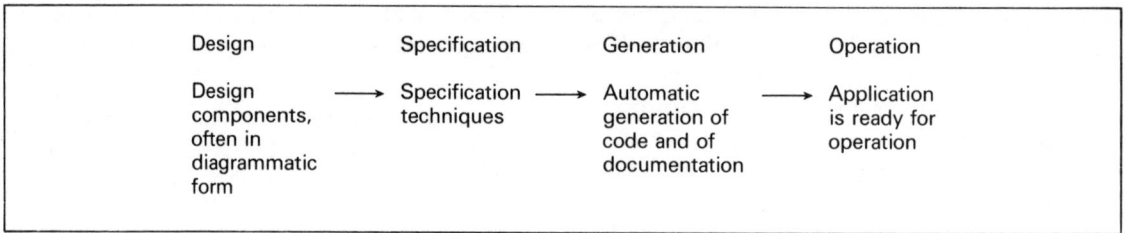

Figure 9.2 *CASE*

relationship diagrams to be produced. These show the relationships between datasets.

★ A dataview diagrammer which can be used to show the navigation (access) paths through the data.

★ A menu diagrammer providing a schematic representation of the application from the users' perspective and allowing the logic of navigation from function to function to be shown. It also deals with the security of the system.

★ Screen painting facilities linked to the data dictionary.

★ Facilities for specifying report layouts, also linked to the data dictionary.

★ An action diagrammer. Customisation of a generated application is allowed through the integrated BUILDER 4GL. The action diagrammer allows the structure of the code and program flow to be diagrammed, syntax to be checked through a language sensitive editor and provides links with the data dictionary.

★ Guidance system, repository and generator:

  ★ The guidance system acts as an intelligent interface between the developers and the central repository.
  ★ At the heart of the central repository is the data dictionary.
  ★ The generator produces BUILDER code which is then automatically compiled into machine code. Documentation is also produced automatically.

★ Other features include the following:

  ★ Links to Vax 3GL code
  ★ Compatibility with RdB and RMS
  ★ PC development.

CASE tools are also offered by Oracle Corporation in the form of SQL∗DESIGN DICTIONARY (SDD) and SQL∗DEVELOP-MENT METHOD. SDD is a multi-user database (built on the ORACLE RDBMS) that can record an organisation's complete information needs, along with design decisions and the implementation details of applications. It performs consistency and quality checking throughout analysis and design and produces documentation. SDD provides a central repository and tools such as entity-relationship modelling, function hierarchies and dataflows. Following the definition of requirements, SDD automatically generates a default database and predicts database size. The developer can fine tune this design. SDD will then create tables, indexes, views, etc. SDD supports Oracle's own SQL∗DEVELOPMENT METHOD (SDM) or James Martin's Information Engineering. SDM is a structured development approach with the following stages:

★ strategy (strategic, top-down view of organisation)
★ analysis
★ design
★ build and document
★ transition
★ production.

The use of CASE tools is surely one of the ways in which application development will proceed in the future. Already many CASE tools are beginning to flood the market in the same way that 4GLs did a year or two ago. Some of these CASE tools used to compete in the 4GL market-place. Often they incorporate a 4GL. Others were once offered as analyst work-benches and have now been extended to include other components. This situation is very similar to the way application generators became 4GLs.

9.2 4GLs and the fifth generation

9.2.1 The fifth generation

In Chapter 1 we defined the fifth generation of computing as being concerned with artificial intelligence (or AI) tools and techniques. AI has started to come out of academic and research institutions and applications of AI are now to be found in a wide variety of situations in business and industry. As we saw briefly in Chapter 5, some 4GLs now provide links to knowledge-based systems or provide natural language interfaces, both of which are associated with AI. In the second part of this chapter we shall take another look at the fifth generation of computing, particularly where it comes together with the fourth generation.

9.2.2 What do we mean by AI?

AI is a very complex but interesting area where much work has been done, but where there is so much still to do. We cannot hope to go into all the issues. See Rich (1983) for further discussion, although there are now many books written about AI which fill in the background to AI research.

Most definitions of AI talk about it as an attempt to make machines do those things previously done only by humans, i.e. tasks requiring intelligence. At one time that would have included such tasks as playing chess but few people would now consider chess playing programs to have intelligence. In other words we are continually striving to make the machine perform more and more difficult tasks and to

move them closer to the way in which humans solve problems. Traditionally, of course, computers were used to perform tasks which were difficult for humans, e.g. number-crunching and repetitive processing tasks. Those actions we as humans take for granted, such as recognising images and understanding the spoken and written word, were not mimicked by computers. AI research is now attempting to make machines cope with such problems. Of course, in some ways it is difficult to define machine intelligence when human intelligence itself is so ill-defined.

After the first flurry of random activity, the study of AI has settled down, developed, and inevitably fragmented into areas of specialisation. Such areas include:

★ natural language understanding
★ speech recognition
★ vision
★ machine learning
★ intelligence in computer-assisted learning
★ intelligent front-ends
★ planning systems.

These areas are not mutually exclusive. They also involve several independent areas of expertise, e.g. cognitive psychology, computer science, linguistics, etc. Common themes include knowledge representation, knowledge manipulation and the human–computer interface.

9.2.3 AI in the real world

At one time AI was of concern only to academics and researchers. Many interesting and successful steps were made but nothing in terms of real applications. However, gradually AI has found its place in industrial and business organisations in such areas as robotics (e.g. car manufacturing), image analysis (e.g. medicine), intelligent computer-aided instruction or intelligent tutoring systems (e.g. education and training), expert or knowledge-based systems now in widespread use (e.g. in finance, medicine, manufacturing and engineering), natural language (e.g. as a front-end to other software), and so on. There are many other applications of AI far too numerous to mention here. Getting to the stage where such systems are in regular everyday use has been a relatively long and slow process, particularly if you consider for example that the first expert system, Dendral, was built in the 1960s! Factors contributing to this emergence are shown in Figure 9.3.

9.2.4 Expert or knowledge-based systems

One of the best-known areas in AI is the expert system. Many people prefer the term knowledge-based system because of the connotations of the word expert. Expert systems are built round a knowledge-base of facts, rules and other information. Often the knowledge-base is built in the form of rules (or production rules). Hence expert systems are often also called rule-based systems. However other forms of knowledge representation may also be used. There must also exist a mechanism for navigating the knowledge-base. This is often given the rather grandiose title of 'inference engine'. There are several major differences between conventional software and knowledge-based systems. These are shown in Table 9.2.

Despite the fact that expert systems are being used successfully in a wide range of application areas there is still a long way go. Improvements are being made all the time but criticisms are still levelled at this type of system. A list of such criticisms appears in Table 9.3. However, expert systems have much to offer – precisely what is shown in Figure 9.4.

9.2.5 4GLs and AI

As we saw in Chapter 5 some 4GLs are now offering natural language facilities or links to knowledge-based techniques.

A. 4GLs and natural language

One important area of AI is natural language. The goal is that the user of a computer system should be freed from the need to learn any computer-based techniques, however simple. The non-procedural syntax of some 4GLs is relatively near to looking like natural language but is still too close to the conventional programming language. Many offer simple techniques which are suitable for a naive user:

★ icons
★ windows
★ menu-selection
★ form-filling.

However, there are situations where the need is for more verbose input. Here, offering a natural language facility rather than a specialised syntax offers obvious advantages.

One of the drawbacks of any system which has to understand natural language input is the size of the vocabularies offered by most languages. It is impossible to provide a totally unbounded system which understands all the words in, say, the English language. Many such systems which are used as an interface to other software, e.g. a natural language query system, operate on a dictionary system. A standard, pre-defined dictionary of a certain number, say 5000, of key-words which the system understands

Table 9.2 The differences between conventional software and knowledge-based systems

Conventional software	Knowledge-based systems
Algorithms	Heuristics
Representation and use of data	Representation and use of knowledge
Repetitive process	Inferential process
Effective manipulation of large databases	Effective manipulation of large knowledge bases
Controlled development cycle	Flexible and pragmatic development cycle
Oriented towards numerical processing	Oriented towards symbolic processing

The emergence of AI has happened for various reasons:
- Growing awareness through various programmes, e.g. financial support for a variety of applications via programmes such as Alvey and for more specific needs through others such as the Training Agency's AI Applications to Learning Programme. These and other initiatives have provided opportunities for further research into the dissemination of information about AI.
- Developments in the technology. The availability of more powerful and more sophisticated machines able to handle the systems being built.
- Wider availability of tools needed to build these systems, e.g. languages, environments, shells, etc.
- Developments and improvements in the tools on offer, e.g. better interfaces, more sophisticated methods of knowledge representation.
- Wider availability of expertise in AI systems.
- Cost-effectiveness through tools and the emergence of techniques, i.e. less *ad hoc* and so less expensive methods.
- Embedding of AI systems into other application areas.

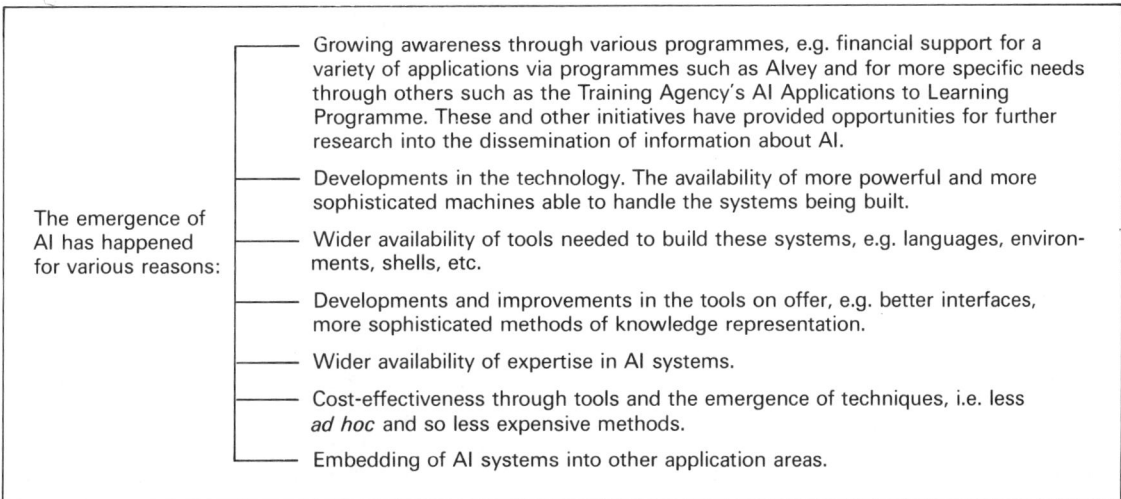

Figure 9.3 *Factors contributing to the emergence of AI*

might be offered. As well as this, it is usually possible for the user to set up a dynamic dictionary of words, specific to their own application. If during a session with the system the user inputs an unknown word they are given the chance to change it, or add it to the dynamic dictionary. Maintenance of the dynamic dictionary hence becomes a crucial task.

One might think that this approach should always be adopted. Despite the fact that some 4GLs offer natural language facilities, e.g. RAMIS's ENGLISH query facility, there are also some drawbacks:

Table 9.3 Some of the criticisms levelled at expert systems

★ Some people feel that we could end up with a situation where expert systems take major, even crucial decisions out of the hands of people.

★ De-skilling, i.e. less qualified/experienced people are allowed to make expert decisions.

★ Legal problems – who takes the blame for erroneous decisions.

★ Lack of knowledge (or deep enough knowledge).

★ 'Explosion' under expansion. (Toy demonstrators do not readily become full-blown, usable systems.)

★ Poor explanation of reasoning – an area which is the basis of much research activity.

★ Lack of any real-world 'common sense'. Often a human expert will overrule the formal method of doing something if it appears unsuited to a particular situation.

★ Do not learn from experience. Machine learning is a separate and very complex issue in AI research.

★ Sharp fall-off in performance at the boundaries of knowledge.

★ Often too slow for a real-time situation, although expert systems are now used in real-time applications. This has become possible as the tools and techniques available have improved. However, there is some confusion here over the use of the term real-time.

★ The need for yet another body of specialist techniques and expertise.

★ Reliability issues.

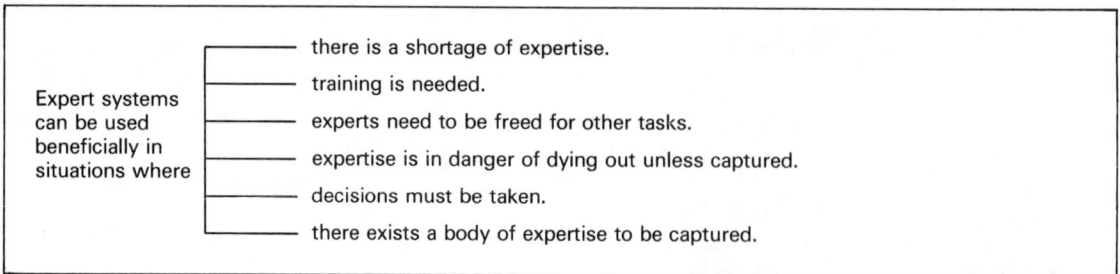

Figure 9.4   *What do expert systems have to offer?*

★ Research into natural language translation is still being undertaken.
★ Natural language translation requires extra resources.
★ It can only be used for a restricted domain.

B. 4GLs and knowledge-based techniques

Expert systems set out to capture the knowledge normally associated with a human expert in some field. They are hence concerned with giving help and advice in specific areas – in much the same way a human expert might. One of the problems we identified earlier is the encoding of sufficient knowledge to make the system respond like a human expert. Often it is desirable to be able to access data stored elsewhere, e.g. in a conventional database. It hence makes sense to link together 4GLs with knowledge-based techniques. Several 4GLs are now offering this facility.

One 4GL providing links to AI techniques is Cullinet's KnowledgeBUILD which provides an optional expert system tool called Application Expert. Data from Cullinet's RDBMS IDMS/SQL may be accessed from Application Expert, as well as RMS files and other SQL-based databases on the VAX.

GURU from MDBS has many of the components found in more conventional (if there is such a thing) 4GLs. These include links to MDBS III databases as well as Ashton Tate's well-known dBASE III and dBASE III Plus, graphics facilities, forms management, query facilities (SQL), text processing, report generation facilities, statistical facilities, a structured 4GL and remote communications facilities.

GURU also provides a natural language interface option and the tools to produce rule-based expert systems. This approach of combining knowledge-based techniques with other tools obviously offers the advantages of allowing the expert system to link to the data and utilise graphics and statistical facilities already in the system.

The AI environments ART and KEE both allow access to data stored in INGRES databases. INGRES also employs AI techniques directly in its Query Optimiser, to determine the optimum sequence for data access.

9.2.6 What next?

There is still a long way to go for 4GLs to be fully developed and no one can predict what form this development will take. However, there is little doubt that many organisations are already reaping the benefits offered by 4GL use and will increasingly do so for some years yet.

One thing which has emerged from our discussions is the integration of previously separate technologies. 4GLs, now recognised as useful and worthwhile tools, put in a CASE environment or linked to AI technology will double their usefulness. This is obviously one way forward.

The fifth generation of computing has begun to emerge into the real world. A host of AI applications are being used with great success in commercial and industrial organisations and AI techniques are also being embedded into applications to provide 'intelligence'. The future will no doubt see an increase in this trend.

9.3 Follow-up questions

9.3.1 Questions

1) Explain why many organisations are still not fully committed to 4GL use.

2) Software tools may be categorised into three distinct types.
   a) Describe these three categories.
   b) Where do 4GLs fit into this categorisation?

3) a) What are the objectives of the CASE tool?
   b) List the basic components of the CASE tool.

c) How do CASE tools differ from the 4GL?

d) What other tools offer automation of at least part of the application development process?

4) What do you understand by the term AI?

5) Explain the reasons why AI has now moved out of research labs and academic institutions into everyday situations.

6) List eight of the criticisms aimed at expert systems. How do you think these problems might be overcome in the future?

7) Explain how 4GLs provide links with the fifth generation.

Appendix A Some current 4GLs

This appendix looks at some of the products mentioned in the text in more detail. These products represent a reasonable cross-section of currently available 4GLs, but are not the only ones which could have been considered. A fuller investigation into the hundreds of 4GLs on the market would constitute another volume to this book. Hopefully the information contained here will help to consolidate some of the ideas in the main text. Further details about any of the products mentioned can be obtained directly from the manufacturer. Examples of code from PROGRESS can be found at the end of this Appendix.

Delta

The company

Unlike some of the other products we have mentioned, the parent company for this product is European, rather than American. The Delta group originated in Switzerland with Delta Software Technologie AG in Schwerzenbach, near Zurich. In 1983 a sister company was formed in West Germany. Delta Software GmbH is to be found in Frankfurt and Dusseldorf. By 1987 Delta Software International Ltd was formed to assume responsibility for the support and distribution of Delta in the UK and Eire. Development of the product Delta is shared by Switzerland, West Germany and the UK. The latest member of the Delta Group is IBSI Delta Atelier Logiciel in Paris, with other companies responsible for the distribution of Delta also to be found in Austria, Sweden, Finland, Portugal, Brazil, Australia, Norway, Italy and Spain.

The product – overview

Delta Application Development System (ADS) is an integrated system consisting of a number of tools which provide support for the development, documentation and maintenance of systems, as well as supporting project management. Both on-line and batch applica-

tions can be developed. Delta provides uniformity in syntax, error-handling and system conventions and generates COBOL or PL/1 programs. Basically Delta consists of the tools listed below. Other tools from the Delta Group are fully compatible with those mentioned below, AMELIO, for example, which takes programs written in COBOL code and turns them into structured Delta syntax, whilst also providing analytical and statistical documentation.

The tools

Delta/DETAB
A decision table processor which allows decision tables to be defined, produced and transformed into programs.

Delta/FDOC
A functional documentation processor which allows for the restructuring and maintainability of documentation by assigning chapter numbers, creating tables of content and an index, and by producing a graphic description of the documentation structure.

Delta/FILE
A data interface tool processor, Delta/FILE generates the framework necessary for file accesses, file descriptions and the access routes, leaving the developer needing only to know which macros to call up. Delta/FGEN supports the generation of record and file descriptions and creates documentation files.

Delta/GRU
Allows for control break processing, a technique found in other tools such as RPG (one of the early report generators). Delta/GRU provides test aids and graphic documentation.

Delta/MACRO
A macro processor allowing programmers to use pre-programmed code in addition to their own. This is the heart of the product and can be used in conjunction with any of the other tools. It is also the mechanism by which code is generated for the different machine environments.

Delta/OSP

For on-line structured programming, allowing the use of standardised program structures. Delta/OSP generates the program framework and the user provides the progam details. Delta/OSP provides a concise, non-procedural method of coding common program types such as MENU, BROWSE, REFERENCE (enquiry), UPDATE and DATA-ENTRY. This tool also supports prototyping.

Delta/PROG

Generates a program framework. Standard macros may be incorporated and additional code inserted.

Delta/PSD

A data-driven design processor allowing for program schema descriptions through the use of a simple non-procedural language. Programs may be designed independently of the detailed code. The design then exists as a Delta document which can be passed to the program. Delta/PSD used with Delta/FILE (INVERT) and Delta/TSP provides for Jackson Structured Programming.

Delta/REPORT

A report generator covering all phases of report design, prototyping, programming and documentation. Delta/REPORT generates source programs in COBOL or PL/1, report layouts and can provide output on microfiche with an index or to a laser printer or on-line in the spooling system.

Delta/SCREEN

A screen painting/generation tool which

★ generates screen maps from screen documentation.
★ takes care of data conversion, padding of fields, numeric field transformations and validation.
★ generates menus for the HELP system.
★ generates the access to screens using standard macros.

★ creates routines for the transfer of data to the output area and controls validation and capture of input.

Delta/SPP

A structured programming processor which enables the application and implementation of structured programming and pseudocode. It

★ checks adherence to structured programming methods.
★ supports testing.
★ integrates with other tools such as Delta/MACRO allowing standard functions to be invoked and Delta/REPORT.

Delta/TSP

A tree structure processor. Like Delta/PSD this is also a program design tool but uses a structured programming syntax. Both design tools support Warnier and Jackson program design techniques.

Delta/XDOC

A cross-reference documentation generator. For each program generated Delta creates a documentation file. Delta/XDOC analyses and extracts information from these documentation files. The information extracted can also be transferred to a data dictionary system if required.

Other features

All of the tools can generate either COBOL or PL/1. The tools may be used in conjunction to code a single program, e.g. Delta/OSP or Delta/PSD for the skeleton structure and Delta/SPP and/or Delta/DETAB for the detailed logic, etc.

Delta Workbench is a full implementation of Delta Application Development System which runs on IBM PCs and compatibles. Workbench employs a menu-driven front-end which has an option for mouse control.

Hardware

Delta can be used on a wide variety of systems:

Bull	IBM	Siemens
Data General	ICL	Tandem
DEC	NCR	UNISYS
Hewlett Packard	Nixdorf	etc.

Services offered

★ Training
★ Documentation
★ Improvements/upgrades
★ A support group for the benefit of customers
★ Maintenance facilities

It is impossible to give full details of all available tools here. For further information about any of the products from the Delta Group contact them directly at the following address(es):

UK   Delta Software International
      1 White Hill
      Chesham
      Buckinghamshire HP5 1AA

Switzerland   Delta Software Technologie AG
               Ringstrasse 7
               CH-8603 Schwerzenbach

Germany   Delta Software GmbH
           Koenigstrasse 84
           Holzbuettgen
           D-4044 Kaarst 2
           West Germany

           Delta Software GmbH
           Schaubstrasse 16
           Sachsenhausen
           D-6000 Frankfurt/Main 70
           West Germany

Ref: Software Development with Delta – Delta Manual no. MA 216 (or MA116 Software Entwicklung mit Delta).

FOCUS

The company

Information Builders Incorporated was founded in 1975. The writers of FOCUS were amongst the first to develop non-procedural language technology. Information Builders has its corporate offices in New York with sales and consulting offices throughout the USA. Overseas affiliates and agents are found in Argentina, Australia, Belgium, Brazil, Canada, Chile, Denmark, Egypt, Finland, France, Germany, Hong Kong, India, Israel, Netherlands, Norway, Peru, Singapore, Spain and Sweden, among other countries. Information Builders (UK) Ltd, set up in 1981, is the UK subsidiary found in London.

The product – overview

FOCUS is a 4GL incorporating a database. When released it was seen initially as an IBM mainframe productivity and prototyping tool, although as the 4GL emphasis shifted in the mid-1980s, it gained strength as an end-user and development tool and now runs on other machine types.

The tools

FOCUS provides a range of tools, some of which are described here.

Database
FOCUS provides a facility to model data by either using relational tables or via network or hierarchical structures. The FOCUS database employs a construct or model called shared-relational structures which draws on all four of the common models, relational, hierarchical, network and inverted files. The optimum order for data retrieval may be specified and any field indexed. Integrity and security features are provided including referential integrity, restricted access, encryption, etc. Distributed database facilities are also offered.

Transaction processing

FOCUS can handle all the tasks needed to build a transaction processing system. Such tasks include data entry, validation, table look-ups, and transaction logging. The interactive database editor allows browsing or maintenance of data without the need to write formal procedures.

Dialogue manager

The FOCUS dialogue manager facility allows the creation of interactive dialogues and menus which can prompt for run-time parameters, invoke stored procedures and execute other applications.

Full screen text editor

The FOCUS full screen text editor (TED) allows the creation or editing of files both within and external to FOCUS. There is a split screen capability which displays up to four files simultaneously. There is also an in-built screen painting facility.

Forms design

FOCUS screen manager (FIDEL) allows the production of screens for data entry or display. Information may be displayed in protected or modified areas. Colour, reverse video, blinking, intensity, noprint and underlining features are available to customise screens. A screen painting facility is also built into the FOCUS TED editor (see above).

Host language interface (HLI)

This enables programs written in such languages as COBOL, FORTRAN and C to access and maintain FOCUS databases.

Graphics

FOCUS graphics facilities allow the production of a variety of graph types, including bar charts, histograms, pie charts and scatter diagrams. The same language used for queries and reporting is also used for graphics.

Financial reporting

Row oriented financial statements such as income statements, balance sheets and budgets can be created with the FOCUS financial reporting language. Using the same basic syntax as the FOCUS report writer, it allows recursive calculations, what-if analyses, etc.

Statistics

FOCUS/STATISTICS offers a complete set of business statistical functions including time series, regression, correlation, variance, exponential smoothing and descriptive statistics, designed to complement the query, reporting and graphics facilities. The statistics functions are fully integrated in the FOCUS environment, allowing easy movement from reports to statistics to graphs.

Spreadsheet

FOCCALC is a spreadsheet facility fully integrated within FOCUS. FOCUS report writing requests may be placed directly into spreadsheet cells as well as data from FOCUS databases and other files. Up to four active windows may be positioned on a screen, including a variety of graph types. FOCALC provides features such as goal seeking, what-if analysis, financial functions, project management and graphics.

Data dictionary

The FOCUS data dictionary (FOCUSDD) is itself written in FOCUS and allows the monitoring, control and auditing of FOCUS systems. Information is held about fields, files and programs and the relationship between these various data elements. FOCUSDD has reporting facilities and a program change log facility as well as utilities for creating file descriptions from the data held in the dictionary. If a master file description is changed, these changes are included in the dictionary when the file is saved, so that the data remains consistent with the latest version of the application.

Other features

PC/FOCUS is a PC implementation of FOCUS. PC/FOCUS multi-user is a simultaneous-user version of PC/FOCUS for local area networks.

Some of the other tools provided by Information Builders are themselves written in FOCUS, as is the FOCUS data dictionary. For example, FOCAUDIT and FOCMAN which are not part of the main FOCUS system. FOCMAN is a project management system and FOCAUDIT is a toolkit for financial auditors.

Hardware

There are versions of FOCUS available for IBM mainframes, DEC VAX computers, Wang VS systems, UNIX systems and IBM PCs and compatibles.

Services offered

★ Education and training
★ Support
★ Documentation
★ Consultancy
★ Quality control

It is not possible to cover all tools in detail here. Further details about any of the tools mentioned and of other products and services offered by Information Builders may be obtained direct from them at the following address:

UK   Information Builders (UK) Ltd
          Station House
          Harrow Road
          Wembley
          Middlesex HA9 6DE

Corporate offices   Information Builders Inc.
                         1250 Broadway
                         New York NY 10001
                         USA

INGRES

The company

Like many of the manufacturers of 4GLs and database products referred to in this book, Relational Technology's corporate headquarters are found in the USA. Relational Technology International Ltd, based in London, is a wholly owned subsidiary of Relational Technology Inc. Other regional headquarters and principal distribution centres are found in Abu Dhabi, Amsterdam, Brussels, Frankfurt, Helsinki, Hong Kong, Madrid, Oslo, Paris, Stockholm, Sydney, Tel Aviv, Tokyo and Toronto, among other places.

INGRES was introduced by Relational Technology in 1981, as one of the first commercial relational database products on the market. INGRES/APPLICATIONS – a 4GL application development system, integrated with the RDMS followed a couple of years later. Relational Technology also provide a distributed relational system.

The product – overview

There are four product groups in the INGRES family:

★ INGRES SQL Relational Database Manager
★ INGRES end-user query and reporting products
★ INGRES/APPLICATIONS 4GL development system
★ INGRES/STAR distributed data management products

Each of these groups is based on SQL and integrated with other INGRES products through the INGRES data dictionary and through common interfaces. Products may be chosen to meet individual requirements.

The tools

INGRES provides a comprehensive range of tools across the product groups and some of these will be described here.

INGRES/RDBMS

This is the RDBMS which allows for the presentation of data in the form of two-dimensional tables. There is no limit on the number of databases and each database can have any number of tables and each table any number of indexes. All databases and tables can be modified dynamically and without affecting existing applications. Data can also be copied to and from the host operating system files.

The RDBMS provides controlled access to data and a range of data integrity and security features including detection of failure and reinstatement of data to its former condition, and data locking. It is supported by advanced query optimisation techniques and a range of productivity tools.

INGRES query optimiser

The query optimiser determines the optimum sequence for data access through the use of AI techniques. It also generates database queries in the form of SQL and responds to queries by generating only essential data elements. Other features include optimisation of physical disk access, processor workload and system response times. Network traffic and use of communication lines are also optimised in the case of networked systems.

INGRES integrated data dictionary

This is an active, integrated data dictionary which interacts with other tools, providing an on-line information resource. The Data Dictionary interacts with applications automatically enforcing security and integrity rules, defines data structures, security rules, integrity rules, screen forms, reports, graphs, charts and applications and allows security privileges at three levels. The security facilities can be built into applications.

INGRES/SQL

SQL provides the interface between database and applications. INGRES/SQL is ANSI Standard SQL and provides an interface to INGRES/RDBMS and other INGRES tools. It can be used interactively or embedded into conventional languages, including Ada, BASIC, C, COBOL, FORTRAN, Pascal and PL/1. INGRES/SQL can be used as an integral part of the INGRES fourth generation application development system and integrates with the data dictionary. It can also be used interchangeably with INGRES/QUEL.

INGRES/QUERY

INGRES/QUERY allows access to data via a fill in the forms mechanism. It enables data to be viewed on-line and allows updates/deletions and insertions. INGRES/QUERY interacts with the user and provides help messages. Like other tools within INGRES it integrates with the data dictionary. Default forms can be customised with INGRES/FORMS and the forms can be used in applications.

INGRES/REPORTS

INGRES/REPORTS allows the generation of simple reports through the completion of questionnaires displayed on the screen. Default reports are customised using interactive screen forms and customised report specifications may be added to the data dictionary. Reports can be built into applications. Help and error messages are available for each option.

Customisation features include many of those discussed in Chapter 4, e.g. page length, underlining, sorting order, totalling, spacing, etc. For more complex reporting procedures INGRES provides INGRES report writer. Report writer statements give control over layout, format and computation. INGRES/SQL data selection statements can be embedded into report writer programs and its interface to INGRES/REPORTS allows existing reports to be used as a model. Like other INGRES tools, the report writer interacts with the data dictionary.

INGRES/VIGRAPH (visual graphics)

INGRES/VIGRAPH allows for graphic output from the INGRES database. It is driven by interactive screen forms and runs on a range of terminals/printers/plotters and provides colour/ shading. Outline sketches can be produced and finished graphs saved in the data dictionary. Defaults can be customised. VIGRAPH's WYSIWYG (What You See Is What You Get) editor lets details of the graphs be customised. INGRES/VIGRAPH can produce line graphs, scatter plots, bar charts and pie charts. Text can be incorporated and default text generated from the definitions in the data dictionary.

INGRES/FORMS

INGRES/FORMS allows the user interface to be customised. All applications may be driven entirely from screen forms. INGRES/FORMS is itself a forms-based application, with help available for each option. INGRES/FORMS is not restricted to INGRES applications and can be used to standardise the interface to applications. The forms can be designed from scratch or through customising existing or default forms. Screen painting is used and visual effects include colours, underlining, blinking, reverse video, etc. INGRES/FORMS interacts with the data dictionary.

INGRES/APPLICATIONS

INGRES/APPLICATIONS provides an interactive, forms-driven method for building applications which interact with the data dictionary to provide on-line access to the definitions. It allows routines to be added to link the selected facilities via the INGRES 4GL. INGRES/SQL statements and 3GL language routines may also be included. INGRES/APPLICATIONS supports prototyping by allowing incomplete applications to be tested interactively and modified as required. Development and production environments are kept separate. All stages of application development are logged in the data dictionary.

INGRES/NET

INGRES/NET allows INGRES data to be used across a network. It is a transparent software layer that conducts the dialogue between INGRES components running on two different machines joined by a network. INGRES/NET runs on a variety of operating systems. Remote systems can have their own facilities for developing and/or running INGRES applications and data security is extended to all remote users. All updates are made on the host system.

INGRES/STAR

INGRES/STAR distributes a database or several databases across a networked system. Different operating systems can be integrated into the network. All users have access to all data, subject to security and share a common data resource. A single data dictionary defines permissions/integrity features. Data locking/failure and recovery features still apply. A distributed optimiser picks the best route for satisfying a multi-site request. As well as INGRES/NET and INGRES/STAR, INGRES Gateways provide access to dBASE files, VAX/VMS files and DB2 and SQL/DS databases.

Other features

INGRES/PCLINK provides PC users with a bridge between tools such as Lotus 1-2-3 and INGRES databases on a host system. PC users can access information in a host database using a visual menu-driven query method. PCLINK automatically reformats data in Lotus 1-2-3, dBASE, WORDSTAR and MULTIPLAN formats on the PC. INGRES/RDBMS is also available for PCs.

Direct access to INGRES data is provided through several software tools, including FOCUS (see earlier description), Datatalker (an English language database query and reporting system), SAS (a statistical package), RS/1 (an interactive graphics and analysis system) and KEE and ART both AI systems.

Hardware

INGRES is available on a variety of hardware types, which include:

Amdahl
Apollo
Apricot
AT&T
Data General

DEC VAX
Hewlett Packard
IBM
IBM PCs and some compatibles.
ICL
NCR
Unisys
etc.

Services offered

★ After sales support including updates
★ Consultancy service
★ On-line customer information
★ INGRES User Association (IUA)
★ Customer training centres
★ Documentation
★ Computer-based training

Further details about any of the tools mentioned here and of other products and services offered by Relational Technology may be obtained direct from them at the following address:

UK   Relational Technology International
           Limited
           Anchor House
           15–19 Britten Street
           London SW3 3TY

ORACLE

The company

ORACLE Corporation was founded in 1977 and implemented the first commercially available relational database system in the form of ORACLE in 1979. ORACLE Corporation's headquarters are found in Belmont, California. The company operates in over thirty different countries. ORACLE Corporation UK Ltd markets the full range of ORACLE products throughout the UK and Eire. ORACLE UK have their headquarters in Richmond, Surrey, with regional offices in Bristol, Manchester and Edinburgh.

The product – overview

ORACLE is a RDBMS integrated with a range of application development tools to provide a fourth generation environment. Tools are available for both end-user and professional. Whilst once offered as a bundled package of tools, ORACLE is now unbundled to provide a more flexible approach for the potential developer. ORACLE Corporation have also moved into the CASE tool marketplace (see Chapter 9).

The tools

ORACLE offers a wide range of development tools. Some are aimed specifically at the end-user, e.g. EASY*SQL, providing ease-of-use facilities such as form-filling or query by example, etc. Other tools, whilst not directly aimed at the end-user, can be used as such, e.g. SQL*FORMS. Finally, some tools are very much for professional developers, e.g. SQL*DESIGN DICTIONARY. It is only possible to give an overview of some of these tools. Further details can be obtained directly from the manufacturers.

The RDBMS

The ORACLE RDBMS is aimed at large databases and multiple users and is based on SQL. A number of features are provided to ensure rapid data access, including data cache, compressed B-tree indexes to optimise data retrieval, data held in compressed form, etc. The RDBMS allows data independence through the separation of the logical and physical views of the database. A range of integrity and security features are offered:

★ record level locks
★ before and after-images
★ roll-back recovery
★ restricted access
★ password stored in encrypted form
★ backup and archival facilities, etc.

SQL*FORMS

An interactive development tool providing screen painting facilities, windows and query by example. Forms-based applications for maintaining and querying the database can be built and modified.

SQL*MENU

SQL*MENU provides a flexible menu environment and is used to control access to applications, hence providing security against uncontrolled use.

SQL*REPORT

This is the report writer used to provide complex reports. Simple reports may be produced via other tools as described. SQL commands may be surrounded by sequencing and text formatting commands to produce a variety of reports.

SQL*PLUS

SQL*PLUS provides conversational interaction with the RDBMS. Tables and views can be modified, data items entered or modified and *ad hoc* queries set-up. This tool also provides report writing facilities.

SQL*CALC

This is a spreadsheet and offers compatibility with Lotus 1-2-3. Data can be retrieved from the ORACLE database, for use within the spreadsheet. SQL can also be used.

SQL*Graph

Allows data from the ORACLE database to be presented graphically. SQL*Graph allows for pie charts, line graphs, bar charts and colour.

EASY*SQL

This tool allows the end-user to utilise SQL through the use of a mouse and graphical presentation. This eliminates the need for the end-user to learn the syntax and commands of SQL.

Other features

SQL*DESIGN DICTIONARY (SDD) and SQL*DEVELOPMENT METHOD were discussed in Chapter 9, under the heading 4GLs and CASE tools (see page 111). Other features include networking and distributed database facilities which are achieved through SQL*STAR and SQL*CONNECT. PC users may also link up to the ORACLE system on a mainframe through SQL*PLUS and EASY*SQL.

Hardware

ORACLE is available on a number of computer systems:

Apollo	Hewlett Packard
AT&T	IBM (mainframes and PCs)
Data General	NCR
DEC	

Services offered

ORACLE UK offers a range of consultancy and training services. The headquarter's address is:

> ORACLE Corporation UK Limited
> Thames Link House
> 1 Church Road
> Richmond
> Surrey TW9 2QE

PROGRESS

The company

PROGRESS was developed by the Progress Software Corporation in the USA. Progress Software (formerly Data Language Corporation) was formed in 1981 and released the first version of PROGRESS in August 1984. The headquarters of Progress Software Corporation are in Boston, Mass. PROGRESS is now being sold worldwide, with services being offered throughout the USA and in Amsterdam, Antwerp, Cologne, Copenhagen, Helsinki, Melbourne, Munich, Oslo, Paris, Reykjavik, Rome, Stockholm, Toronto, Vienna and Zurich among other places.

The product – overview

PROGRESS is a general purpose application builder offering a RDBMS used primarily for the development of business applications. It offers a range of facilities for prototyping and application development. It is suited to both end-users and professionals, offering both ease-of-use facilities and more sophisticated options. PROGRESS offers a subset of the facilities discussed in Chapters 4 and 5. It has five basic components:

★ a RDBMS
★ a data dictionary
★ an application development language
★ a screen and report formatter
★ a procedure editor.

Optional facilities include:

★ a query/run-time system
★ a developers tool-kit
★ PROGRESS FAST TRACK – a recent addition to the available PROGRESS components, intended to speed up the development process.

These optional facilities will not be discussed here. Details may be obtained direct from the company.

SQL is to be offered from Version 5 of PROGRESS.

The tools

The RDBMS
PROGRESS offers its own RDBMS as an integral part of the product. It provides for variable length fields and records in combination with compressed multi-field B-tree indexes, hence allowing fields to occupy only the number of bytes required to contain that data. The user is allowed to work with one database at a time. PROGRESS supports very large databases.

Files, fields and indexes may be changed at any time without database dump/reorganisation and without affecting existing application procedures. A field's length as defined in the data dictionary is its default length for screens and reports. Security and recovery features include:

★ automatic concurrency control
★ backout of all incomplete transactions upon system failure
★ roll forward recovery
★ optional transaction log file.

The data dictionary
The PROGRESS data dictionary manages the structure of the database. It is a central storage facility for database descriptions, formatting and validation. The data dictionary also holds information about defaults, help messages, etc. All database definitions are stored dynamically and may be changed by users with the appropriate authorisation. Data can be validated automatically and parent–child relationships allow the user to enforce referential integrity. User access is controlled. Other features include the ability to access data stored in other file structures, e.g. dBASE. Bulk load/dump facilities allow the validation and editing of data from other systems.

The application development language
PROGRESS is a 4GL combined with a relational database system. Some of the tools within the PROGRESS system are also written in PROGRESS, e.g. the data dictionary. Access to routines written in other languages, e.g. C, is also possible. Examples of code written in PROGRESS are included in Appendix B.

PROGRESS allows you to develop applications in an interactive, interpretive manner. Each block of instructions may be checked and if no errors are found PROGRESS compiles the code. The application is stored as compiled code which obviously improves performance. Compiled and non-compiled code may be mixed.

The application language calls upon the other parts of the product. For example, it accesses the data dictionary to locate files and fields etc., it calls up the screen and report formatter to create screens and reports, stores data in and retrieves data from the RDBMS. The statements of the application development language are entered, edited and executed via the procedure editor.

Screen and report formatter

PROGRESS automatically formats screens and reports without separate formatting specifications, allowing manual intervention where required. Default designs may be supplemented, modified or replaced. The screen and report formatter is integrated with the data dictionary. Data entry screens and reports are generated automatically through the use of various simple commands. Reports can define control-break groups to provide subtotals, grand totals and a range of aggregate functions. Page headers and footers can also be defined. Windows, colour and other video attributes are available. A windowing capability is provided.

Procedure editor

PROGRESS provides a full screen syntax checking editor. The editor is integrated with the compiler and other components of PROGRESS. These will be called upon as necessary in the process of building, testing, executing and modifying PROGRESS programs. New PROGRESS procedures are typed in using the interactive editor. Existing procedures can be recalled for editing and testing.

Hardware

PROGRESS is portable across many different types of computer systems, but has not really been aimed at mainframe host systems, such as the IBM range of mainframe computers. PROGRESS can be found on the following machine types among others:

Altos	Motorola
Apollo	NCR
AT&T	Nixdorf
DEC	Prime
Fortune	Pyramid
Hewlett-Packard	Sun
IBM PC	Unisys
ICL	etc.

Services offered

★ Maintenance
★ Training
★ Telephone support
★ Marketing support

Progress Software's address is:

UK   Progress Software Limited
        Slington House
        Rankine Road
        Basingstoke
        Hants, RG24 0PH

The code

The code in Appendix B was produced by a student as part of a fourth-year undergraduate project to compare and evaluate various available 4GL products. Each product was used to produce a prototype student records system. With PROGRESS the initial prototype took a very short time to build (approx two weeks of the student's scheduled project time, 6–10 hours per week). Whilst this code does not represent a final system, it is useful to see what can be done in a very short time when the right tools are available. A lot more headway was made using PROGRESS than with some of the other products the student considered.

The prototype system

The objective of the prototype was to build a computerised student records system. The system was to allow the following to be added, modified, deleted, displayed and printed as required:

★ student's personal details
★ exam marks
★ course details.

As the objective was to build a prototype in a short time the screens and reports produced are largely defaults rather than tailored.

As can be seen, PROGRESS requires code to be written in its application development language. The examples of code which follow help to underline the differences between this and writing in COBOL, say. A routine such as

FORM HEADER "STUDENT DETAILS"
    WITH CENTERED.

VIEW.
for each stupersn:
    DISPLAY stuid stuname stusex studob
        stuaddrs courseid WITH CENTERED.
END.

produces the student details as shown on page 136. Other examples of code are also given.

Appendix B A prototype student records system written in PROGRESS

```
┌─────────────────────────────────────────────────────────┐
│                                                           │
│              STUDENT RECORDS SYSTEM                       │
│                                                           │
│                                                           │
│                    MAIN MENU                              │
│                                                           │
│        1) Student personal details                       │
│                                                           │
│        2) Student exam results                            │
│                                                           │
│        3) Details of courses                             │
│                                                           │
│        4) Help                                            │
│                                                           │
│        5) EXIT from system                                │
│                                                           │
│                                                           │
│        Selection:                                         │
│                                                           │
└─────────────────────────────────────────────────────────┘
```

```
/*MAIN-MEN.P*/
/*This routine displays the main menu and reads user
choice*/


DEFINE VARIABLE Selection AS INTEGER FORMAT "9".

REPEAT ON ENDKEY UNDO, RETRY:
  FORM
  SKIP(2)"              MAIN MENU              "
  SKIP(2)"    1) Student personal details     "
  SKIP(2)"    2) Student exam results         "
  SKIP(2)"    3) Details of courses           "
  SKIP(2)"    4) Help                         "
  SKIP(2)"    5) EXIT from system             "
```

```
WITH CENTRED TITLE "STUDENT RECORDS SYSTEM".
UPDATE SKIP(2) SPACE(1) selection AUTO-RETURN WITH
SIDE-LABELS.
HIDE.

        IF selection EQ 1 THEN RUN S-MENU1.P.
ELSE IF selection EQ 2 THEN RUN RES-MENU.P.
ELSE IF selection EQ 3 THEN RUN COR-MENU.P.
ELSE IF selection EQ 4 THEN RUN HELP-1.P.
ELSE IF selection EQ 5 THEN QUIT.

ELSE MESSAGE "Incorrect selection
- please try again".
END.
```

MAIN MENU HELP

1) Student personal details
   This option gives access to student's personal details such as:
   ID CODE, NAME, ADDRESS, SEX, D.O.B., COURSE.

2) Student exam results
   This option gives access to students exam results. The results for a
   particular student may be obtained if that student's ID CODE is
   known. Results for a particular course may be obtained if the
   COURSE ID is known.

3) Details of courses
   This option gives access to course details such as: COURSE ID,
   COURSE NAME.

```
/*HELP-1.P*/
/*This routine gives the user main menu help*/


FORM
SKIP(2)"    1) Student personal details                    "
       "       This option gives access to student's
               personal details such as: ID CODE,
               NAME, ADDRESS, SEX, D.O.B., COURSE.          "
SKIP(1)"    2) Student exam results                          "
       "       This option gives access to student's
               exam results. The results for a
```

```
                         particular student may be obtained
                         if that student's ID CODE is known.
                         Results for a particular course
                         may be obtained if the COURSE ID is
                         known.                                    "
SKIP(1)"        3) Details of courses                             "
         "             This option gives access to course
                         details such as: COURSE ID,
                         COURSE NAME.                              "

WITH CENTERED TITLE "MAIN MENU HELP".
VIEW.
```

STUDENT'S PERSONAL DETAILS

MENU

1) Add a new record

2) Update a record

3) Delete a record

4) Display one record

5) Display all records

6) Print all records

7) Return to Main Menu

Selection:

```
/*S-MENU1.P*/
/*This routine displays the menu of STUDENT PERSONAL
DETAILS options and accepts the user selection*/

DEFINE VARIABLE Selection AS INTEGER FORMAT "9".

REPEAT:
 FORM
 SKIP(2)"                     MENU                      "
 SKIP(1)"    1) Add a new record                        "
```

```
SKIP(1)"    2) Update a record         "
SKIP(1)"    3) Delete a record         "
SKIP(1)"    4) Display one record      "
SKIP(1)"    5) Display all records     "
SKIP(1)"    6) Print all records       "
SKIP(1)"    7) Return to Main Menu     "
WITH CENTERED TITLE "STUDENT'S PERSONAL DETAILS".
UPDATE SKIP(2) SPACE(1) selection AUTO-RETURN WITH
SIDE-LABELS.
HIDE.
        IF selection EQ 1 THEN RUN S-ADDSTU.P.
ELSE IF selection EQ 2 THEN RUN S-UPDATE.P.
ELSE IF selection EQ 3 THEN RUN S-DELETE.P.
ELSE IF selection EQ 4 THEN RUN S-ONEREC.P.
ELSE IF selection EQ 5 THEN RUN S-DETS1.P.
ELSE IF selection EQ 6 THEN RUN S-DETS2.P.
ELSE IF selection EQ 7 THEN RUN MAIN-MEN.P.
ELSE MESSAGE "Incorrect selection - please try
        again".
END.
```

```
                    ADD NEW RECORD

        ID: L01                 NAME: RUSH D.
ADDRESS: 28C OLD BLDG.          SEX: M
   D.O.B.: 11/11/1966           COURSE: D01

        ID: L02                 NAME: WADE S.
ADDRESS: 22, OLD BLDG.          SEX: M
   D.O.B.: 11/11/1966           COURSE: H01

        ID: L03                 NAME: PETERS M.
ADDRESS: 204, NEW BLDG.         SEX: M
   D.O.B.: 11/19/1965           COURSE: D01

        ID: L04                 NAME: MILES R.
ADDRESS: 23, OLD BLDG.          SEX: M
   D.O.B.: 10/15/1966           COURSE: H02

        ID: L05                 NAME: KING M.
ADDRESS: 25, OLD BLDG.          SEX: M
   D.O.B.: 11/11/1966           COURSE: H01
```

```
/★S-ADDSTU.★/
/★This routine allows the user to enter new student
details to the file of student personal details.
Relevant details are also added to the results file★/

FORM HEADER "ADD NEW RECORD" WITH CENTERED.
VIEW.
REPEAT:
 INSERT stupersn WITH 2 COLUMNS CENTERED.
 DO:
  CREATE results.
  results.studid=stupersn.studid.
 END.
END.
```

UPDATE RECORD					
ID	NAME	SEX	D.O.B.	ADDRESS	COURSE ID.
L01	RUSH D.	M	11/11/1966	28C OLD BLDG.	D01
L02	WADE S.	M	11/11/1966	22, OLD BLDG.	H01
L03	PETERS M.	M	11/19/1965	204, NEW BLDG.	D01
L04	MILES R.	M	10/15/1966	23, OLD BLDG.	H02
L05	KING M.	M	11/11/1966	25, OLD BLDG.	H01

```
/★S-UPDATE.P★/
/★This routine allows the user to select and update a
student personal details record. If student id is
altered then student exam results file is updated to
include the new student id★/

FORM HEADER "UPDATE RECORD" WITH CENTERED.
VIEW.
REPEAT:
 PROMPT-FOR stupersn.studid.
 FIND stupersn USING studid.
 DISPLAY studid stuname stusex studob stuaddrs
 courseid WITH CENTERED.
 UPDATE studid stuname stusex studob stuaddrs
 courseid.
 FIND results WHERE results.studid=stupersn.studid.
 results.studid=stupersn.studid.
 results.courseid=stupersn.courseid.
END.
```

```
STUDENT DETAILS

STUDENT'S ID: 666

NAME: BLOGGS K.

SEX: M

D.O.B.: 11/11/1968

ADDRESS: 42, NEW RD.

COURSE: HND COOKERY

COURSE ID: H02

RESULTS YEAR[1]: 95.00      RESULTS YEAR[2]: 67.00
RESULTS YEAR[3]: 32.00      RESULTS YEAR[4]: 23.00
RESULTS YEAR[5]: 0.00
```

```
/*S-ONEREC.P*/
/*This routine displays all details for a user
selected student. Details are held in PERSONAL,
RESULTS, and COURSES files*/


DEFINE VARIABLE student AS CHARACTER FORMAT "(3)"
LABEL "STUDENT'S ID".

REPEAT:
 FORM WITH CENTERED TITLE "STUDENT DETAILS".
 UPDATE SKIP(1) student AUTO-RETURN WITH SIDE-LABELS.
 VIEW.

 FIND stupersn WHERE stupersn.studid=student.
 DISPLAY SKIP(1).
 DISPLAY stuname LABEL "NAME".
 DISPLAY SKIP(1).
 DISPLAY stusex.
 DISPLAY SKIP(1).
 DISPLAY studob.
 DISPLAY SKIP(1).
 DISPLAY stuaddrs.
```

```
DISPLAY SKIP(1).
FIND courses WHERE courses.courseid
=stupersn.courseid.
DISPLAY corname LABEL "COURSE".
DISPLAY SKIP(1).
DISPLAY courses.courseid LABEL "COURSE ID".
DISPLAY SKIP(1).
FIND results WHERE results.studid=stupersn.studid.
DISPLAY period LABEL "RESULTS YEAR".
END.
```

STUDENT DETAILS

ID	NAME	SEX	D.O.B.	ADDRESS	COURSE ID.
666	BLOGGS K.	M	11/11/1968	42, NEW RD.	H02
AAA	ANDERS A.	F	11/11/1986	123, KEW GDNS.	D01
AS2	NUNNEY I.	M	12/03/1959	3, SWAN LANE	D01
D43	JOHNSON J.	F	02/11/1968	23, LONG LANE	H03
D44	DEAN M.	F	11/11/1966	122 MERP LANE	H02
D45	JACKSON J.	F	02/11/1968	23, OLD RD.	D01
F55	NERTY M.	M	11/11/1966	12, VERDER HOUSE	H02
G45	SMITH L.	F	11/11/1967	BURNT DOWN	D01
H34	SMITII L.	M	11/11/1967	BUCK HOUSE	H02
L03	PETERS M.	M	11/19/1965	204, NEW BLDG.	D01
L04	MILES R.	M	10/15/1966	23, OLD BLDG.	H02
L05	KING M.	M	11/11/1966	25, OLD BLDG.	H01
L99	SMITH G.	M	07/04/1965	12, ROSE RD.	D01

```
/*S-DETS1.P*/
/*This routine displays the personal details of all
students*/


FORM HEADER "STUDENT DETAILS" WITH CENTERED.
VIEW.
FOR EACH stupersn:
 DISPLAY studid stunsme stusex studob stuaddrs
 courseid WITH CENTERED.
END.
```

```
                    STUDENT EXAM RESULTS


                            MENU

            1) Update student exam results

            2) Display a student's results

            3) Display a course results

            4) Display all results

            5) Print all results

            6) Return to Main Menu


            Selection:
```

```
/*RES-MENU.P*/
/*This routine displays RESULTS menu and accepts
user's selection*/


DEFINE VARIABLE Selection AS INTEGER FORMAT "9".

REPEAT:
FORM
SKIP(2)"                    MENU                    "
SKIP(1)"    1) Update student exam results         "
SKIP(1)"    2) Display a student's results         "
SKIP(1)"    3) Display a course results            "
SKIP(1)"    4) Display all results                 "
SKIP(1)"    5) Print all results                   "
SKIP(1)"    6) Return to Main Menu                 "

WITH CENTERED TITLE "STUDENT EXAM RESULTS".
UPDATE SKIP(2) SPACE(1) selection AUTO-RETURN WITH
SIDE-LABELS.
HIDE.
        IF selection EQ 1 THEN RUN R-UPDATE.P.
ELSE IF selection EQ 2 THEN RUN R-ONESTU.P.
ELSE IF selection EQ 3 THEN RUN R-COURSE.P.
```

```
ELSE IF selection EQ 4 THEN RUN R-ALLSTU.P
ELSE IF selection EQ 5 THEN RUN R-PRNALL.P.
ELSE IF selection EQ 6 THEN RUN MAIN-MEN.P.
ELSE MESSAGE "Incorrect selection - please try
     again".
END.
```

UPDATE STUDENT EXAM RESULTS						
STUDENT	COURSE	YEAR [1]	YEAR [2]	YEAR [3]	YEAR [4]	YEAR [5]
D04	H02	56.00	65.00	0.00	0.00	0.00
L05	H01	76.00	98.70	78.90	0.00	0.00
L03	D01	34.00	35.00	0.00	0.00	0.00

```
/*R-UPDATE.P*/
/*This routine allows the user to update selected
students' exam results*/


FORM HEADER "UPDATE STUDENT EXAM RESULTS" WITH
CENTERED.
VIEW.
REPEAT:
 PROMPT-FOR results.studid.
 FIND results USING studid.
 DISPLAY studid courseid period WITH CENTERED.
 UPDATE period.
END.
```

STUDENT EXAM RESULTS						
STUDENT	COURSE	YEAR [1]	YEAR [2]	YEAR [3]	YEAR [4]	YEAR [5]
L03	D01	34.00	35.00	0.00	0.00	0.00
L04	H02	56.00	65.00	0.00	0.00	0.00
L05	H01	76.00	98.70	78.90	0.00	0.00

```
/*R-ONESTU.P*/
/*This routine displays exam results for user selected
students*/


FORM HEADER "STUDENT EXAM RESULTS" WITH CENTERED.
VIEW.
REPEAT:
 PROMPT-FOR results.studid.
 FIND results USING studid.
 DISPLAY studid courseid period WITH CENTERED.
END.
```

	COURSE RESULTS				
	COURSE REQUIRED: D01				
STUDENT	YEAR [1]	YEAR [2]	YEAR [3]	YEAR [4]	YEAR [5]
D44	0.00	0.00	0.00	0.00	0.00
D45	0.00	0.00	0.00	0.00	0.00
F55	0.00	0.00	0.00	0.00	0.00
G45	0.00	0.00	0.00	0.00	0.00
H34	0.00	0.00	0.00	0.00	0.00
L03	34.00	35.00	0.00	0.00	0.00
L99	0.00	0.00	0.00	0.00	0.00
M55	0.00	0.00	0.00	0.00	0.00
N02	0.00	0.00	0.00	0.00	0.00
N03	0.00	0.00	0.00	0.00	0.00
N04	0.00	0.00	0.00	0.00	0.00
N05	0.00	0.00	0.00	0.00	0.00
N06	0.00	0.00	0.00	0.00	0.00
Q01	0.00	0.00	0.00	0.00	0.00

```
/*R-COURSE.P*/
/*This routine allows the user to select a course and
displays the exam results of all students on that
course*/


DEFINE VARIABLE course AS CHARACTER FORMAT "X(3)"
LABEL "COURSE REQUIRED".
```

```
REPEAT:
 FORM
 WITH CENTERED TITLE "COURSE RESULTS".
 UPDATE SKIP(1) course AUTO-RETURN WITH SIDE-LABELS.
 VIEW.


 FOR EACH results:
  IF results.courseid=course THEN DISPLAY studid
  period WITH CENTERED.
 END.
END.
```

	ALL EXAM RESULTS					
STUDENT	COURSE	YEAR [1]	YEAR [2]	YEAR [3]	YEAR [4]	YEAR [5]
111	H03	95.00	34.00	23.00	0.00	0.00
666	H03	95.00	67.00	32.00	23.00	0.00
A01	H03	0.00	0.00	0.00	0.00	0.00
AAA	H03	0.00	0.00	0.00	0.00	0.00
AS2	H03	0.00	0.00	0.00	0.00	0.00
D43	H03	0.00	0.00	0.00	0.00	0.00
D44	D01	0.00	0.00	0.00	0.00	0.00
D45	D01	0.00	0.00	0.00	0.00	0.00
F55	D01	0.00	0.00	0.00	0.00	0.00
G45	D01	0.00	0.00	0.00	0.00	0.00
H34	D01	0.00	0.00	0.00	0.00	0.00
L03	D01	34.00	35.00	0.00	0.00	0.00
L04	H02	56.00	65.00	0.00	0.00	0.00
L05	H01	76.00	98.70	78.90	0.00	0.00
L99	D01	0.00	0.00	0.00	0.00	0.00

```
/*R-ALLSTU.P*/
/*This routine displays exam results for all
students*/


FORM HEADER "ALL EXAM RESULTS" WITH CENTERED. VIEW.
FOR EACH results:
 DISPLAY studid courseid period WITH CENTERED.
END.
```

```
                        POLYTECHNIC COURSES


                              MENU

                   1) Add a new course

                   2) Update course details

                   3) Delete a course

                   4) Display one course

                   5) Display all courses

                   6) Print all courses

                   7) Return to Main Menu


              Selection:
```

```
/*COR-MEN.P*/
/*This procedure displays the COURSES menu and accepts
the user's selection.*/


DEFINE VARIABLE Selection AS INTEGER FORMAT "9".

REPEAT:
 FORM
 SKIP(2)"              MENU                "
 SKIP(1)"   1) Add a new course           "
 SKIP(1)"   2) Update course details      "
 SKIP(1)"   3) Delete a course            "
 SKIP(1)"   4) Display one course         "
 SKIP(1)"   5) Display all courses        "
 SKIP(1)"   6) Print all courses          "
 SKIP(1)"   7) Return to Main Menu        "

 WITH CENTERED TITLE "POLYTECHNIC COURSES". UPDATE
 SKIP(2) SPACE(1) selection AUTO-RETURN WITH
 SIDE-LABELS.
 HIDE.
```

```
        IF selection EQ 1 THEN RUN ADD-CORS.P.
ELSE IF selection EQ 2 THEN RUN CHG-CORS.P. ELSE IF
selection EQ 3 THEN RUN DEL-CORS.P. ELSE IF
selection EQ 4 THEN RUN ONE-CORS.P. ELSE IF
selection EQ 5 THEN RUN DIS-CORS.P. ELSE IF
selection EQ 6 THEN RUN PRN-CORS.P. ELSE IF
selection EQ 7 THEN RUN MAIN-MEN.P.

ELSE MESSAGE "Incorrect selection - please try
again".
END.
```

ADD NEW COURSE	
ID	COURSE
M01	Bsc. PHYSICS
M02	Bsc. GEOGRAPHY
M03	Bsc. NEEDLEWORK
M04	Bsc. ECONOMICS
M05	Bsc. MEDICINE
M06	Bsc. SURGERY

```
/*ADD-CORS.P*/
/*This routine adds new courses to the file*/


FORM HEADER "ADD NEW COURSE" WITH CENTERED.
VIEW.
REPEAT:
  INSERT course WITH CENTERED.
END.
```

UPDATE COURSE	
ID	COURSE
M01	HND PHYSICS
M02	HND GEOGRAPHY
M03	HND COOKERY ADVNCD

```
/*CHG-CORS.P*/
/*This routine changes course details*/

DEFINE VARIABLE oldcor AS CHARACTER FORMAT "X(3)".

FORM HEADER "UPDATE COURSE" WITH CENTERED.
VIEW.
REPEAT.
 PROMPT-FOR courses.courseid.
 FIND courses USING courseid.
 oldcor=courses.courseid.
 DISPLAY courseid corname WITH CENTERED.
 UPDATE courseid corname.
 FOR EACH stupersn:
 IF stupersn.courseid=oldcor THEN
    stupersn.courseid=courses.courseid.
END.
FOR EACH results:
 IF results.courseid=oldcor THEN
    results.courseid=courses.courseid.
 END.
END.
```

```
                    DELETE A COURSE

   ID     COURSE               Enter "y" to delete this course

   M03    HND COOKERY ADVNCD   N
   M02    HND GEOGRAPHY        Y
   M01    HND PHYSICS          Y
```

```
/*DEL-CORS.P*/
/*This routine deletes a course from COURSES*/

DEFINE VARIABLE Delete AS LOGICAL FORMAT "Y/N".

FORM HEADER "DELETE A COURSE" WITH CENTERED.
VIEW.
REPEAT:
 PROMPT-FOR courses.courseid.
 FIND courses USING courseid.
 DISPLAY courseid corname WITH CENTERED.
 Delete=NO.
 UPDATE Delete LABEL
  "Enter ""y"" to delete this course".
 IF Delete THEN DELETE courses.
END.
```

```
COURSE DETAILS

ID      COURSE

M04     Bsc. ECONOMICS
M05     Bsc. MEDICINE
D01     Bsc. MATHEMATICS
```

```
/*ONE-CORS.P*/
/*This routine displays details of user selected
course*/

FORM HEADER "COURSE DETAILS" WITH CENTERED.
VIEW.
REPEAT:
 PROMPT-FOR courses.courseid.
 FIND courses USING courseid.
 DISPLAY courseid corname WITH CENTERED.
END.
```

```
COURSES

ID      COURSE

D01     Bsc. MATHEMATICS
D02     Bsc. HISTORY
H02     HND COOKERY
H03     BCS YEAR 1
J01     HND COMPUTING
M03     HND COOKERY ADVNCD
M04     Bsc. ECONOMICS
M05     Bsc. MEDICINE
M06     Bsc. SURGERY
```

```
/*DIS-CORS.P*/
/*This routine displays details of all courses*/

FORM HEADER "COURSES" WITH CENTERED.
VIEW.
FOR EACH courses:
 DISPLAY courseid corname WITH CENTERED.
END.
```

References

Adamski, L. (June 1985), 'The Prototyping Process', *Systems International.*

Albrecht, A. J. and Gafney, J. E. (1983), 'Software Function, Source Lines of Code and Development Effort Prediction: A Software Science Validation', IEEE Transactions on Software Engineering, SE-9(6), pp. 639–48.

Benyon, D. and Skidmore, S. (eds) (1987), *Automating Systems Development*, Plenum Publishing.

Boehm, B. W. (1976), 'Software Engineering', IEEE Transactions on Computers, C-25(12), pp. 1226–41.

Bratko, I. (1986), *Prolog Programming for Artificial Intelligence*, Addison-Wesley.

Butler, M. (July 1988), 'Talking Some Sense into the 4GL Business', *Dec User*, pp. 29–39.

CCTA Report (July 1986), *Application Generator Assessment, Evaluation and Selection.*

Chard, R. A. (1985), *Evaluating Program Generators for Micros*, NCC.

Chorafas, D. N. (1986), *Fourth and Fifth Generation Programming Languages:* vol. 1, *Integrated Software, Database Languages and Expert Systems*, McGraw-Hill.

Christoff, K. (September 1985), 'Building a Fourth Generation Environment, *Datamation.*

Clocksin, W. F. and Mellish, C. S. (1984), *Programming in PROLOG*, 2nd edn, Springer-Verlag.

Cobb, J. (July 1985), 'In Praise of 4GLs', *Datamation.*

Cullum, R. (February 1985), 'Iterative Development', *Datamation.*

Daniels, A. and Yeates, D. (1988), *Basic Systems Analysis*, 3rd edn, Pitman.

Date, C. J. (1986), *An Introduction to Database Systems*, 4th edn, vol. 1, Addison-Wesley.

DeMarco, T. (1978), *Structured Analysis and System Specification*, Yourdon Inc.

DTI/NCC (1987), *The Starts Guide*, 2nd edn, vol. 1.

Fawcett, S. (November 1985), 'Users Force Changes to Role of DP Departments', NCC Survey, *Computing.*

Forage, G. E. and Wilkes, J. F. (eds) (1985), *Fourth Generation Languages and Advanced Software Development Aids*, Advanced Technology Series, Inbucon Management Consultants Ltd.

Gooding, C. (27 June 1986), 'Getting It Right Before Deciding', *Financial Times.*

Grant, F. (July 1985), 'The Downside of 4GLs', *Datamation.*

Grindley, K. (1986), *Fourth Generation Languages:* vol. 1, *A Survey of Best Practice* (The Grindley Report), IDPM Publications.

HMSO (1983), *Application Generation: Rapid Development of Application Systems Without Conventional Programming*, HMSO Publications.

Jones, G. (1987), *Programming in Occam*, Prentice-Hall.

King, M. J. and Pardoe, J. P. (1985), *Programming Design Using JSP: A Practical Introduction*, Macmillan.

Lantz, K. E. (1986), *The Prototyping Methodology*, Prentice-Hall.

Lee, M. (March 1986), 'Slow Response to Formal Methods', *Computing.*

Leonard, J., Pardoe, J. P. and Wade, S. (July 1988), 'Software Maintenance: Cinderella Is Still not Getting to the Ball', *Software Engineering*, IEE/BCS Conference Publication no. 290.

Lobell, R. F. (1983), *Application Program Generators*, NCC.

McFadden, F. R. and Hoffer, J. A. (1985), *Database Management*, Benjamin Cummings Publishing.

Martin, J. (1976), *Principles of Database Management*, Prentice-Hall.

    (1977), *Computer Database Organisation*, Prentice-Hall.

    (1982), *Applications Development Without Programmers*, Prentice-Hall.

    (1985), *Fourth Generation Languages:* vol. 1, *Principles*, Prentice-Hall.

    (1986), *Fourth Generation Languages:* vol. 2, *Representative 4GLs*, Prentice-Hall.

Martland, D., Holloway, S., and Bhabuta, L. (eds) (1986), *Fourth Generation Languages and Application Generators*, Unicom Applied Information Technology Reports Series, Technical Press.

Norton, M. (October 1988), '4GL Survey', *Informatics.*

Patman, B. (1986), 'An Introduction to Systems Design Techniques', in Martland *et al.* (1986).
Perrot, R. H. (1987), *Parallel Programming,* Addison-Wesley.
Prizant, A. (December 1986), '4GLs: Proceed with Caution', *IBM Computer Today.*
Ratcliff, B. (1987), *Software Engineering: Principles and Methods,* Blackwell Scientific Publications.
Read, N. and Harmon, D. (1981), 'Assuring MIS Success', *Datamation.*
Rich, E. (1983), *Artificial Intelligence,* McGraw-Hill.
Riddle, W. E. and Fairley, R. E. (eds) (1980), *Software Development Tools,* Springer-Verlag.
Rogers, J. B. (1986), *A Prolog Primer,* Addison-Wesley.
Sammet, J. E. (1969), *Programming Languages: History and Fundamentals,* Prentice-Hall.
Sanschagrin, M. P. (May 1986), 'Maintenance Tools for a Fourth Generation Language', *Software Maintenance News.*
Sommerville, I. and Morrison, R. (1987), *Software Development with Ada,* Addison-Wesley.
Stahl, B. (April 1986), 'The Trouble with Application Generators', *Datamation.*
Steele, R. (January 1987), 'Bringing 4GLs down to Earth', *IBM Computer Today.*
Sutherland, J. (October 1988), 'Asking for It' (survey), *Datalink.*
Teorey, T. J. and Fry, J. P. (1982), *Design of Database Structures,* Prentice-Hall.
Unicom Seminar Proceedings (1988), *Fourth Generation Systems: Their Scope, Application and Methods of Evaluation.*
Watt, J. (1987), *Applied Fourth Generation Languages,* Sigma Press.
Yourdon, E. (June 1986), 'What Ever Happened to Structured Analysis?' *Datamation.*

Manufacturers' materials for the following products (and related tools):

CORVISION
DELTA
EASYTRIEVE PLUS
FOCUS
GENER/OL
GURU
INGRES
KnowledgeBUILD
MANTIS
MIMER
ORACLE
PROGRESS
RAMIS
UNIFACE

Answers to questions

Chapter 1

1) a) First generation – binary or machine code.
   Second generation – assembly languages, binary digits of the first generation are replaced by mnemonic codes. Both first and second generation known as low-level languages.
   Third generation – typically the high-level languages such as COBOL and FORTRAN.
   Fourth generation – often called non-procedural languages, but not all 4GLs can be classified in this way.
   b) Main differences between first to fourth generation include increased portability, freeing of the programmer from having to understand the workings of the machine, more natural notation and the move towards non-procedural languages.

2) The fifth generation is to do with artificial intelligence (AI) and employs radically different tools and techniques from the previous generations.

3) High-level indicates a notation nearer to that of the human programmer.

4) 3GLs are easier to use and learn, offer a more natural notation, are further removed from the machine, offer savings in time and effort, are easier to change.

5) Disadvantages include training required, roots in batch processing environment, can offer different facilities despite standardisation, programs tend to be huge and difficult to modify/maintain.

6) Application packages are restricted to solving specific problems, are not easily modified and may not perform to user's standards.

7) Procedural – the programmer has to define what is required and how it will be carried out by writing a sequence of executable statements.
   Non-procedural – only the what is specified not the how.

8) Some people define 4GLs as non-procedural. Although not a complete definition most 4GLs offer some non-procedural components.

Chapter 2

1) Changes include wider availability of computing power, decrease in hardware costs, increased demand for information, applications and computer personnel, increase in speed and power of computers, increase in complexity of applications.

2) a) The traditional systems life-cycle provides a framework in which applications may be developed. Its stages are outlined in Figure 2.4 and Table 2.1, pages 19 and 18 respectively.
   b) Disadvantages include inflexibility, costs and development time, systems produced do not match requirements, resultant maintenance problems, etc.

3) a) Application backlog refers to the inability of DP to keep up with the request for applications and the resulting wait.
   b) Requirements specification is the document produced post analysis containing the user's requirements for a system.
   c) Culture of complexity refers to the idea that if computing professionals give the impression that computing is a highly specialised and difficult task it will remain just that.
   d) Redundancy of data describes how in a file environment the same data may be kept on several different files. Databases help to eliminate this redundancy.

4) a) Software maintenance is caused by bugs in code, systems not matching requirements, changes in requirements, legislation, procedures or hardware. It is costly, time-consuming and can degrade code.

b) Corrective maintenance, the process of finding and correcting errors post-implementation.
Adaptive maintenance, changing software to adapt to environmental changes.
Perfective maintenance, enhancements to both the functionality and the efficiency of code.

c) Preventive maintenance tries to improve the maintainability of the software or provide a better basis for enhancements.

5) a) Problems include the application backlog, use of life-cycle approach, communication problems, maintenance, slow adoption of structured methods, development times and costs, etc.

b) Solutions could include end-user computing, increased resources, structured techniques, formal methods, database implementation, etc.

c) They tend to be partial solutions, each tackling a different problem or different ends of the same problem.

Chapter 3

1) 4GLs are high-productivity tools offering ease-of-use facilities which are helping to solve some of the problems of the computing industry.

2) Difficult because the technology is still evolving, there are no standards, experts find it difficult to agree and there is a diversity of 4GL products.

3) 4GLs offer non-procedural facilities, ease-of-use components, portability, fast development, increased productivity, etc.

4) a) The pure 4GL is the totally non-procedural product offering a template approach.

b) The hybrid 4GL offers a mixture of procedural and non-procedural facilities.

c) The dedicated 4GL is meant for a specific purpose, e.g. decision support.

d) The general-purpose 4GL can be used for a wide range of applications.

e) The full-function 4GL can be used to replace COBOL, for example.

5) a) The end-user 4GL would offer non-procedural techniques, e.g. screen painter, report generator, etc. and ease-of-use, e.g. menu selection, use of windows, etc.

b) The professional tool would extend these techniques and offer more conventional facilities, e.g. procedural language.

Chapter 4

1) DBMS, data dictionary, query and report facilities.

2) a) Advantages include preventing possible duplication of data, more likely to fit in with corporate policy, flexibility.

b) Aids portability, ensures integration.

3) List should include DBMS (possibly relational), alternative data structuring, intelligence, integrity, security and recovery features, links to external DBMSs, dynamic reorganisation, active integrated data dictionary and alternate indexing.

4) a) Relational model offers ease of use, as well as ease of representation, security and implementation and data independence.

b) Yes, some data is not best represented by this approach. Also some organisations may have a commitment to other data structures.

5) a) Integrity features may include integrity checks such as limit or range checks, masks and referential integrity as well as transaction integrity and concurrency control.

b) Security features include authorisation, e.g. passwords and user names, privileges, restricted access and encryption.

c) Recovery features include back-ups of database/files, restart and recovery, checkpoints, journal facilities, before and after imaging.

6) a) A data dictionary is a central repository of data about data, i.e. metadata.
   b) Other terms include directory, library, catalogue and encyclopaedia.
   c) Same reasons as for questions 2a and 2b.

7) Query facilities include: query language, natural or English language, query through form-filling. A standard query language such as SQL may be offered. Reporting facilities may be offered through a language (procedural or non-procedural), menus, form-filling and similar techniques or natural language.

Chapter 5

1) Features might include screen painting, statistical and graphics facilities, on-line help, text editing, PC development, etc.

2) a) Links may be offered through interfaces to existing code or through internal production of 3GL code.
   b) Because of the commitment in most organisations to 3GL code, even if only in maintaining older applications.

3) a) 4GLs utilise compilation, interpretation and generation techniques.
   b) Interpretation is useful for interactive techniques and prototyping, but is less efficient than compilation. Generation allows for the automatic production of code but may produce less efficient programs. Some generated code may need further translation.

4) Fixed processing cycles – the technique whereby certain routine operations are combined to produce a standard program which is automatically incorporated into the 4GL application. This technique varies from 4GL to 4GL; many don't incorporate it at all. It constrains the programmer to a certain way of working.

Chapter 6

1) 4GL development approaches include within traditional life-cycle, replacement approach, such as that suggested by Grindley, DP professionals and end-users working together as a team, end-user development and prototyping.

2) The life-cycle approach is based upon a pre-specification, everything produced in one go approach. This involves large project teams and little user involvement. On the other hand 4GL development encourages user involvement, prototyping, smaller development teams and a piecemeal approach.

3) a) Prototyping is the process of building and refining a model of the system being constructed.
   b) Throwaway prototyping is where the prototype is used to develop an understanding of requirements or test feasibility of proposals. It is then discarded and the system is rebuilt. In evolutionary prototyping the prototype evolves into the system.
   c) Advantages include: greater end-user involvement, provision of a working model, allowance for changes to be made, confirmation that system can be produced, etc. It also helps tighten up thoughts on the system and produce the right system first time.
   d) Disadvantages include: it requires acceptance, commitment, co-operation and control, has greater visibility and may produce less efficient systems.

4) Tools for prototyping include data dictionary to act as a single repository, screen painting facilities to allow quick screen definition, reporting facility for the specification and production of reports, a DBMS, and a high-level language for fast interactive coding. All of these aid fast development, making changes, interactive testing and moving data around system.

5) 4GLs have changed the complexity, the timing, the nature and the areas of maintenance.

6) a) Advantages of standards include improvements in efficiency and effectiveness, aid to training, control, supervision, communication and safety, promotion of good practices and ideas, etc.

   b) Standards are found in hardware, software, documentation, design methodologies, safety/security.

   c) As yet little but they are as valid in a 4GL environment as any other. Organisational standards could be set to cover, documentation, database design, content, format and naming of procedures, etc.

Chapter 7

1) Effects may include improvements in competitiveness, changes in departmental structures and organisational roles, setting up of a corporate strategy for application development and provision of additional services, e.g. information centre.

2) a) The Data Administrator and the Database Administrator or Manager.

   b) The emphasis on information provision and the use of database systems.

   c) Functions of the Data Administrator include identification of company-wide information requirements, education and training, selection of data analysis techniques, standards, control and monitoring, privacy, security and integrity issues, etc. Functions of the Database Administrator include standards, database design and development, education and training, user support, security, integrity and control.

3) a) The analyst is not only required to perform the usual tasks of analysis and design, but possibly also to build the complete application. Some analysts may have difficulty with the programming

tasks. Greater knowledge of the application area is also required. The role is one of the analyst/programmer.

   b) The programmer is having to work closer to the end-user. 4GL use also requires the programmer to adopt a different way of working and may constrain programming skills.

4) a) 4GLs affect hardware resources for various reasons: inefficiency of some products, more systems and programs are developed, prototyping, end-user computing, on-line systems, peak-time usage, etc.

   b) Possible steps include: optimise database design, restrict file creation and up-date privileges, run jobs at off-peak times, monitor usage, choose applications according to pre-defined criteria.

5) a) End-user computing is possible/desirable because software package selection should involve end-users, end-user tools now exist, e.g. some 4GLs, increased computer awareness and literacy.

   b) Advantages include: increases the number of people producing systems, releases DP professionals from more trivial tasks, helps reduce the application backlog, allows users to put tools to full use, gives users a better insight into the computing task.

   c) Disadvantages include: need for careful control and for professional input, proliferation of hardware and software and insufficient expertise.

6) a) The information centre not only provides computing services but helps end-users to make the best use of computing facilities for themselves.

   b) The main objectives: help end-users make effective use of information technology, provision of training, control of end-user computing, communication with users to establish requirements, promotion of good practices, giving advice on hardware and software purchase and developing tools to aid end-user computing.

c) The DP department was there to produce applications for users, not really to help and assist them in using computing facilities for themselves.

Chapter 8

1) a) Advantages include: alternative development approaches allowed, increased productivity, faster systems development, systems developed match requirements closer, programs have a longer life and are easier to change, greater involvement for end-users, ease-of-use, are up-to-date tools, improved documentation, smaller development teams, improved requirements analysis, etc.

b) As described in Chapter 8.

2) a) Disadvantages include: diversity of products on offer, settling down period, lack of impartial help/advice, inefficiency, unidentified training needs, approaches adopted, interfacing to 3GL code, integration, etc.

b) As described in Chapter 8.

3) Organisations can minimise the disadvantages by the approach they adopt to selecting and using the 4GL, e.g. proper evaluation, setting of objectives, monitoring of usage, etc.

4) Selection should start with a search of the literature to find 4GLs which meet basic requirements. From this a shortlist of perhaps three can be selected. More rigorous evaluation of the shortlisted products should then take place against predetermined criteria. Other customers should be contacted, manuals looked at and evaluation software considered. The origins of the product and company should be considered and future developments looked for.

Chapter 9

1) Organisations may be too committed to 3GL code, have had bad experiences of 4GL use, be aware of their disadvantages, not want to further add to growing backlogs and maintenance, not have experienced staff or prefer the tools they already use and have used for many years.

2) a) Categories are cognitive, notational and augmentive.

b) 4GLs are augmentive tools.

3) a) CASE tools aim to automate the complete development cycle from analysis to production of code.

b) Basic components would include analysis tools and diagrammatic techniques, a data dictionary, code generation facilities, a screen painter, a report generator and a dialogue specifier.

c) The 4GL may just be one component of the CASE tool. 4GLs are aimed more at 'back-end' automation.

d) 4GLs and analyst workbenches.

4) AI involves trying to make computers cope with tasks normally thought of as requiring (human) intelligence or to solve problems in a way that is similar to how people solve problems.

5) Reasons include: growing awareness, wider availability of tools and techniques, developments in technology, embedded applications, and more expertise available.

6) Criticisms include: problems of decision-making, de-skilling, legal blame, lack of knowledge, poor explanation of reasoning, lack of common sense, reliability, speed and performance.

7) Through natural language interfaces or links to knowledge-based (expert) systems.

List of trademarks

A large number of products are referred to in this book. The names of such products are usually registered trademarks or trademarks and are acknowledged as being the property of their relative owners. As many trademarks and owners as possible are listed here and whilst every care has been taken in compiling this list inevitably some omissions may occur. Also, some changes may have occurred since this list was compiled.

Trademark	Owner
ADABAS	Software AG
APPLICATION EXPERT, Cullinet, KnowledgeBUILD, IDMS/SQL, ADS/Online, IDMS/R	Cullinet Software Inc.
ART	Interference Corporation
CORVISION, BUILDER, Cortex, APPLICATION FACTORY	Cortex Corporation
CRYSTAL	Intelligent Environments Ltd.
DATACOMB/DB	Applied Data Research Inc.
DATATALKER	Natural Language Inc.
dBASE III, dBASE III Plus	Ashton Tate
DEC, Digital, RdB, VAX, VMS, RMS	Digital Equipment Corporation
IBM, DB2, SQL, VSAM, IBM PC	International Business Machines
DELTA ADS, AMELIO	Delta Software Technologie AG
EASYTRIEVE PLUS, GENER/OL, EASYTRIEVE PLUS.PC., THE CORPORATE TIE	Pansophic Systems Incorporated
FOCUS, FIDEL Screen Manager, FOCUS TED Editor, FOCUS/STATISTICS, FOCCALC, FML, FOCAUDIT, PC/FOCUS, FOCTALK, LEVEL5	Information Builders Inc.
GURU, MDBS III	MDBS Inc.
HARVARD PRESENTATION GRAPHICS	Software Publishing Corporation
Honeywell	Honeywell Inc.
ICL	International Computers Ltd
INFORMIX	Informix Software Inc.
INGRES, INGRES/VIGRAPH, INGRES/PCLINK, INGRES/STAR, INGRES/APPLICATIONS, INGRES/DBMS, INGRES/SQL, INGRES/QUERY, INGRES/FORMS, INGRES/NET, INGRES/REPORTS, INGRES Gateways etc.	Relational Technology International
INTELLECT	Intellect Software International
KEE	Intellicorp

LEONARDO	Creative Logic
Lotus 1-2-3	Lotus Development Corp.
Cincom, MANTIS, SPECTRA, SUPRA, TOTAL, ULTRA	Cincom Systems Inc.
MIMER	Mimer Software
NCR	The NCR Corporation
MULTIPLAN	Microsoft Corporation
ORACLE, SQL*FORMS, SQL*PLUS, SQL*REPORT, SQL*MENU, SQL*DESIGN DICTIONARY, SQL*CALC, SQL*Graph, SQL*DEVELOPMENT METHOD, EASY*SQL, SQL*STAR, SQL*CONNECT	Oracle Corporation
POWERHOUSE	Cognos Ltd
PROGRESS	Progress Software Corporation
RAMIS Information System, RAMIS/PC Workstation, FREE-LINK, OMNILINK	On-Line Software International Inc.
RS/1	BBN Software Products
SAS	SAS Institute
UNIFACE	Inside Automation BV
UNISYS	Unisys Inc.
UNIX	AT&T Bell Labs
WANG	WANG Laboratories Inc.
WORDSTAR	Micropro International Corporation
XI PLUS	Expertech

Index

Index compiled by Peva Keane